HOMEW🍎RK

U.S. History
(1865–Present)

From Reconstruction Through the
Dawn of the 21st Century

RON OLSON

CAREER
PRESS
Franklin Lakes, NJ

HOMEWORK HELPERS: HISTORY (1865-PRESENT)
EDITED BY JODI L. BRANDON
TYPESET BY EILEEN DOW MUNSON
Cover design by Lu Rossman/Digi Dog Design NYC
Printed in the U.S.A. by Book-mart Press

To order this title, please call toll-free 1-800-CAREER-1 (NJ and Canada: 201-848-0310) to order using VISA or MasterCard, or for further information on books from Career Press.

CAREER
PRESS

The Career Press, Inc., 3 Tice Road, PO Box 687,
Franklin Lakes, NJ 07417
www.careerpress.com

Library of Congress Cataloging-in-Publication Data

Olson, Ron, 1959-
    Homework helpers. U.S. history (1865-present) : from Reconstruction through
the dawn of the 21st century / by Ron Olson.
        p. cm.
    Includes bibliographical references and index.
    ISBN-13: 978-156414-918-3
    ISBN-10: 1-56414-918-8
        1. United States—History—1865—Study and teaching. 2. United States—
History—1865—Problems, exercises, etc. I. Title. II. Title: U.S. History (1865-
present). III. Title: From Reconstruction through the dawn of the 21st century.

E661.O47 2007
973.8—dc22

                                                                        2006038183

Dedication

I wish to dedicate this book to two unique teachers. First of all, I would like to acknowledge my ninth-grade German teacher, Frau Hollinger, at Socorro High School, who took an active interest in "Wolfgang" and instilled in me the joy and love of learning. Secondly, I would like to acknowledge my history professor, Monroe Billington, at NMSU, whose love of history and dedication to teaching still inspires me in my job as a teacher today.

Acknowledgments

To several of my friends who have been a great safety net of encouragement throughout this process: Brian and Colleen Redpath, Ray and Mary Armstrong, Scott and Patti Barringer, Scott and Diane Holtz, Dana Roth, Steve and Gail Capatch, and Dana and Sonya White.

To three of my fellow AP teachers who have also been a great safety net of encouragement and friendship throughout this process: Nancy Potter, Steve Armstrong, and Carolyn Callaghan.

To Grace Freedson for her support in arranging the opportunity for me to work on this project. It is good to finally see this book published!

And, last, but not least, my two "guard dogs" who kept watch over me as I spent countless hours in my office at my iMac typing and researching. Madison, my Springer Spaniel, and Sparky, my Cocker Spaniel, followed me everywhere and stayed close by my side during the entire process (it's too bad they can't read!).

Contents

Introduction

Welcome to *Homework Helpers: U.S. History!*

This series (Book One and Book Two) was written with you, the student, in mind. It is my hope to make the study of U.S. history a bit easier. This series reviews U.S. history: **Book One** covers 1492 to the end of the Civil War in 1865, and **Book Two** covers Reconstruction in 1865 to the present. It is meant to help you master the material from a U.S. history course and to help prepare you for review exams such as the SAT II U.S. History exam and the Advanced Placement U.S. History exam.

The vast amount of material you are presented with in a U.S. history course may seem a bit overwhelming, but don't be intimidated. It can be a daunting task to think about people, places, and things from the times of Columbus and the founding of the colonies all the way to the events of 9/11 and the War on Terrorism. That's a lot of history! If you learn to use a few tools along the way, you can begin to manage the vast amount of historical information. Although some dates and people are very important, it is a good idea to focus on themes and trends and make connections that way.

Many state and national exams ask about the names of leaders or the succession of major battles in a war, but they generally won't ask specific questions about numerous facts. Wars are often presented as being "sandwiched" between two bookends: the events leading up to and the events following the war. It is vital that you be aware of modern times and current affairs so that you can analyze current situations and make connections to past events that shed light on the present. That said, many state and national exams generally include a limited number of questions from 1988 to the present, given the relative "newness" of the presidents and the lack of time necessary for thorough historical analysis.

Each chapter includes a Review Exam. Buy a notebook to record your answers to these exams. The correct answers and explanations are included for each exam. After you complete a Review Exam, go back and check your answers. If necessary, go back and review the material again and repeat the test. Practice does make perfect!

Each chapter begins with a brief time line of six major events meant to help you keep events in a chronological perspective.

Each chapter also contains a "Trends and Themes of the Era" meant to provide an overview of the "big ideas" for the time frame covered in that chapter. These are good ideas to help "anchor" your review of the material.

The introductory paragraph in each chapter begins with three key words that act as a road map for that particular chapter. As you read the chapter, look for these concepts to be developed. Also, the introduction serves as a quick overview of the entire chapter, giving you a broad look at the "landscape" of that particular chapter. As you read each lesson within the chapter, the details will be filled in.

Several different thematic maps are included to help guide you in the review of material (and to ensure that you are not geographically illiterate!). Visualize important details on the maps such as the names of places and the development of a particular theme for a map (land usage, trails, acquisitions, and so forth). Take time when you are presented with a map to **STOP** and **STUDY** the map. Ask yourself very basic, yet important questions: What information does this map provide? How does this map relate to the important information in the chapter?

As you read this book, keep in mind several of the broad themes that begin occurring and look for various **trends over time**: economic trends, political trends, important legislative acts, tariffs, economic depressions (panics), labor trends, foreign policy issues, domestic policy issues, court cases, immigration, and women and minorities in history. After reading a few chapters, you want to be able to make comparisons over periods of time from one decade to another, or looking at trends over a 40- to 50-year period. Test yourself by designing your own time line with eight to 12 significant items from those few chapters. Keep these in your notebook, too.

In order to guide your study of history you need to *read the material in this book carefully*! It is a story—take time to enjoy it! Don't read all of the material in one setting, and don't be afraid to mark up the text with a highlighter or pencil. Take time to digest the material in each mini-lesson in the chapters. Pace yourself. Remember that good comprehension of a subject matter comes after sufficient review. If you can, work on the material from this review book for a short period of time each night. I hope that this book helps bring comprehension, confidence, and enthusiasm to your study of history.

Reconstruction (1865–1877)

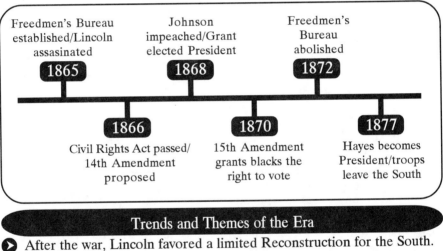

Freedmen's Bureau established/Lincoln assasinated

1865

Johnson impeached/Grant elected President

1868

Freedmen's Bureau abolished

1872

1866

Civil Rights Act passed/ 14th Amendment proposed

1870

15th Amendment grants blacks the right to vote

1877

Hayes becomes President/troops leave the South

Trends and Themes of the Era

▶ After the war, Lincoln favored a limited Reconstruction for the South. Congress, however, was dominated by Radical Republicans, who favored a harsher Reconstruction plan to punish the South for secession and for slavery.

▶ After Linsoln's assassination, Congress overwhelmed Andrew Johnson, who had taken over as president, and instituted punitive Reconstruction policies.

▶ Blacks in the South, freed during the Civil War, gained considerable rights during radical Reconstruction. Through both legal and illegal means, white Southerners fought against granting these rights.

▶ After the failure of radical Reconstruction, Southerners used court rulings and legislation to institutionalize segregation and discrimination against blacks.

Restore, rebuild, and retreat! After four years of civil war, it was time to rebuild the nation. The war was disastrous for the South; the economy, landscape, and race relations lay in ruins. The task of rebuilding meant not only helping to heal the nation's wounds, but also restoring the Confederate states to the Union and transforming Southern society. The long-term consequences of the war left serious social, political, and economic challenges to address. What would freedom mean for the four million former slaves? How would the South be brought back into the Union? Lincoln's plan for Reconstruction can best be summed up in his second inaugural address: "With malice toward none; with charity for all; with firmness in the right, as God gives us to see the right, let us strive on to finish the work we are in; to bind up the nation's wounds...." What began as a plan to bind the nation's wounds developed into a serious political battle not only between the Radical Republicans and the Democrats but also between the executive and legislative branches of government. The chance to rebuild Southern society ultimately ended with the failure of Reconstruction. The increased segregation in Southern society, the Democrat's return to power in the South, and the retreat of Northerners signaled the end of Reconstruction, laying the foundation for new problems that wouldn't be fully resolved until well into the 20th century.

Lesson 1-1: Reconstruction: Executive or Legislative Decision?

Unlike the Radical Republicans in Congress, who wanted to severely punish the Confederate states, Lincoln proposed a more forgiving and flexible plan for Reconstruction. In December 1863, Lincoln issued the Proclamation of Amnesty and Reconstruction, also known as the **10 Percent Plan**, which pardoned any former Confederate who would take an oath to support the Constitution. The pardon offer wasn't extended to officers in the Confederate armed forces above certain ranks, or to those who had resigned Union government posts to aid in the rebellion. In each state, when one-tenth of the voting population had taken the oath of loyalty to the Union and established a new government, Lincoln would recognize that government.

Lincoln's plan was marked by a lack of vindictiveness to bring the South back. He argued that the Southern states had never left the Union because secession was illegal. Lincoln felt that the executive branch was responsible for dictating Reconstruction terms. He could use pardons to bring back the rebel states. Lincoln's lenient plan ended with an assassin's bullet on April 14, 1865, leaving the issue of Reconstruction unresolved.

Southerner **John Wilkes Booth** was upset about the events of the Civil War and devised a plot to assassinate the president, vice president, and secretary of state on April 14, 1865, in order to throw the government into chaos and allow for a resurgence in the South. (General Lee had just surrendered to General Grant at Appomattox on April 9th.) The plan was for Booth to kill Lincoln in the Ford Theater while he was watching a performance of *Our American Cousin*. Conspirator George Atzerodt was to kill Vice President Johnson at his home, and conspirators Lewis Powell and George Herold were to kill Secretary of State William Seward. On April 11th, Booth and his fellow conspirators listened to Lincoln give a speech about civil rights and voting rights for blacks. The speech greatly angered Booth and the plan was put into place. Booth fatally shot Lincoln, and Powell and Herold wounded Seward and others in his house by stabbing them, but Atzerdot did not follow through with his plan. Booth himself was caught and shot for his crimes, and his conspirators were all caught and hanged. The government was not thrown into chaos, and the business of Reconstruction was underway.

Radical Republicans in Congress denounced Lincoln's plan for being too easy on the South and for not securing any rights for freed slaves. The **Radical Republicans,** whose leaders included Charles Sumner, George Julian, and Thaddeus Stevens, were the most militant antislavery wing of their party. They believed that when the Southern states seceded, those states ceased to exist. They feared any attempts of Confederates to regain political power. Many in Congress felt that the president was exceeding his authority by using his executive privilege to control Reconstruction efforts. They also thought that Congress, not the president, should dictate the terms by which the nation would reunite, and they wanted the Republican Party to be established as the dominant force in Southern life. Their efforts to reshape Southern society also included a firm stance on free labor and education and civil rights for freed blacks.

It became Congress's duty to set in motion the terms of Reconstruction and re-admission of the Southern states to the Union. Radical Republicans felt that Congress should revolutionize Southern life. They wanted to redistribute the plantations' wealth to blacks and whites loyal to the Union. They felt that Confederacy leaders shouldn't be allowed to return to power, and that the federal government should give blacks full equality by ensuring voting rights.

In July 1864, Congress proposed its own plan for Reconstruction by passing the **Wade-Davis Bill,** which declared that each Confederate state would be run by a military governor. After half of each state's eligible voters took an oath of allegiance to the Union, a state convention could be called to overturn secession and outlaw slavery. Lincoln's veto set the stage for a heated debate on who should be in charge of Reconstruction—the president or Congress—and Reconstruction stalled, with Congress and the president deadlocked over the terms of the Confederate states' readmission.

The Radical Republicans succeeded in dictating some terms of Reconstruction. In March 1865, Congress established the **Freedmen's Bureau**, offering education, employment, economic relief, and legal aid to freed slaves. The Freedmen's Bureau helped build hospitals and supervised the founding of black schools throughout the South. Along with establishing the Freedmen's Bureau, Congress passed the **13th Amendment**, which abolished slavery. The amendment was ratified in December 1865.

After Lincoln's assassination, Vice President Andrew Johnson, a Southern Democrat who opposed secession, became president. When Johnson became president, he forged ahead with a slight modification of Lincoln's Reconstruction plan without facing any Congressional opposition. He strongly supported states' rights and didn't favor political rights for freedmen. Under Johnson's plan, nearly all Southerners were pardoned by taking an oath of allegiance to the Union. Johnson's plan further required reconstructed state governments to denounce secession and ratify the 13th Amendment.

In practice, however, Johnson's Reconstruction plan sought to rebuild the Democratic Party, promote the planter elite, and allow the executive branch to control the terms of Reconstruction. Furthermore, he pardoned many powerful ex-Confederates and allowed reconstructed Southern governments to be dominated by proslavery forces such as Confederate army officers, plantation owners, and former government officials. His amnesty offer to Southerners outraged the Radical Republicans, and he lost their support. Johnson felt that he, rather than Congress, should firmly control the terms of Reconstruction. By the end of 1865, 10 of the 11 states had met his lenient plan, and "restoration" was at hand.

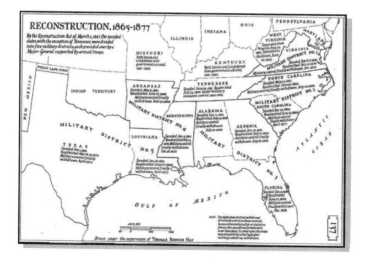

Lesson 1-2: The Terms of the Radical Republicans

Congress reconvened in December 1865 and immediately challenged Johnson's Reconstruction plan. Radical Republicans, led by Senator **Charles Sumner** and Representative **Thaddeus Stevens,** set out to dismantle Johnson's plan and to dictate Reconstruction on Congress's own terms, calling for black voting rights, confiscation of Confederate estates, and military occupation of the South. To accomplish this, they had to gain the support of moderate Republicans.

Congress then passed two bills by overriding Johnson's vetoes: the **Civil Rights Act of 1866**, granting blacks full citizenship and civil rights, and an extension of the Freedmen's Bureau. (This was the first time a presidential veto had been overridden on a major piece of legislation.) Congress began to exert its authority over the president.

To give the Civil Rights Act constitutional protection, in 1866 Congress passed the **14th Amendment**, declaring all persons born or naturalized in the United States to be citizens of their states and of the nation, and prohibiting states from denying citizens equal protection and due process of the law. Congress thus reversed the *Dred Scott* decision (1857), which had denied blacks citizenship. The 14th Amendment defined national citizenship for the first time, making anyone born in the United States automatically a citizen. This signaled a dramatic shift in power from the states to the federal government. In the 1866 congressional elections, the Republicans made the proposed amendment part of their party platform. The opposition from Johnson backfired, and the Republicans retained large majorities in both houses of Congress.

Now that Radicals were in charge, they wanted to secure passage of the 14th Amendment with the **Reconstruction Act of 1867**. Except for Tennessee, the South was divided into five military districts, with a major general controlling each region through martial law. To get out of military control, a state had to adopt a constitution, allow blacks the right to vote, and ratify the 14th Amendment. Congress wanted to firmly dictate the terms of Reconstruction policies and seemed obsessed with a need to defeat the president. In June 1868, seven ex-Confederate states voted to ratify the amendment, and it finally had the necessary amount of votes needed for passage.

Lesson 1-3: Impeachment Crisis

In March 1867, the same month Congress passed the Reconstruction Act, it passed two bills to limit President Johnson's authority. Johnson was at odds with Congress on Reconstruction, and he took a narrow view of the legislation. The **Tenure of Office Act** prohibited the president from removing civil officers without Senate approval, and the **Command of the Army Act** prevented the president from issuing military orders except through the commanding general, Ulysses S. Grant, who couldn't be removed without the Senate's approval.

In August 1867, with Congress out of session, Johnson suspended Secretary of War **Edwin Stanton**, a Radical Republican appointed by Lincoln, and replaced him with Grant. Stanton then remained barricaded in his office for nearly two months. Republicans in Congress refused to approve Johnson's replacement and called for impeachment on the grounds that Johnson had violated the Tenure of Office Act and was now guilty of "high crimes and misdemeanors." (Johnson's violation served as an excuse for Congress to launch impeachment proceedings. The real motivation was to remove a president hostile to Congressional Reconstruction.)

On February 24, 1868, the House of Representatives adopted 11 articles of impeachment against Johnson. In the trial before the Senate, they tried to prove he was obstructing legislation, which was a political rather than a criminal offense. The final vote after the nearly three-month-long trial fell one vote short of removing Johnson from office. No indictable crime had been committed. Although Johnson remained in office for the rest of his term, he was virtually a lame-duck president.

Lesson 1-4: Congressional Reconstruction Continues

The **15th Amendment,** proposed in 1869 and passed in 1870, guaranteed the right to vote to any citizen regardless of race, color, or previous condition of servitude. The amendment aimed to promote black suffrage in the South, and to guarantee it in the North and West. The last Southern states awaiting readmission (Texas, Mississippi, and Virginia) were required to ratify the new amendment as a condition for readmission to the Union. Susan B. Anthony and others from the women's movement opposed the amendment because it still excluded women from voting.

Also working to undermine the 15th Amendment was the **Ku Klux Klan (KKK)**. Founded in 1866 in Tennessee by Nathan Bedford Forest, it operated in all Southern states by 1868, conducting raids to intimidate black voters as part of its campaign to assert white supremacy in the South. Along with these raids, the Klan orchestrated lynchings and floggings of blacks.

In May 1870, to counter the Klan's threats to black suffrage and to bolster the Fifteenth Amendment, Congress passed the Enforcement Acts of 1870 and 1871, which protected black voters. Congress also passed the Ku Klux Klan Act in 1871 to authorize the president to use federal troops and emergency measures to overthrow the Klan. As incidences of vigilantism increased, the Klan and other secret societies maintained a strong presence in many areas and remained focused on restoring white supremacy by intimidating blacks. They wanted an ordered society and feared the new roles of blacks in a white society.

Reconstruction-Era Constitutional Amendments at a Glance

13th Amendment	Abolished slavery	• Prevented Southern states from reestablishing the institution of slavery after the end of the Civil War.
14th Amendment	Defined U.S. citizenship and provided for equal protection of the law for all citizens	• For the first time the federal government, not the states, defined citizenship by stating that all persons born in the United States were citizens. • Provided due process and equal protection of the laws for all citizens.
15th Amendment	Gave the right to vote to all males, regardless of race or color	• Guaranteed black men the right to vote but failed to grant the right to vote to women.

Lesson 1-5: Free Blacks in a White Society

Freed slaves worked to build new lives for themselves after the Civil War. They lacked land and cash as they began a new chapter in their lives, but they now had the freedom to move, to unite broken families, to legally marry, to get an education, to establish their own churches, and to own land.

The first task for many was simply to reunite families torn apart by the years of slavery. Others began making plans to move. As one black preacher urged his listeners, to be truly free "you must move away from the shadow of the Great House." Although a black migration began, many blacks remained near the areas they had lived in as slaves.

After the war ended, many freed blacks were led to believe that the government would grant them "40 acres and a mule." Near the end of the Civil War, General Sherman had issued **Field Order 15**, which divided up land south of Charleston into 40-acre parcels for individual freed families. He also had indicated that the army might lend the families mules to help at the beginning of the planting season. But even though more than 20,000 families cultivated land once owned by Confederates, the War Department rescinded the decree and allowed whites to reoccupy their former lands.

The Freedmen's Bureau was created as an agency of the War Department to provide help for refugees, settle freedmen on lands, put people back to work, issue rations, and build hospitals and schools. Its initial emphasis was protecting freedmen's rights and regulating working conditions. In 1869, due to a lack of funding, Congress ordered the bureau to shut down. By 1872, the Freedmen's Bureau was out of business, and its demise signaled the beginning of the Northern retreat from Reconstruction.

Many of the "reconstructed" Southern governments enforced **black codes** in an attempt to create a subjugated black work force. Most states outlawed interracial marriage and jury service by blacks, and banned blacks from testifying against whites or bearing arms. Most codes also imposed a curfew on blacks and limited their access to public institutions. South Carolina further required licenses for blacks who wanted to enter nonagricultural employment. Radical Republicans claimed that the South was perpetuating slavery under another name and that the black codes were simply being used to control former slaves. President Johnson defended the codes along with his overall plan for Reconstruction.

Destitute and unemployed, many blacks moved to cities in search of work. As a result of this migration, the population of urban blacks in the South increased by 75 percent in the late 1800s. Other freedmen tried to establish farms of their own, but, lacking resources and equipment, were forced to rent out land as tenant farmers under the **sharecropping system**. By the end of the 1860s, the sharecropping system had replaced slave-filled plantations as the driving force behind the Southern economy. Under this system, freedmen and poor whites rented out plots of land from plantation owners. In exchange for use of the land, shelter, and farming equipment, these laborers, known as sharecroppers, gave the landowner up to one-half of their crop yield. The system ensured that the sharecropper could never raise enough money to gain real financial independence.

Opponents accused the new Southern governments of being unsound and corrupt, and many of the government workers took bribes and exchanged favors for votes. Democrats called the Southern moderates who cooperated with Republicans **scalawags** and labeled the Northern opportunists **carpetbaggers** (an unpleasant title meant to suggest that the Northerners came to the South just to gain easy political power and wealth through bribes).

During Reconstruction, nearly 2,000 black men served as local elected officials. Many of them had been free before the war and had worked as teachers, clergy, and skilled artisans. Sixteen black Southerners were elected to Congress. The first black elected to the Senate was **Hiram Revels** from Mississippi. (He occupied the seat formerly held by Jefferson Davis.) Blacks also began their long loyalty to the Republican Party by voting as a bloc for the next 50 years. Congress responded to increased violence in the South by passing the **Civil Rights Act of 1875**. It prohibited discrimination against blacks in places of public accommodations and guaranteed freedmen's right to serve on juries. But the new law didn't stop Southerners from enacting more discriminatory laws. In 1883, the Supreme Court overturned the act by declaring that the states, not Congress, could redress a "private wrong or a crime of the individual." Once again, it was left up to the states to determine the rights of individuals.

Lesson 1-6: Compromise and Retreat

During the 1870s, the Radical Republicans lost influence in Congress with the deaths of two key leaders, Charles Sumner and Thaddeus Stevens, and many others become more moderate in their views. The Radicals' demise, along with reports of corruption in reconstructed governments, sapped Northerners' enthusiasm for Reconstruction. At the same time, economic panic and political scandal diverted the nation's attention.

Another factor contributing to the end of Reconstruction was the rulings of the Supreme Court. In a series of decisions, the Court reversed many of the trends the Radicals had introduced.

Society in the South After Reconstruction

Although blacks in the South gained freedom, they hardly gained equality. Despite the Radical Republicans' efforts at Reconstruction, many Southern blacks struggled with poverty, illiteracy, and unemployment. As Reconstruction waned, the freedmen's condition only worsened. The Freedmen's Bureau closed, voting restrictions such as **poll taxes** and **literacy tests** proliferated, and racial violence spread. Blacks were required in many places to pay a tax in order to vote, and after Reconstruction it was used a means of getting around the 14th Amendment by further denying civil rights to blacks. Other communities added literacy tests that proved a person could read and write well enough to interpret portions of the federal or a state constitution. A **grandfather clause** stated that a literacy test for blacks could be waived if that person's grandfather had been a registered voter prior to the passage of the 15th Amendment. Once in place, these measures, along with continued intimidation from the KKK, dramatically limited the numbers of black voters.

Discrimination in the South further intensified with the passage of **Jim Crow laws** in the 1880s. Jim Crow laws segregated many public accommodations, such as trains, steamboats, streetcars, and schools, and restricted or forbade black access to other facilities, such as theaters and restaurants. The

Supreme Court upheld such segregation in *Plessy v. Ferguson* (1896), which declared "separate but equal" facilities to be constitutional. This decision cleared the way for decades of demoralizing discrimination against blacks.

The Supreme Court Weighs In

As the North's resolve in dealing with Reconstruction waned, the Supreme Court hampered the federal government's ability to promote civil and political equality. In a series of cases in the 1860s and 1870s, the Supreme Court established a narrow reading of the 14th and 15th amendments.

In what were known as the *Slaughterhouse Cases* (1873), the Court's decision was a very narrow interpretation of the 14th Amendment. In 1869, Louisiana created a 25-year monopoly by granting one company the right to slaughter livestock. Other butchers sued, claiming their rights had been violated by the state. The Court stated that the Fourteenth Amendment protected only the privileges of "national citizenship," and declared that the Louisiana legislators' ruling on the slaughterhouse operators didn't deprive them of their property without due process.

The Court's ruling that the 14th Amendment protected only the rights of national citizenship, not state citizenship, later allowed for a number of restrictions on state voting privileges. In *U.S. v. Cruikshank* (1876), the Court overturned the conviction of three men who had been charged with violating their victims' civil rights. The ruling meant that individuals would have to look to the states for protection of their rights. In *U.S. v. Reese* (1876), the Court's ruling also limited the scope of the 15th Amendment, stating that it didn't confer the right of suffrage on anyone, but merely prohibited barring suffrage based on race, color, or previous condition of servitude. This gave states the ability to legally deny people the right to vote by using nonracial reasons.

Lesson 1-7: Distractions of Corruption and Dissent

In 1868, Ulysses S. Grant, the Union Civil War hero, defeated the Democratic candidate, Horatio Seymour, for president. Grant's two terms in office were shadowed by numerous scandals, including the 1869 Black Friday scandal, the 1875 Whiskey Ring, the 1876 Belknap scandal, and the infamous **Credit Mobilier** scandal in 1872. In the Black Friday incident, Grant's brother-in-law conspired with two powerful industrialists to corner the gold market. In the Whiskey Ring, Grant's personal secretary was found guilty of taking bribes from a group of distillers seeking to evade millions of dollars in taxes. In the Belknap scandal, Grant's secretary of war, William E. Belknap, was impeached for accepting bribes to sell Native American trading posts in Oklahoma. Credit Mobilier was a company created by the Union Pacific Railroad, and the board of directors from the company and the railroad ran both boards. The company paid bribes to congressmen to prevent an investigation into its dealings. In 1872, these transactions, involving Vice President Colfax and Congressman James A. Garfield of Ohio, became public knowledge. The House of Representatives condemned Oakes Ames, one of the directors of the company, considered impeaching Colfax, and published the names of lawmakers with whom Ames had dealt. The widespread corruption in Grant's administration weakened the Republican Party and diverted the nation's attention from Reconstruction.

Approaching the election of 1872, dissident Republicans split off from the party to protest Grant's corruption and formed a new political party called the Liberal Republicans. Liberal Republicans opposed corruption and favored sectional harmony. The new party joined with the Democrats and nominated Horace Greeley for president. Though Greeley was a determined campaigner, he lost resoundingly to Grant. Despite Grant's victory, however, the division in the Republican Party was a clear sign of congressional Reconstruction's loss of momentum.

The Panic of 1873

In Grant's second term in office, the nation faced serious economic woes. What began as a European economic downturn soon spread to the United States. As a result of over-expansion by railroad builders and businessmen, the nation's economy collapsed in what is known as the **Panic of 1873**. During the next five years, the stock market crashed and the largest bank in the nation failed, as did many smaller banks and firms. More than 18,000 businesses failed, and 25 percent of railroads shut down. The economic panic, coupled with Grant's many political scandals, distracted the nation from Reconstruction and would allow Southern Democrats to edge their way back to power in the South.

Lesson 1-8: The End of Reconstruction

The 1872 split in the Republican Party hastened the collapse of Republican rule in the South. Moderates in Congress pushed through Amnesty Acts allowing almost all ex-Confederate officials to return to politics and hold office. Using tactics such as promising tax cuts and engaging in outright violence and intimidation, Democrats took control of one state after another. Some Republicans gave up and moved back North; others defected to the Democratic Party. By 1877, Democrats had gained enough votes to win state elections in every one of the former Confederate states.

Democrats called their return to power Redemption. Once under Democratic control, the Southern states cut expenses, ended social programs, and revised their tax systems to grant relief to landowners. In turn, many blacks migrated northward to escape the discriminatory policies of the Redeemed South. In 1879, 4,000 blacks from Mississippi and Louisiana alone reached Kansas to settle on land outside the grasp of Southern Democrats.

Reconstruction-Era Legislative Acts at a Glance

Freedmen's Bureau - 1865	Provided for education, relief, labor, and resettlement for blacks	• This act directly involved the federal government in assisting blacks to transition from slavery to freedom. • This act was abolished for lack of funding in 1872.
Civil Rights Act - 1866	Granted blacks full citizenship and civil rights	• This act directly involved the federal government in securing civil rights for blacks. • This act was passed over Johnson's veto.
Military Reconstruction Act - 1867	Divided the South into five military districts and set out new rules for readmission of states to the Union	• This act put the Radical Republicans firmly in charge of dictating the terms of Reconstruction.
Tenure of Office Act - 1867	Stated that the president could not remove an approved presidential-appointed official without consent of the Senate	• This act attempted to give the Congress more authority over presidential appointments. • This act led directly to Johnson's impeachment in 1868.
Enforcement Acts of 1870 and 1871 and the Klan Act of 1872	Attempted to protect black voters and black civil rights including authorizing the president to use federal troops and emergency measures against the Klan	• These acts were another attempt of the federal government to protect the rights of blacks that were being denied by the states.
Civil Rights Act - 1875	Prohibited discrimination against blacks in places of public accommodations and guaranteed freedmen's right to serve on juries	• Because it was not enforced, the new law didn't stop Southerners from enacting even more discriminatory laws against blacks. • This act was overturned by the Supreme Court in 1883.

The South was allowed to pursue a racial agenda consistent with its political, economic, and social interests. Southern Democrats maintained themselves in power, and the Civil War became the "glorious lost cause" and Reconstruction became the story of Redemption.

In the 1876 election, Republicans nominated moderate Rutherford B. Hayes and Democrats nominated Samuel J. Tilden for president. Although Tilden won the popular vote, Republicans challenged the election returns from South Carolina, Florida, and Louisiana when Tilden remained one vote short in the Electoral College. The election results were disputed, and a 15-member commission was established with five senators, five representatives, and five judges (seven Republicans, seven Democrats, and the Supreme Court Justice). The final vote from the commission was eight to seven in favor of Hayes.

To prevent Democrats from obstructing Hayes's path to the White House, Republicans promised that, in return for the presidency, Hayes would remove federal troops from South Carolina and Louisiana. They also promised no further opposition to white Southern governments, finances for the plans for a railroad from Texas to the West Coast, and extra money for internal improvements in the South for roads, bridges, and harbors. In return, the South agreed to treat blacks fairly and respect their rights.

Congress never carried through on all of the economic promises, and Southern Democrats never pressed it to do so. After he assumed office, Hayes abided by the so-called **Hayes-Tilden Compromise** and removed federal troops from the last two occupied states in the South. By January 1877, Democrats had won control of all Southern state governments, and Redemption was complete. Southern governments, under Democratic rule, re-imposed laws severely restricting black suffrage and civil rights. Reconstruction was officially over.

Review Exam

Multiple Choice

1. President Lincoln's plan for Reconstruction required that the president be in charge of the Reconstruction plan and that _____.
   a) 75 percent of all adult white males to take a loyalty oath and blacks be given the right to vote
   b) 10 percent of all adult white male taking a loyalty oath
   c) those taking the loyalty oath be pardoned
   d) B and C only

2. "With malice toward none; with charity for all; with firmness in the right, as God gives us to see the right, let us strive on to finish the work we are in; to bind up the nation's wounds...."
   These words best sum up _____'s views of Reconstruction.
   a) President Andrew Johnson
   b) Charles Sumner
   c) Thaddeus Stevens
   d) President Abraham Lincoln

3. The Radical Republicans' response to Reconstruction was that _____.
   a) they should work together with the president to establish a workable plan
   b) they alone should set the terms and conditions of Reconstruction
   c) the president should present his plan first to Congress for approval
   d) the Democrats should develop a separate plan

4. All of the following were major components of the Radical Republican plan for Reconstruction EXCEPT _____.
   a) the Democratic Party was to be an integral part of politics in the South
   b) blacks were to be given the right to vote and provided with educational opportunities
   c) Congress should dictate the terms of Reconstruction
   d) Southern life would be reshaped to fit the "ideals" of the Radical Republicans

5. As part of Andrew Johnson's presidential plan for Reconstruction, he _____.
   a) allowed Confederate leaders to regain political power
   b) imposed a harsher plan than Lincoln
   c) sought to work with the Congressional leadership in developing a joint plan
   d) agreed reluctantly to blacks receiving the right to vote

6. The 14th Amendment was significant in that it _____.
   a) defined citizenship as those born in the Untied States
   b) allowed limited segregation
   c) granted citizens equal protection and due process of law
   d) A and C only

7. Part of the Reconstruction Plan enacted by Congress _____.
   a) required the ratification of the 14th Amendment
   b) placed all Southern states under military rule

c) provided for suffrage for all blacks with the 15th Amendment

d) A, B, and C

8. All of the following people or groups did not support the 15th Amendment EXCEPT _____.

   a) Susan B. Anthony and others in the women's movement, because it still excluded women from voting

   b) the KKK, who used scare tactics to keep blacks from voting

   c) the Radical Republicans in Congress, because they opposed President Johnson's attempt to pass this amendment

   d) white Southerners, who did not want to share political power with blacks

9. The method of sharecropping in the South provided _____.

   a) blacks a process of eventually receiving free land

   b) a system of blacks renting out land as tenant farmers

   c) a system of economic freedom for blacks

   d) an end to slave labor because blacks could now become wage earners

10. Black codes sought to segregate life in the South by all of the following EXCEPT _____.

    a) allowing blacks to testify on juries

    b) not allowing blacks to bear arms

    c) allowing blacks limited access to public institutions

    d) limiting jobs for blacks

11. In an effort to get around the 15th Amendment and limit blacks voting, Southern states began to enact _____.

    a) poll taxes for voting purposes

    b) literacy tests for prospective voters to prove that they could read and write

    c) grandfather clauses to exempt those whose grandfather had been a registered voter prior to the passage of the 15th Amendment

    d) A, B, and C

12. Congress was able to successfully override a presidential veto when President Johnson attempted to veto the _____.

    a) Civil Rights Act of 1875   c) Civil Right Act of 1866

    b) Freedmen's Bureau   d) 13th and 14th amendments

13. In their goals for Reconstruction, the Radical Republicans _____.
    a) sought to punish the South for its actions in the Civil War
    b) sought ways to compromise with Southern legislators by means of Reconstruction legislation
    c) sought to quickly readmit Southern states
    d) were willing to consider a moderate approach on Reconstruction bills being proposed in Congress

14. The Freedmen's Bureau lasting contribution for blacks during Reconstruction was that of _____.
    a) providing blacks with a means for gaining an education
    b) establishing economic freedom for most of the blacks in the South
    c) support of numerous congressional black candidate
    d) the establishment of hospitals and churches for blacks

15. Signs that Reconstruction efforts were weakening by the 1872 presidential election could be seen by all of the following EXCEPT _____.
    a) lack of funding and the closure of the Freedmen's Bureau
    b) corruption and scandal in Grant's presidential term
    c) the return of the Democratic Party to Southern politics
    d) the weakening of the efforts of the KKK

16. The election of 1876 all but ended Reconstruction, as evidenced by _____.
    a) the contested results in the presidential election that ultimately gave the advantage to Hayes
    b) the removal of troops from the South
    c) black codes restricting civil rights of blacks throughout the South
    d) A, B, and C

17. The impeachment proceedings against President Johnson were significant for all of the following reasons EXCEPT that _____.
    a) The House of Representatives succeeded bringing 11 articles of impeachment against the president mainly for obstruction of justice (it was motivated by political reasons)
    b) Although he was impeached by the House, the Senate failed by one vote in removing President Johnson from office
    c) The charges in the House of Representatives failed to meet the Constitutional test of "high crimes and misdemeanors"
    d) The trial focused on President Johnson's dismissal of Secretary of War Edwin Stanton, a Radical Republican who Johnson wanted to fire

Matching

a. Wade-Davis Bill	j. Democratic Party
b. Credit Mobilier	k. Civil Rights Act of 1875
c. Hiram Revels	l. carpetbaggers
d. Panic of 1857	m. 13th Amendment
e. Reconstruction Act of 1867	n. Nathan Bedford Forest
f. Freedmen's Bureau	o. Field Order 15
g. Tenure of Office Act	p. Jim Crow Laws
h. Secretary of War Edwin Stanton	q. scalawags
i. 15th Amendment	r. John Wilkes Booth

_____18. divided the South into five military districts

_____19. declared that the Confederate states would be run by a military governor and made ratification of the 14th Amendment mandatory

_____20. prohibited the president from removing civil officers without Congressional approval

_____21. offered education, employment, economic relief, and legal aid to freed slaves

_____22. the first black elected to the Senate (he occupied the seat formerly held by Jefferson Davis from Mississippi)

_____23. removed from office in 1867 by President Johnson, which greatly angered Congress as a violation of the Tenure of Office Act

_____24. Southern moderates who cooperated with Republicans during Reconstruction

_____25. allowed for segregation of public accommodations in the South and was upheld by the Plessy v. Ferguson Supreme Court decision in 1896

_____26. blacks believed that it would provide them with "40 acres and a mule" after the end of the war

_____27. Northerners who went to the South during Reconstruction

_____28. abolished slavery

_____29. founder of the Ku Klux Klan

_____30. by the end of Reconstruction in 1876, this political party had once again been restored to power in the South

____31. devised a grand scheme in 1865 to assassinate Lincoln and to have fellow conspirators kill the vice president and secretary of state

____32. granted suffrage to any citizen regardless of race, color, or previous servitude

____33. prohibited discrimination against blacks in places of public accommodation

____34. a political scandal involving the Union Pacific Railroad and its board of directors in which bribes were paid to congressmen to prevent an investigation

____35. during Grant's second term in office, the nation suffered serious economic problems with a stock market crash, business failures, and rising unemployment that served to distract the president and Congress from dealing further with Reconstruction

Short Response

36. Compare and contrast the presidential and congressional plans for Reconstruction. As Congress began asserting its authority over the president in carrying out Reconstruction, how did this challenge the relationship between Congress and the president?

37. How did the courts begin to restrict the aims of Reconstruction?

38. How did the concepts of *restore*, *rebuild*, and *retreat* reflect the views of Reconstruction?

Answers begin on page 279.

The Wild, Wild West

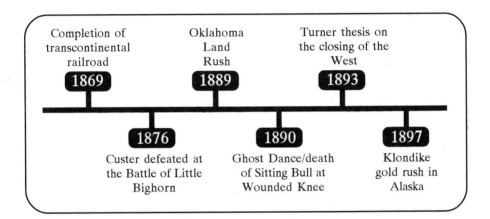

Completion of transcontinental railroad
1869

Oklahoma Land Rush
1889

Turner thesis on the closing of the West
1893

1876
Custer defeated at the Battle of Little Bighorn

1890
Ghost Dance/death of Sitting Bull at Wounded Knee

1897
Klondike gold rush in Alaska

Trends and Themes of the Era

> The first transcontinental railroad, and the others that followed, united the nation economically, geographically, and socially.

> Monopolistic practices corrupted railroads in the late 1800s.

> Traditional roles of Native Americans continued to be challenged as more natives were forced to relocate to reservations.

> The Cattle Kingdom saw thousands of farmers driving cattle to profitable markets, only to see this way of life greatly challenged by harsh weather (1886) and the invention and patent of barbed wire (1874).

> Gold and silver ore deposits in various locations in the West brought about a "boom-and-bust" cycle for population growth in the region.

> The Homestead Act of 1862 helped to usher in a wave of settlers in search of land in the West.

Rails, roundups, and reservations! Even before Horace Greeley popularized John Soule's 1851 quote, "Go west, young man," the West lured the imagination of Americans. The many decisions to go west and the transformation of the landscape and people's lives remains a vital experience in American culture of the 19th century. Once railroads connected the country in 1869, the wheels were set in rapid motion to dramatically reshape the political, economic, geographic, and social climate of the region. Cowboys, frontier settlers, immigrant laborers, buffalo soldiers, miners, entrepreneurs, Native Americans, and others all left their marks in this region. The allure of new land and new opportunities "out west" developed a rugged individualism deep in the American psyche. This began to be challenged with the 1890 census results proclaiming the disappearance of the frontier line. Three years later, historian **Frederick Jackson Turner** developed a unique concept of the frontier experience in his 1893 thesis, "The Significance of the Frontier in American History," by discussing the closing of the frontier. According to Turner, "the frontier is gone, and with its going has closed the first period of American History." Despite the fact that indeed change was once again imminent with the dawn of the 20th century, the events of the West crafted a unique saga of American expansion in the 19th century.

Lesson 2-1: Golden Spikes and the Iron Horse

Before railroad expansion west of the Mississippi, the trip from Missouri to Oregon or California could take as long as six months. With the transcontinental railroad, it took one week. This rapid expansion of railroad mileage after the Civil War would eventually see the United States lead the rest of the world, with more than 250,000 miles of track by World War I. Cities in the East were connected with cities in the West.

During the Civil War, Northern congressmen were free to promote their version of a railroad bill, which would have a northern route (eventually making Chicago a major hub for railroad activity). The **Pacific Railroad Act** (1862) granted a contract to the **Union Pacific** to build west from Omaha, Nebraska, and to the **Central Pacific** to build east from Sacramento, California. The bill included the creation of federally chartered corporations that would receive free public lands and generous loans to secure the building of the railroad. The companies were offered $16,000 per mile over the plains, $32,000 per mile over plateaus, and $48,000 per mile over hills and mountains. For every mile each company completed it gained 22 sections of land in states and 40 sections of land in territories along the route; by the end, they had received nearly 45 million acres of land. Promoters could sell land and buy stock, and corrupt accounting procedures and bribery allowed huge profits. A golden spike driven in with a silver hammer at **Promontory Point** in Utah on May 10, 1869,

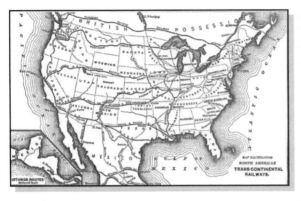

officially united East and West. The new railroad attracted settlers, miners, hunters, and tourists to the region, and they arrived thanks to the "iron horse" steam engines.

Immigrants completed much of the work on the first transcontinental railroad. Chinese immigrants were used as cheap labor for the Central Pacific; Irish immigrants, Civil War veterans, and others were used as laborers for the Union Pacific.

After the completion of the transcontinental railroad in 1869, many of the Chinese scattered with several ending up in San Francisco. Anti-Chinese sentiment began to grow mainly out of a resentment of the economic situation in California because many Chinese were industrious workers, and many felt that the Chinese could not assimilate into American society and were taking jobs away from other people in California. After pressure from Californians, in 1882 Congress adopted the **Chinese Exclusion Act**, which barred the further entry of Chinese laborers into the country.

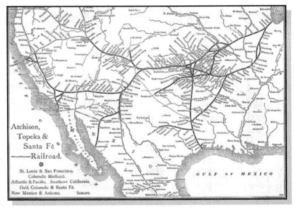

Soon after the completion of the first transcontinental railroad in 1869, other railroads began to crisscross the west. By 1883, work was completed on the second transcontinental railroad, the **Southern Pacific**, enabling it to connect San Francisco to New Orleans. The **Atchison, Topeka and Santa Fe Railroad** saw its construction begin in 1869 from Atchison, Kansas, and within the next 30 years, it built and controlled more than 9,000 miles of rail throughout the western region. The **Great Northern**, was the northernmost railroad in the United States and ran more than 1,700 miles from St. Paul, Minnesota, to Seattle, Washington. Major towns began to spring up along the routes allowing places including Dodge, Albuquerque, El Paso, Denver, Portland, Seattle, and San Francisco to be connected.

The railroad companies were responsible for a series of vast improvements. Telegraph communication along with rail travel quickly became the backbone of the nation. Companies such as the **Baldwin Locomotive Works** built powerful steam engines for the various railroads. Standardization became the key to success for the railroads. To end confusion over the width of the various railroads, railroad companies agreed to adopt a standard gauge of 4′ 8 ½″. To expedite the shipment of raw materials and finished goods on return trips, railroads developed a system of four time zones to establish a common reference of time, no longer depending on "God's time." Other additions to the rails included air brakes, signal systems, and refrigerated cars. **George Pullman** took advantage of this new form of travel and helped design elaborate dining and sleeping cars at the Pullman Palace Car Company, just south of Chicago. By the early 1880s, more than two-thirds of all railroads were using Pullman Cars.

In addition to a wide range of innovations, the rail lines held a tremendous amount of political and economic power because of their control of transportation. Rail companies aggressively competed by using such tactics as undercutting competitors, forcing competitors into bankruptcy, buying out competitors, offering cut-rates for shipping goods, and granting kickbacks to politicians, enabling the larger rail lines to form monopolies and control the trade along a variety of trunk lines.

This monopolistic trend of the rail lines was also a common feature in other businesses across America in the late 19th century. By the mid-1890s, more than one-third of all railroad mileage was tied up in foreclosure or bankruptcy proceedings. Investment bankers took over failing railroads and controlled trade, prices, and profits. Entrepreneurs including **J.P. Morgan**, **Cornelius Vanderbilt**, and **Jay Gould** took over many weakened railroads by reorganization and refinancing. Because of these actions, the federal government responded by passing the **Interstate Commerce Act** in 1887, which attempted to regulate the railroad practices by requiring that shipping rates be "reasonable and just"and published, and not allowing secret rebates and price discrimination against smaller markets. During the following two decades, 16 cases involving this regulation went before the Supreme Court—and the railroads won 15 of the cases! Not until President Teddy Roosevelt encouraged Congress to pass the **Hepburn Act** in 1906 were railroad practices further regulated by the federal government.

Lesson 2-2: Changing Cultural Identity of Native Americans

Near the end of the Civil War, the Native American population in the West topped 360,000 and comprised groups such as the Plains Indians, Pawnees, Apaches, Hopi, Zuni, Navajo, Pueblo, Cherokee, and Sioux. Most groups held a reverence for the land, crops, and animals, and had a great fear of whites. The tribes were trying to preserve their way of life despite further expansion in the West. As more whites moved West, native American tribes began to fear for their own futures. Many whites felt that their livelihood, land, and profit was limited by the presence of the tribes.

Over the years, Native Americans were killed in direct warfare with whites, and devastating diseases took a horrible toll on their population. As they became increasingly dependent on trade with white men, traditional Native American ways of life suffered.

Traditional roles within the Native American society were also challenged. As whites continued moving west after the introduction of the railroad, it upset the migratory patterns of buffalo and the patterns of the hunt. The destruction of the buffalo nearly wiped out the Native Americans of the Plains. In the mid-1860s bison numbered between 13 and 15 million. In the 1870s and 1880s, rail tourists had "bagging parties" from railroad cars and simply shot buffalo for sport. (William Cody got his nickname "**Buffalo Bill**" after killing more than 4,300 bison in eight months.) By the mid-1880s, buffalo became nearly extinct, greatly impacting tribes that were dependent upon the buffalo.

Last Stands

The **Massacre at Sand Creek**, Colorado, in 1864 symbolized the hostile relations between tribes and the white man. In this case, Cheyenne Indians who did not want to fight as the whites raided the area (in search of gold) were relocated to Sand Creek. In an effort to make the Native Americans suffer further, Col. John Chivington and his troops decided to take away this last piece of Cheyenne land, which was supposed to be a safe haven, by descending on the group of more than 500 Cheyenne while they were sleeping. The attack ended with more than 200 deaths, mostly women and children. Chivington was treated as a hero in his hometown of Denver, Colorado, although others were outraged at the incident.

Chief Sitting Bull and George Armstrong Custer met at the infamous **Battle of Little Big Horn** in 1876. Once gold was discovered in the Black Hills region of South Dakota in 1874, Custer led the survey in the region. The discovery of gold placed increased pressure to rid the region of Native Americans. At the Battle of Little Bighorn on June 25, 1876, Custer's force of 600 troops arrived a day early and stumbled on an encampment of more than 2,500 Sioux and Cheyenne. In the ensuing battle, Custer and one-third of his soldiers were killed, and Chief Sitting Bull and Chief Crazy Horse emerged victorious. The Native Americans used this opportunity to achieve a short-lived victory over the encroachment of the white man in the region. Retribution from the whites was swift. A year later, Chief Crazy Horse surrendered to the army and, in the process of preparing to move him and his troops to a military outpost in Nebraska, Chief Crazy Horse was killed. After the battle, Chief Sitting Bull was pursued by U.S. troops and fled to Canada. He returned to Montana in 1881 and surrendered to the army. Following two years of imprisonment, he was allowed to travel as an attraction for Buffalo Bill's Wild West Show. After a short time on tour, he returned to a reservation in South Dakota. In 1890, during the spread of the Ghost Dance, policemen were sent to arrest Chief Sitting Bull in order to prevent another uprising. During a struggle with his supporters and the tribal police, he was shot in the head by a Lakota policeman.

In 1877, the Nez Perce and **Chief Joseph** in the Idaho region were being forced by the federal government to relocate to a reservation. Chief Joseph and others from the tribe were pursued by the army as they trekked through Washington, Oregon, and Idaho toward the Canadian border. After 75 days and 1,300-plus miles of travel, and running low on food and supplies, Chief Joseph surrendered in Montana just 40 miles from the Canadian border with his famous oration: "I am tired; my heart is sick and sad. From where the sun now stands I will fight no more forever." The federal government then shipped them to Indian Territory in Oklahoma, where disease and starvation killed more than one-third of the remaining survivors. In 1885, Chief Joseph and his followers were allowed to return to the Northwest.

After being pursued throughout the region, **Chief Geronimo**, a prominent Apache leader, was forced to surrender to the army in 1886. He and his followers were sent to Florida and eventually ended up being forced a year later to relocate again to Indian Territory in Okalahoma. Geronimo lived here until his death in 1909.

White Men and the Reservation Policy

As they were forced to relocate to reservations, Native Americans were deprived of their traditional lands and way of life. In this process, they became increasingly dependent upon the federal government, and in turn the federal government grew increasingly insensitive to the way of life of the tribes. The reservation terms were easily violated by the railroads. As gold was discovered in some regions, and as more settlers went west in search of land for settlement, Native Americans were simply seen as "in the way of progress." Caring for the tribes was a major role of the Bureau of Indian Affairs, whose main goal was to "civilize" the native tribes.

The **Dawes Act** enacted in 1887 allotted 160-acres plots of reservation land to individuals. This was seen as a way to assimilate Native Americans into white society by breaking up the reservations and converting them into herders and farmers. The federal government sold the remainder of reservation land to settlers. Most of the land given to the Native Americans was difficult to use for herding and farming. Once-proud nomadic Native American tribes were forced to change their way of life: Children were clothed and educated in the ways of the "white man," and Native American religious and sacred ceremonies were banned. Nomadic tribes were confined to territory within their reservations. Resistance was all but futile.

The last symbolic act of violence against an independent way of life was at Wounded Knee, South Dakota, in 1890, when at least 200 Native American men, women, and children were machine gunned while some of the Sioux were chanting the **Ghost Dance** (an attempt to bring Native Americans back from the dead in order to drive out the white man). They believed that Ghost Dance shirts would protect them from harm. These Sioux Indians were still determined to preserve their tribal ways and a sense of themselves as a separate people. In the end, the **Wounded Knee Massacre** resulted in the deaths of Sitting Bull, other warriors, and several soldiers, and the massacre of innocent men, women, and children. The use of violence continued as the Natives were forced to continue assimilation into white society.

In her 1881 work, *A Century of Dishonor*, author **Helen Hunt Jackson** detailed the mistreatment of Native Americans by the federal government, challenged the reservation policy, and detailed accounts of broken treaties and broken promises between the federal government and various tribes. Her work highlighted the ongoing problems of Native American assimilation and an increased white presence in the West.

Lesson 2-3: Cattle Kingdom

Towns and stockyards thrived on the business of the ranchers whose longhorns were driven to market. Several trails, including the Chisholm Trail and Goodnight-Loving Trail were used to get upwards of 5 million longhorns to railroads for transport to Chicago meatpacking plants. The long trip could take three months and included crossing rivers, searching for grasslands for the cattle, and dealing with rustlers, Native Americans, and the unpredictable climate. **Joseph Glidden**'s 1874 patent of his design of barbed wire on range lands eventually ended the long cattle drives by the mid-1880s.

Cattle Trails of the Western U.S.

This cattle work on the open range elevated the cowboy to folk hero status. Many cowboys were former Confederate soldiers, and almost one-third of the cowboys were black. The demanding work included rounding up the herds in the spring, branding newborn calves, and selecting the steers to send to market. During the early to mid-1880s, ranchers came to expect profits of nearly 40 percent. By the mid-1880s, overproduction, increased competition, sagging prices, lack of grass to feed all of the cattle, and devastating diseases wiped out many cattle. Range wars erupted between big corporations and independent ranchers.

Devastating blizzards in 1886 and 1887 severely challenged this way of life. The blizzards buried cattle in snowdrifts, and the summer weather brought no relief, as carcasses floated downstream or were found cut up in barbed wire. Severe heat and drought dried up water holes and scorched grasslands, and in some places the losses amounted to up to 90 percent. The days of long cattle drives and open range ranching were over.

Lesson 2-4: Boom-and-Bust Cycle

The gold rush that started with the discovery of gold at Sutter's Mill in California in 1848 sparked decades of searching for mineral wealth in the West. Gold was discovered near **Pike's Peak** in Colorado in 1859 and led to another "gold rush" to the West. Thousands of people flocked to the Rocky Mountains region in search of wealth and several mining towns sprung up, including Denver. The **Comstock Lode** of silver ore was discovered in Nevada in 1859 and again brought people West. Gold was discovered in the Black Hills of South Dakota in 1874 and resulted in the removal of the Lakota Indians from the region. The last of the big gold discoveries was in the Klondike region of Alaska in 1896. Word of the discovery spread quickly and sparked the massive **Klondike Gold Rush** to the region in 1897 and 1898. People rushed to ports in San Francisco and Seattle to head North in search of gold.

All of these mineral discoveries brought about a massive boom-and-bust cycle in the West. Overnight mining camps and company towns sprung up. Gambling halls, saloons, banks, and other businesses became fixtures in the towns. Many local economies became increasingly dependent upon the mining industry and susceptible to the ups and downs in the market. People were lured to various regions in search of instant wealth. Women were attracted to the West for a variety of reasons. One of the biggest benefits women gained in the West was the right to vote when Wyoming, Colorado, Idaho, and Utah took the lead in granting female suffrage.

Lesson 2-5: Settlers and Culture

Rugged individuals settled this region. They gathered buffalo chips for fuel, lived in sod houses, remained isolated from neighbors, and faced long, harsh winters and hot summers with a mix of fierce rainstorms, grasshoppers, and tornadoes. They endured the hard work of raising crops and animals on the homestead.

The **Homestead Act of 1862** promised 160 acres of free land to settlers who lived on it, cultivated it, and kept up improvements for five years. More than 83 million acres of land were ready for settlement, mainly in Central Plains and upper Midwest areas along with some land in California, Colorado, Washington, and Wisconsin. Between 2 and 6 million farms established and developed the Midwest region as the "world's breadbasket" due to the large amount of grains grown on the farms. New technology greatly aided the farmers (plows, reapers, harvesters, patents on inventions, barbed wire, and scientific studies of soil, grains, and climate). Due in large part to the growth and importance of agriculture in this region, the Department of Agriculture was established as a cabinet office in 1889.

Grangers, led by Oliver Kelley in 1867, at first sought to enhance the lives of isolated farmers through social, educational, and fraternal activities. It grew to more than 800,000 members by 1875 and admitted men and women equally for membership. They then became concerned for the plight of the farmers and advocated measures before state and federal legislatures benefiting the farmers and their families.

The **Oklahoma Land Rush**, the last and largest land rush, occurred on April 22, 1889. Thousands gathered to claim more than 2 million acres of land at noon. In excess of 100,000 "boomers" gathered in pursuit of their dream of land ownership. This land rush marked the end of the opening of the West.

In 1872, **Yellowstone National Park** in Wyoming became the first national park created to preserve land in the west for future generations. Other national parks soon followed: Yosemite and Sequoia in California in 1890, and Mt. Rainier in Washington in 1899.

Buffalo Soldiers also played a unique role in life in the West. In 1866, Congress reorganized the peacetime army and created two segregated regiments of black cavalry, the Ninth and 10th United States Cavalry Infantry Regiments. The Cheyenne and Comanche soon nicknamed these soldiers "Buffalo Soldiers." The army troops were then stationed to forts out West where they were involved in clashes with Native Americans, subdued Mexican revolutionaries, outlaws, and rustlers, explored and mapped regions of the Southwest, and established frontier outposts around which future towns and cities grew. Despite the harsh assignments and isolated regions, these soldiers served with distinction and had the lowest rate of desertion in the entire army.

The myth of the West was portrayed in popular "dime novels" and newspaper stories that featured wild stories about Deadwood Dick, Wild Bill Hickock, Buffalo Bill, Billy the Kid, Calamity Jane, Annie Oakley, and others. To showcase this excitement, William Cody began a 20-year run of his traveling show **Buffalo Bill's Wild West Show**. It included live performers and animals, reenactments of Custer's Last Stand, Native American attacks on stagecoaches, visits by Sitting Bull and other Native Americans, and cowboys and cowgirls showing off their skills.

Review Exam

Multiple Choice

1. Frederick Jackson Turner's 1893 essay on the closing of the frontier was important in that _____.
    a) it basically declared that the frontier era was now over
    b) it discouraged any further settlement in the West
    c) people began to lose interest in the lifestyle and life in the West
    d) America lost its enthusiasm for exploration and discovery

2. Improvements by the railroads included _____.
    a) standard gauge of 4 feet 8 1/2 inches
    b) the establishment of time zones
    c) air brakes, sleeper cars, and refrigerated railcars
    d) A, B, and C

3. The cattle boom came to an end in large part due to _____.
    a) severe weather conditions (droughts and blizzards) as well as overgrazing and the use of barbed wire on range lands
    b) railroad transportation proving to be too expensive to transport animals to market for slaughter
    c) the reduction in the number of ranchers willing to risk raising cattle
    d) too many ranchers leaving the range to move to the big cities in search of work

4. The Chinese Exclusion Act in 1882 was significant in that it _____.
   a) enacted a 10-year moratorium on Chinese immigration
   b) no longer allowed Chinese immigrants to immigrate to America
   c) put strict quotas in Chinese immigration
   d) also included Japanese immigrants not being allowed to immigrate to America

5. The Homestead Act of 1862 was important in enticing settlers to the West because _____.
   a) it promised 160 acres of free land to settlers
   b) settlers were required to live on the land, cultivate it, and keep up improvements on it for five years
   c) it increased the number of settlers moving West
   d) A, B, and C

6. The Central Pacific and Union Pacific railroads were in fierce competition to build the transcontinental railroad because _____.
   a) the expense of labor was rising and difficult to acquire
   b) stockholders were demanding increased profits
   c) the federal government was awarding several square miles of public lands for each mile of track completed
   d) land was becoming scarce because of increased cattle ranching

7. In addition to the Central Pacific and Union Pacific railroads, the _____.
   a) Southern Pacific Railroad route connected New Orleans to San Francisco
   b) Atchison, Topeka and Santa Fe Railroad connected areas from Kansas throughout parts of the Southwest
   c) Great Northern Railroad connected St. Paul, Minnesota, to Seattle, Washington, and provided a route for transportation of farm goods
   d) A, B, and C

8. Men such as J. P. Morgan, Cornelius Vanderbilt, and Jay Gould were involved in railroad activities for all of the following reasons EXCEPT that they sought _____.
   a) to control the price of shipping to maximize profits
   b) to acquire weaker railroads while in bankruptcy
   c) limited competition from a variety of companies
   d) personal wealth from their acquisitions (and were sometimes referred to as "robber barons")

9. All of the following were factors in the increasing amount of deaths of Native American tribes in the Great Plains region EXCEPT _____.
   a) harsh conditions when Native Americans were forced to relocate and settle in different regions
   b) the spread of diseases, including smallpox, and the lack of immunities to fight these diseases
   c) increased starvation with the demise of the buffalo herds
   d) decreased violence between Native Americans and whites

10. The goal of the Dawes Act in 1887 was to _____.
   a) destroy traditional tribal customs and assimilate Native Americans into white society
   b) slow Native American assimilation into white society
   c) protect Native American customs and homelands
   d) abolish the reservation system

11. In addition to the discovery of gold at Sutter's Mill in California in 1848 that led to the gold rush in 1849, minerals (gold or silver) were also discovered and began similar rushes and a "boom-and-bust" cycle _____.
   a) at Pikes Peak near Denver, Colorado, in 1859
   b) at the Comstock Lode in Nevada in 1859
   c) in the Klondike region in Alaska in 1898
   d) A, B, and C

12. All of the following add to the romanticized lifestyle of the West EXCEPT _____.
   a) families living off of the land and surviving harsh conditions sometimes in isolation from others
   b) the popularity of the West in "dime novels" and traveling shows such as Buffalo Bill's Wild West show
   c) the dangerous lifestyle of cowboys on the range
   d) Buffalo Soldiers serving with distinction at outposts in the West

13. _____ became a major hub for railroad activity and the meatpacking industry during the later years of the 19th century.
   a) New Orleans   c) Dallas
   b) Chicago   d) Denver

14. Oklahoma was the site of _____.
   a) the largest and last of the land rushes in 1889, in which 2 million acres of land was opened for settlement

b) a new railroad to serve portions of the Southwest

c) the last stand of Native American tribes in the West

d) a gold rush in the Black Hills region

15. _____ did not grant suffrage to women after 1865 in an effort to lure more women to settle out West.

a) Wyoming

c) California

b) Colorado

d) Idaho

16. The "boom-and-bust" cycle as seen out West is generally most closely associated with _____.

a) the cattle industry

b) railroad construction

c) the reservation policy for Native Americans

d) mining

17. The lifestyle of the Plains Indians was greatly altered by the _____.

a) harsh climatic conditions due to extended droughts

b) near-destruction of the buffalo

c) construction of several railroads across the West

d) desire to live quiet lives on reservations

Matching

a. Pacific Railroad Act

b. Massacre at Sand Creek

c. Ghost Dance

d. Helen Hunt Jackson

e. Interstate Commerce Act (1887)

f. Joseph Glidden

g. Grangers

h. Chief Geronimo

i. Hepburn Act of 1906

j. Battle of Little Bighorn

k. Baldwin Locomotive Works

l. Chief Crazy Horse

m. Chief Joseph

n. Buffalo Bill's Wild West Show

o. Promontory Point

p. George Pullman

q. Wounded Knee Massacre

r. Chisolm Trail

s. Yellowstone National Park

_____18. leader of the flight of the Nez Perce toward Canada in 1877 (who surrendered in Idaho)

_____19. author of *A Century of Dishonor*, which detailed the mistreatment of Native Americans by the federal government and highlighted the ongoing problems of assimilation

_____20. organization started by Oliver Kelly to give farmers an outlet for social, educational, and fraternal activities

____21. one of the last Native Americans to succumb to white conquest and was eventually relocated to territory in Oklahoma

____22. attempted to regulate railroad practices by regulating shipping rates charged by the railroads

____23. area where the Central Pacific and Union Pacific met on May 10, 1869, symbolizing the completion of the transcontinental railroad

____24. recipient of a patent for his invention of barbed wire

____25. 1862 legislation that granted a contract to the Union Pacific and Central Pacific railroad companies to construct a transcontinental railroad

____26. an attempt among the Sioux to bring Native Americans back from the dead in order to use them to drive out the white man

____27. was killed when his tribe was being moved to a military outpost in Nebraska

____28. the first national park created to preserve the nation's natural resources (it also led to the creation of other national parks)

____29. further regulated railroad practices with federal guidelines that strengthened the Interstate Commerce Act

____30. one of a few companies that built steam engines used on the railroads across the country

____31. a major cattle route from San Antonia, Texas, leading north to Oklahoma and Kansas

____32. 1864 raid in Colorado that served as another use of brutality to rid the Western region of Native American tribes; more than 200 Native Americans were killed in this attack

____33. resulted in the death of Sitting Bull and other warriors during the Ghost Dance in 1890

____34. 1876 raid in which General Custer was greatly outnumbered and eventually killed by Sioux and Cheyenne Indians

____35. took advantage of increased travel on railroads and developed the sleeping cars for railroad companies

____36. William Cody's traveling show

Short Response

37. How was the myth of the American West developed?

38. How did the concepts of *rails, roundups, and reservations* change the character of the American West?

Answers begin on page 281.

The Era of Big Business: America in the Gilded Age

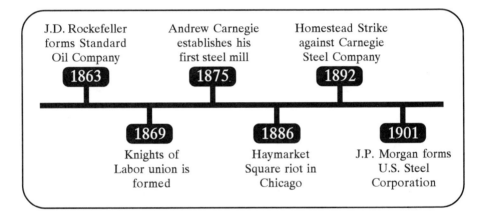

J.D. Rockefeller forms Standard Oil Company
1863

Andrew Carnegie establishes his first steel mill
1875

Homestead Strike against Carnegie Steel Company
1892

1869
Knights of Labor union is formed

1886
Haymarket Square riot in Chicago

1901
J.P. Morgan forms U.S. Steel Corporation

Trends and Themes of the Era

▶ First in the form of massive corporations and then in even larger trusts, big business built up monopolies over markets and made enormous profits.

▶ Big business drove industrialization and helped foster a belief in America as the land of opportunity, where anyone who worked hard could get rich, but it also created a vast gulf between the rich and the poor.

▶ At first, the government followed a laissez-faire policy with big business, but as business abuses increased state governments and then the federal government passed regulatory legislation.

▶ Labor unions began to push their demands for safety, better wages, and shorter hours. Various strikes erupted across the country. Union demands were increasingly associated with violence and with resistance from labor leaders.

Growth, wealth, and challenges! Mark Twain is responsible for naming this period the Gilded Age. It was indeed a "golden time" of tremendous economic growth and technological innovations. America and its big cities became the destination of millions seeking to make new lives for themselves. The large cities bustled with excitement and economic opportunities for a better life. Big businesses, trusts, and monopolies began to dominate everything from railroads to oil to steel. Business leaders exerted a tremendous impact on the economy and on the lives of virtually every American. Beneath the "gilded" surface loomed serious problems, as the income gap widened based on skill, gender, race, and region, and as state and federal government attempted to regulate business activity. The "captains of industry" were becoming exceedingly rich and powerful, while others labored tirelessly just to survive. America was seen as being the land of opportunity, but at what cost?

Lesson 3-1: Big Labor and Economic Growth

Business ruled during the years after the Civil War, and a new industrial economy developed, governed by gigantic corporations. In 1860, the United States was the fifth-leading industrial power in the world, and by the 1890s it was the leading industrial nation, producing more than one-third of the world's goods. The entire U.S. economy was growing, especially manufacturing, agriculture, and railroads. Railroads were the largest consumers of coal, the largest carriers of people and goods, and the largest single employers of labor.

Just before the Civil War, Congress passed legislation allowing businesses to form corporations. Afterwards, these corporations dominated much of American business. The economy's rapid growth produced large-scale corporations as technological innovations spread. Chicago became the country's second-largest industrial area, and the home of food, metal, transportation, and corporate headquarters. New York, the largest city in America, was the site of finance, publishing, advertising, and fashion industries, as well as transportation and corporate businesses.

Firms felt pressure to cut costs and boost profits in order to compete. **Vertical integration** allowed a business to acquire the resources it needed to produce and market a product from start to finish, whereas **horizontal integration** allowed a business to acquire competitors at a low rate, diminishing competition and permitting sales with minimal competition. Some companies used both vertical and horizontal integration to create monopolies and control prices to maximize profits.

Businesses also formed **combinations**, creating loose alliances of enterprises under a large national organization. In addition, a business could create a **consolidation**, blending several companies into one corporation and raising large sums of money by selling stock certificates. Market control meant that a corporation could set prices for a product, and then amass incredible fortunes.

These corporations, and the businessmen who ran them, became extremely wealthy and powerful at the expense of the many poor workers. Much of the public saw the leaders of big business as **robber barons** who exploited workers in order to accumulate fortunes. Small business owners complained about monopolies, and many citizens feared big business. Despite these concerns, the **"captains of industry"** set out to not only make a fortune for themselves but to transform the U.S. business climate.

Lesson 3-2: Big Men in Business

John D. Rockefeller dominated the industrial world with his **Standard Oil Company**, formed in 1863 in Cleveland, Ohio. "Black gold fever" took hold, as Rockefeller's goal was to cut costs in order to raise revenue and maximize profits. Rockefeller created a cartel, a group of independent business organizations to cooperate and control production. He maintained control over oil wells, oil refiners, pipelines, distribution, sales, and advertising. By 1880, he controlled 90 percent of the nation's oil refining capacity and, over the next few years, his company dominated the nation's petroleum industry. Rockefeller, a titan in the business realm, stated, "The day of combination is here to stay…. Individualism has gone, never to return."

Rockefeller formed the Standard Oil Trust to get around state laws that prohibited a company in one state from owning stock in and operating a company in another state. Individuals exchanged their stock for trust certificates from Standard Oil, so Standard Oil controlled the individual companies but didn't own them.

Rockefeller closed old plants and built larger and newer ones. He threatened his rivals, bribed politicians, conspired with railroads for rebates to lower his transportation costs, and undercut the competition. He also exported his product abroad to other countries in the Standard Oil infamous, and easily recognizable, 5-gallon tin. His business dealings allowed him to accumulate more than $800 million in his lifetime, making him the richest man in America.

Rockefeller was also one of the first major philanthropists in the United States, establishing several important foundations. He donated more than $540 million to charitable purposes, including the University of Chicago and the Rockefeller Institute for Medical Research, which he founded. Most of his philanthropic endeavors were aimed mainly at education and medical science. One of the medical accomplishments included the foundation of the Rockefeller Sanitary Commission in 1909, whose work brought about eradication of the hookworm disease in the South and found a cure for yellow fever.

Andrew Carnegie, a poor immigrant from Scotland, served as a symbol of the rags-to-riches success story. He became one of the richest men in the world with his company, Carnegie Steel. He started out as a bobbin boy in a textile mill in 1848 earning $1.20 per week and attending night school to learn bookkeeping. At age 24, Carnegie's hard work paid off when he was appointed superintendent of the Pennsylvania Railroad's western division. With his earnings and investments, his income rose to more than $56,000 a year.

Seeing the Bessemer process (blowing hot air into a furnace to get impurities out of iron) in Britain led Carnegie in 1875 to buy a steel mill and establish a steel railroad rail mill in Pittsburgh, in the midst of an economic depression. Over the next 25 years, by adding more mills and by taking advantage of boom-and-bust cycles in the economy, he saw steel and coal production skyrocket. Carnegie was a shrewd businessman who undercut the competition, maintained business efficiency, kept labor costs low, and acquired government contracts. He secured his business operations by applying vertical integration to his operations.

The expansion and use of steel for rails, skyscrapers, John Deere and McCormick's machinery, barbed wire, the Washington Monument, and bridge cables, such as those used in building the Brooklyn Bridge in 1883, helped Carnegie increase his market dominance. By 1900, his company, the largest industrial company in the world, was worth nearly $500 million, and it produced more than one-third of all steel output in America. In 1901, Carnegie sold his interests in his company to J. P. Morgan's Federal Steel to form **U.S. Steel Corporation**, the first billion-dollar corporation in U.S. history. Carnegie's profit on the merger was more than $225 million. Carnegie retired and spent the rest of his life as a philanthropist, giving nearly $350 million to 3,000 public libraries, several universities, and other interests for the public good. According to Carnegie, "The man who dies rich dies disgraced."

J. P. Morgan made his fortune by merging companies to form large corporations, and he also headed an investment house, J. P. Morgan & Company. When the Sherman Antitrust Act of 1890 outlawed corporations owning other companies, Samuel Dodd came up with the idea of a "holding company," a corporation of corporations with the power to hold shares of other companies. Morgan then became responsible for reorganizing several important American enterprises, such as railroads, coal companies, General Electric, AT&T, and International Harvester. Morgan's investment deals also caused the disappearance of more than 1,200 companies.

Jay Gould used shady financial deals, bribes, threats, and conspiracies to accumulate his railroad wealth. He bought and sold railroads, watered their stock, and milked the assets. He was even involved in a failed attempt to corner gold on the stock market in 1869. Gould's dealings earned him a reputation as a **robber baron** who gained control of weak properties and turned them into a profit for his own gain.

In 1867, **Cornelius Vanderbilt** took over the New York Central Railroad and merged it with other railroads to form the New York Central Railroad System. By the time of Vanderbilt's death in 1877, he operated more than 4,500 miles of track and was worth more than $100 million. He was a hard-working, fierce competitor who was willing to cut prices to get business. His railroad innovations included replacing old iron tracks with steel tracks, along with using air brakes and Pullman Palace Cars on his lines.

Vanderbilt was never known for philanthropic activities, although he did donate $1 million to Central University, which later became Vanderbilt University. When he died, he was the richest man in the United States. Cornelius Vanderbilt left the bulk of his fortune, $95 million, to his son William, who is remembered for remarking, "The public be damned," when a reporter asked him whether railroads should be run for the public benefit.

Lesson 3-3: The Government and Big Business

The government and much of the nation believed in the principles of **laissez-faire** economics which stressed that the economic market should run freely without government interference. According to the theory, free, unregulated markets led to competition, which in turn led to fair prices for consumers.

The plight of the poor during the Gilded Age was minimized by the tenets of **social Darwinism** in the late 1800s. social Darwinism adapted Charles Darwin's theory of evolution, "survival of the fittest," to the business world, arguing that competition was necessary to foster the healthiest economy, just as competition in the natural world was necessary to foster the healthiest, or fittest, species. By this reasoning, government shouldn't protect the poor because the poor were weak and unfit, and they imperiled the nation's financial health. The rich, meanwhile, were strong, hard-working citizens who bettered the nation, so they shouldn't be subject to government regulation. Prominent social Darwinists included Herbert Spencer and Andrew Carnegie, whose essay promoting a free market economy, "The **Gospel of Wealth**," was published in 1889. It spoke of the need of the wealthy few to manage wealth for the underprivileged who did not have wealth and who could not manage money themselves.

By the 1880s, however, it was beginning to become clear that the markets were *not* free. Corporations had grown so big and powerful that they were controlling entire markets, forcing smaller companies out of business and setting high prices. Consumers became enraged over the high prices that monopolies had set, and small businesses demanded protection from being squeezed out of the market. Railroad monopolies were overcharging small-time customers, especially farmers, even as they gave rebates to powerful politicians and favored clients.

In 1887, Congress passed the **Interstate Commerce Act** to try to stop railroads from engaging in price discrimination, establishing the government's right to regulate private industry to serve the public interest. In 1888, legislative committees in Congress began to investigate and expose the business practices of the robber barons. Congress created the **ICC (Interstate Commerce Commission)**, the first federal regulatory agency to regulate railroad practices across state lines.

Although presidents made few attempts to enforce the decision, in *Munn v. Illinois* **(1876)**, the Supreme Court at first allowed state **Grangers**, a group of farmers united to improve the economic and social position of the nation's farmers, to regulate storage and freight rates. Later, however, the courts began to lean more toward having the federal government control interstate commerce. Railroads challenged the grange commissioners' rulings, and in 1886, the Supreme Court ruled that states couldn't set rates on interstate commerce. In fact, the railroads won 15 of the 16 cases before the Supreme Court. In 1906, the **Hepburn Act** finally gave the ICC power to set rates.

In 1890, Congress passed the **Sherman Antitrust Act**, which outlawed "every contract or combination in the form of a trust in restraint of trade or commerce." The act regulated business practices that squelched competition, including buying out competitors. Though the act eventually became extremely important in regulating business, in its early years it was rarely enforced.

In the 1890s, courts invoked the Sherman Antitrust Act to restrain laborers' right to strike, ruling that strikes violated the act's prohibition against "a conspiracy in restraint of trade." Big business benefited from the pro-business stance of the judiciary and its unwillingness to restrict commercial behavior.

Not until the early 1900s did government begin to enforce the Sherman Antitrust regulatory policies in full. Between 1898 and 1902, 2,600 firms vanished (1,200 in 1899 alone). During the panic of 1893, 500 banks and 150,000 businesses failed, 3 million people were unemployed, and one-fourth of the railroads were taken over by entrepreneurs (Vanderbilt and Morgan), so that seven powerful companies owned more than two-thirds of the nation's railroad tracks.

The lack of antitrust enforcement would lead Congress to pass two additional laws in 1914. The **Clayton Antitrust Act** outlawed trusts, price fixing, agreements to control supply and price of a product, and abuse of power to form or maintain a monopoly. In addition, Congress established the **Federal Trade Commission** to enforce antitrust laws.

Lesson 3-4: Labor Problems and Unrest

Although labor unions began forming in the early 1800s, they didn't gain any significant membership base or bargaining power until the 1860s and 1870s. The harsh, even hazardous working conditions drove laborers to organize into unions. One of the first major labor unions to unite several smaller unions was the **National Labor Union**, headed by **William Sylvis**, in 1866. During its brief history, the union managed to attract a membership of more than 640,000 before the death of its leader and its own demise. Its major goal was to get Congress to pass an eight-hour workday for workers. The efforts failed, but other unions would also include wages and workday length in their dealings with businesses.

Another major labor union, the **Knights of Labor**, founded in 1869 by **Uriah Stephens**, demanded equal pay for women, an end to child labor, an eight-hour workday, and a progressive income tax, among other reforms. The union also began to condemn the concentration of vast amounts of wealth in the hands of a few big business leaders. **Terence Powderly** assumed leadership of the union a decade later and encouraged immigrants, blacks, Hispanics, and women to join. In 1885, the group staged a successful strike against railroad robber baron Jay Gould in Missouri. On the strength of this victory, the Knights' membership and political power grew. The Knights successfully supported a number of politicians for election and forced laws favorable to workers through Congress, but, by the mid-1890s, the union's membership had declined, along with its influence.

Chicago's bloody **Haymarket Square Riot** in 1886 at McCormick Harvester (one of the city's largest employers) was sparked by the company locking out 1,400 Knights of Labor workers over their wage and labor demands. The riot on the evening of May 3rd began when the company tried to bring in scabs to replace the union laborers. The gathering of 3,000 workers was peaceful until someone threw a bomb that exploded in front of the advancing police, killing seven policemen and injuring 70 others. When the police retaliated, four men were killed and hundreds were hustled off to jail. Ten men were indicted for conspiracy to murder, and seven were sentenced to death. Public outrage at the Chicago bombing shook the entire labor movement. Prominent leaders of the Knights of Labor were convicted of inciting the riot, and public support for the labor unions plummeted.

To salvage the labor movement, craft laborers who had been members of the Knights of Labor broke off and formed the **American Federation of Labor (AFL)**. The Knights of Labor had boasted an open membership policy and sweeping labor goals, but the AFL catered exclusively to skilled laborers, restricted membership for blacks and women, and focused on smaller-scale, more practical issues: increasing wages, reducing hours, and imposing safety measures. **Samuel Gompers**, the AFL's leader from 1886 to 1924, guided the powerful union's focus and membership growth.

More radical labor organizations also emerged, most notably the **Industrial Workers of the World (IWW)**. Nicknamed the Wobblies, the union was founded in 1905 by **William "Big Bill" Haywood** in Seattle, Washington. Union members were miners, lumberers, and cannery and dock workers. The union also included women, blacks, and immigrants. The Wobblies never grew to more than 30,000 members before fading in influence in the post-war years.

Other Notable Strikes During the Gilded Age

- The railroad strike of 1877 followed the onset of a national economic recession that same year. The B & O and other railroads went on strike to protest wage cuts. Traffic stopped at more than 50,000 miles of railroad. Workers for nearly every rail line struck, provoking widespread violence and requiring federal troops to subdue the angry mobs. President Hayes finally sent in troops to end the strike. The strike prompted many employers to get tough with labor by imposing anti-union policies: They required workers to sign contracts barring them from striking or joining a union. Some employers even hired private detectives to root out labor agitators and private armies to suppress strikes.

- Workers staged the 1892 **Homestead Strike** against the Carnegie Steel Company in Pennsylvania to protest a pay cut and a 70-hour workweek. In 1892, workers went on strike when Henry Clay Frick planned to cut wages, lock out members of the union, and hire scabs in their place. Frick also installed armed guards from the Pinkerton Detective Agency. Three detectives and six workers were killed in a riot. The National Guard was called in to suppress the violence, and the company hired non-union workers to break the strike. The strike continued until November, when the union lost support and gave in to the company. (It would be more than 40 years before steelworkers began to mobilize again.)

- In 1894, in the midst of the economic panic gripping the country, the **Pullman Strike** took place. **Eugene Debs** led thousands of workers in a strike against the Pullman Palace Car Company outside Chicago after wages were slashed by 25 to 40 percent. Railroad traffic was crippled across the western half of the nation as the movement of livestock, goods, and the mail virtually came to a standstill. The courts ruled that the strikers had violated the Sherman Antitrust Act and issued an injunction against them. President Cleveland sent in federal troops to end the strike when the strikers refused to obey the injunction (which claimed that the strike was obstructing the movement of mail). Debs was arrested, strikers were blacklisted, and federal troops marched in. In the ensuing frenzy, 13 died and 53 were injured. The Supreme Court later upheld the use of injunctions against labor unions, giving businesses a powerful new weapon to suppress strikes. (Organized labor began to fade in strength and didn't resurge until the 1930s.)

On Sunday, November 5, 1916, about 300 members of the IWW boarded two boats and headed north from Seattle to Everett. What was to be a planned demonstration for free speech ended up with seven dead and more than 25 wounded. National Guard troops were called in. This "massacre," along with other episodes of violent actions of labor unions across the nation, continued to add to the public perception of violence with labor unions. As a result of the violence and radical ideas, unions would struggle for public, business, and government acceptance until the 1930s.

Between 1880 and 1905, union activity in the United States led to well more than 35,000 strikes. As did the Haymarket riot and others, these demonstrations sometimes erupted in violence, which alienated much of the American public. Popular support for unions plunged, and employers were free to exact severe retribution on striking workers. Scab laborers willing to cross picket lines were hired. Some even agreed to "yellow dog contracts" that stated they would not join a union. Although various strikes were used by unions, they were able to make small inroads in the eyes of the public in advancing the labor cause.

Despite the violence and other problems plaguing the unions, Congress began to be influenced by labor's demands. Congress created the Bureau of Labor in 1884, passed a bill making the first Monday in September a national holiday called **Labor Day**, and created the cabinet Office of Labor in 1903.

Review Exam

Multiple Choice

1. The "Gilded Age" generally refers to the time period when all of the following were true EXCEPT _____.
   a) America experienced a time of great economic growth in the last two decades of the 19th century
   b) population grew in the big cities with people in search of work and as immigrants streamed into the country
   c) the income gap between the rich and the workers greatly widened as the "captains of industry" amassed great amounts of wealth and workers struggled to make a living wage
   d) all serious problems of business regulations were resolved

2. American economic growth was aided by _____.
   a) new inventions and patents
   b) increasing the output of businesses so that the United States would become the leading economic producer of goods by the 1890s
   c) manufacturing, agriculture, and transportation improvements
   d) A, B, and C

3. Horizontal integration in a business involved _____.
   a) broad investments
   b) acquisition of competitors and minimizing competition
   c) the spread of competition between a variety of businesses
   d) agreements between management and employee unions

4. Vertical integration in a business involved controlling _____ in order to produce and market goods while maximizing profits.
   a) resources   c) distribution
   b) manufacturing   d) A, B, and C

5. John D. Rockefeller was a "captain of industry" with his company, Standard Oil, for all of the following reasons EXCEPT _____.
   a) cost-cutting measures to increase revenue
   b) dominating the petroleum industry with his one company controlling 90 percent of the industry
   c) new agreements with labor unions
   d) maintaining tight controls over oil wells, oil refineries, distribution, sales, and advertising

6. As a result of the growth of corporations in the country, _____.
   a) huge amounts of capital were invested and many technological advances were made
   b) labor unions were able to get fair wages for workers
   c) companies where held libel for their actions
   d) wealth was shared equally in the workplace

7. The economic term *laissez-faire* symbolized economics during the Gilded Age, as evidenced by _____.
   a) business leaders wanting a free market economy operating with minimal government interference
   b) the growth of government regulations controlling business practices
   c) regulation markets and controlling competition between businesses
   d) the lack of competition, which drove up prices

8. Andrew Carnegie is often seen as a prime example of the "rags to riches" story in the Gilded Age because he _____.
   a) began as a poor Scottish immigrant and worked his way up through the system

b) became a multi-millionaire due to his hard work and wise investments

c) enhanced his image by becoming involved with several philanthropic endeavors

d) A, B, and C

9. Social Darwinism argued that _____.
   a) competition in the business world was a bad thing
   b) competition among businesses was indeed the best way to promote a healthy economy
   c) the "survival of the fittest" concept would apply to business practices: The strong will survive and the weak will fade away
   d) B and C only

10. The Sherman Antitrust Act of 1890 was significant in that it _____.
    a) gave the government minimal control with business regulations
    a) established a five-year moratorium on business consolidations
    c) was an attempt to regulate business practices that unfairly squeezed out competition by outlawing "every contract or combination in the form of a trust in restraint of trade or commerce"
    d) allowed a level of cooperation between government regulators and business leaders

11. The National Labor Union, Knights of Labor, the IWW, and the American Federation of Labor were _____.
    a) never successful in addressing workers concerns
    b) all working towards achieving better conditions for workers in an often-hostile work environment
    c) not in agreement about the use of strikes to achieve their goals
    d) all in agreement about membership into the unions

12. The Haymarket Square Riot in Chicago in 1886 was the scene of violence when all of the following events occurred EXCEPT _____.
    a) the Knights of Labor held successful negotiations with McCormick Harvester about labor concerns
    b) the strike grew violent when a bomb was thrown into the crowd of 3,000-plus
    c) scab laborers were brought in to replace striking workers
    d) seven policemen were killed and 10 men were indicted for murder (with seven of them being sentenced to death)

13. The major purpose of the formation of labor unions during the Gilded Age was to _____.
   a) combat harsh and often-hazardous working conditions
   b) use strikes, if necessary, as a means of getting concessions from businesses
   c) unite workers in a common organization with a common cause: better benefits for workers (especially the demand for an eight-hour workday)
   d) A, B, and C

14. Strikes and continued incidences of violence in the labor movement _____.
   a) brought about needed changes in the workplace
   b) brought limited changes to workers and their needs in the workplace
   c) weakened the unions in their dealings with companies
   d) succeeded in new laws especially for wages and number of hours worked

15. In response to repeated acts of violence at various strikes across the country, _____.
   a) presidents Hayes and Cleveland ordered in federal troops to break up two railroad strikes
   b) strikers were often arrested, fired from jobs, and replaced with scab workers
   c) Carnegie hired armed guards from the Pinkerton Detective Agency and stationed them in the workplace
   d) A, B, and C

16. _____ became the first billion-dollar corporation formed in American in 1901.
   a) Standard Oil Company   c) McCormick Harvester
   b) U.S. Steel   d) Pullman Palace Car Company

17. As part of the Gospel of Wealth and philanthropic endeavors _____.
   a) Andrew Carnegie donated millions to establish libraries, several universities, and other interests "for the public good"
   b) J. D. Rockefeller donated millions to help found the University of Chicago and the Rockefeller Institute for medical research
   c) Cornelius Vanderbilt responded with the phrase "the public be damned" when a reporter asked him whether railroads should be run for the public benefit (he felt very little public responsibility)
   d) A, B, and C

Matching

a. robber barons

b. Jay Gould

c. combinations

d. William "Big Bill" Haywood

e. J. P. Morgan

f. Cornelius Vanderbilt

g. consolidations

h. Hepburn Act

i. Interstate Commerce Commission

j. Federal Trade Commission

k. wobblies

l. Eugene Debs

m. Labor Day

n. Clayton Antitrust Act

o. Homestead Strike

p. Uriah Stephens

q. William Sylvis

r. Railroad Strike of 1877

s. Samuel Gompers

_____18. loose alliances of enterprises under a large national organization

_____19. made his fortune as a head of an investment house by merging several smaller companies to form large corporations

_____20. the first federal regulatory agency to regulate railroad practices across state lines

_____21. the joining of several companies into one giant corporation and selling stock for profit

_____22. a new holiday created by the federal government in 1903 along with creating a cabinet level office for labor

_____23. established by Congress to enforce antitrust laws

_____24. business leaders who exploited workers and smaller businesses in order to accumulate vast amounts of wealth

_____25. founder of the IWW trade union in 1905 in Seattle, Washington

_____26. made questionable deals to amass his wealth in the railroad industry for purely personal gains

_____27. 1906 government regulation that allowed for the regulation of railroad rates

_____28. used his railroad acquisitions to form the New York Central Railroad system and never used personal wealth for philanthropic endeavors

_____29. nickname of the Industrial Workers of the World (IWW) trade union that was often associated with violence by some of its members

____30. outlawed trusts, price fixing, and agreements to control supply and the price of a product

____31. a major strike involving the B & O railroad and several other railroads upset about wage cuts

____32. leader of the AFL union for nearly 35 years

____33. socialist leader who led the Pullman Strike in 1894

____34. founder of the Knights of Labor union in 1869

____35. involved workers at the Carnegie Steel Company when they protested a cut in pay and increase in working hours

____36. founder of the National Labor Union in 1866

Short Response

37. What was the relationship between business leaders and unions during the Gilded Age?

38. How did "big business" shape the economy during the Gilded Age?

39. How did the concepts of *growth, wealth, and challenges* describe what is known as the Gilded Age in America?

Answers begin on page 282.

America in the Gilded Age: Politics, Innovations, and Growth

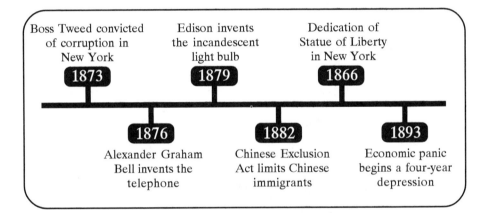

Boss Tweed convicted of corruption in New York — **1873**

Edison invents the incandescent light bulb — **1879**

Dedication of Statue of Liberty in New York — **1866**

1876 — Alexander Graham Bell invents the telephone

1882 — Chinese Exclusion Act limits Chinese immigrants

1893 — Economic panic begins a four-year depression

Trends and Themes of the Era

▶ National politics was dominated by a strong Congress, a perception of "weak" presidents, and the rise of third-party challenges.

▶ Local political parties, or "machines," controlled politics. Politics and politicians were often corrupt, complicit with big business interests.

▶ Technology, in the form of railroads and other innovations, helped drive industrialism, and it became essential to American economic success.

▶ Industrialism attracted rural Americans and European immigrants to U.S. cities. As a result, the United States shifted from an agrarian to an urban society.

▶ Millions of immigrants from Europe, Asia, and Latin America entered the nation during this period as America became a melting pot of people who would dramatically change the cultural climate of America.

Dreams, opportunities, and roadblocks! The Gilded Age challenged the powers of government and big business. The era was a time of tremendous economic growth, population increases in the big cities, rising immigration, and technological innovation. The American Dream of hope and prosperity was symbolized by large cities, bustling businesses, and France's gift of the Statue of Liberty. America's population surged with a dramatic influx of immigrants, and millions were drawn from rural communities and foreign countries with hopes for better jobs and better lives. Yet beneath the thinly layered "gilded" surface loomed challenges to the political and social lives of millions of Americans. Problems of party politics, a rise in nativism, the widening income gap between rich and poor, and the excesses brought on by massive industrialization also emerged. America, the land of opportunity and rags-to-riches stories, would soon face several challenges arising from industrialization.

Lesson 4-1: Politics in an Era of Challenges

Local politics were marked by **machine politics**, so called because the system and the party, rather than individuals, held power. In virtually every region of the United States, local "machines" controlled voter loyalty by distributing political and economic benefits such as offices, jobs, and city contracts. Machines were presided over by party bosses, professional politicians who dominated city government. These bosses usually controlled the jobs of thousands of city workers and influenced the activities of schools, hospitals, and other city-run services. Machine politics thrived on corruption.

William Marcy "Boss" Tweed symbolized political corruption in New York City, and **Tammany Hall** was the Democratic political machine that dominated New York City politics for decades. As chairman of the Tammany general committee, Boss Tweed gained absolute power in the city Democratic Party, controlling nominations and patronage. Votes were openly bought as the corruption continued. The Tweed Ring ran the city without interference and defrauded it by $30 million through padded charges and tax favors. Eventually, Tweed was brought to trial in 1873 on forgery and larceny counts and was given a 12-year prison sentence for his corruption. He served one year and was released. He was then re-arrested on new corruption charges. He escaped from jail, fled to Cuba, and was extradited back to the United States in 1876, and eventually died in jail in New York City.

U.S. Presidents

The presidents of this period were generally weak and pro-business. Late-19th-century politics generated lots of public participation and interest, with 80 percent of eligible voters voting. (However, women were still excluded from voting, and the Supreme Court's 1874 *Minor v. Happersett* ruling stated that the Constitution didn't confer suffrage on women.)

Rarely did either party control the presidency and Congress at the same time. The Republican Party mostly dominated the presidency until the Great Depression in 1932. Congress was the foremost branch of government in the late 19th century with its focus on the budget, cabinet appointments, debate on public issues, and control of legislation. Congress saw its role as establishing policy and the president's role as enforcing policy. Many presidential campaigns waved the "bloody shirt" in an effort to focus on pensions for Civil War veterans, even though the number of veterans was declining and pensions were increasing. Republicans *and* Democrats favored a limited role for the federal government in regulating the economy. The era's economic growth persuaded both parties that limited interference with business was working.

Presidents of the Gilded Age

- **James Garfield**, elected in 1880, was fatally shot four months after taking office.

- **Chester Arthur**, Garfield's vice president, served as president from 1881 to 1885. Congress, spurred on by Arthur's reputation as a corrupt politician and a supporter of machine politics, passed the **Pendleton Act** to create a system based on merit and professional civil service.

- **Grover Cleveland** served as president from 1885 to 1889. He pushed for a reduction in tariffs, and in 1887, he signed the **Interstate Commerce Act** into law.

- **Benjamin Harrison** was president from 1889 to 1893. A pro-business Republican, he supported high protective tariffs and brought about a severe economic depression beginning in 1893 (*The Panic of 1893*).

Grover Cleveland won a second term from 1893 to 1897. He is the only president to have served two terms out of sequence. His second term was dominated by efforts to deal with the economic depression that started in 1893, under Benjamin Harrison.

Lesson 4-2: The Struggles of Farmers

Farmers found themselves on the bottom rungs of the economic ladder after the Civil War. Struggling to pay off mounting debts as land prices rose and crop prices plummeted, farmers demanded help from state and federal governments. When none came, Midwestern farmers banded together in 1867 to form the **Grange**. By 1875, the Grange had more than 800,000 members.

The Grange offered farmers education and fellowship through biweekly social functions, where farmers shared their grievances and discussed agricultural and political reforms. To increase farm profits, Grangers negotiated deals with machinery companies and set up cooperatives and grain storage facilities. They also fought against railroad companies for hiking prices on short-distance shipments and played a big role in the passage of the 1887 Interstate Commerce Act.

By 1880, the Grange had faded and was replaced by the **Farmers' Alliance**. Beginning in Texas in the late 1870s, alliances spread throughout the South and Northwest. By 1890, the alliances embraced a membership of 1.5 million nationwide and proved to be powerful political forces. Alliance-supported candidates did well throughout the Great Plains and the South in the 1890 elections.

The **Colored Farmers' Alliance**, founded in Texas in 1886, was the largest organization of primarily black farmers and agricultural laborers in the late 19th century. It aimed to encourage self-help, promote education, and develop economic cooperation, in addition to organizing boycotts and calling for strikes. By 1891, membership was estimated at 1.2 million. In September 1891, the group organized a cotton pickers strike throughout the South for higher wages that ended with lack of support from black farmers and white violence against the strikers. After the strike, membership in the organization began to decline.

Political Activism: Farmers and Labor Unite

The **Populist Party**, started by members of the Farmers' Alliance, also drew support from urban laborers. The party was founded in St. Louis, Missouri, in 1892, to represent farmers and other workers battling against the well-established interests of railroads, bankers, corporations, and the politicians who supported their interests. At the party's founding convention on July 4th, members adopted the **Omaha Platform** to express their basic beliefs in such issues as government ownership of the railroads and telegraphs, immigration restriction, a graduated income tax, secret ballots, direct election of senators, eight-hour workdays, and free coinage of silver. The platform also supported political reform in the form of initiatives, referendums, and recall elections. Although the platform wasn't adopted then, many of the issues would become the focus of Progressive political reform measures in the following decade.

The Populist Party supported policies that would make debts easier to pay off and raise crop prices. Although the Party's 1892 presidential candidate didn't do well, two governors, several congressmen and senators, and state legislators were elected by the party. The party also began to face opposition from Southern Democrats.

Lesson 4-3: The Panic of 1893

The **Panic of 1893** reflected deep concern not only for farmers and working Americans, but also about the role of the federal government in people's lives. Famine, drought, heat waves, mortgage problems, and low crop prices plagued farmers. What began as a stock market downturn in February 1893 resulted in the market hitting bottom by May 5th on "Industrial Black Friday," leading to the worst economic crisis in the country's history until the Great Depression. Recovery wouldn't kick in until 1897. Several well-known railroads went bankrupt. By midsummer, factories and mines had closed, businesses faced failure, and the unemployment rate had risen to 2 million (15 percent of the workforce). Within a year, the Gross National Product (GNP) dropped and unemployment climbed to 3 million (20 percent of the workforce).

In the midst of the Panic of 1893, Jacob Coxey, a populist businessman from Ohio, proposed a government works program for the unemployed and organized a march to Washington to support his ideas. **Coxey's Army** marched through Ohio and Pennsylvania, and into Maryland, attracting attention and support. (Other armies formed in various parts of the country.) When Coxey reached Washington, D.C., police and soldiers met the crowd of more than 600 marchers and arrested Coxey, beat bystanders, and herded the group into detention camps. Coxey spent 20 days in jail and wasn't allowed to address Congress.

Reaction showed up in the congressional election of 1894, when Democrats suffered the greatest loss of congressional seats in history. President Cleveland was blamed for the country's ills in the midst of the depression. The problems caused a split in the Democratic Party, giving the Populists some marked gains. As a result, it made the Republican Party the majority party in the country. The Republicans also began to promote government action in the lives of ordinary Americans, resulting in a trend that would influence the reforms of the Progressive Era and the Great Depression.

Silver or Gold?

During the Panic unemployment soared, worker strikes spread, and support grew for the Populists. The Populists portrayed Cleveland as a pro-business Republican who neglected the poor, and they began rallying for the next election.

In the 1896 election, the Populists joined with the Democratic Party to support **William Jennings Bryan**. Republicans backed **William McKinley**, who ran on a pro-business platform and supported high protective tariffs. Six years earlier, as a representative in Congress, McKinley had engineered the passage of the **McKinley Tariff** (1890), a protective tariff that raised the price of imports by nearly 50 percent. Tariffs on imported goods provided revenue for the federal government and protected American industry from European competition. High-tariff advocates claimed that tariffs promoted industrial growth, stimulated employment, provided government revenue, and protected the domestic market. Low-tariff advocates contended that tariffs inflated corporate profits, restricted competition, increased consumer prices, violated laissez-faire, and restricted foreign trade.

The silver issue versus the gold standard became the focal point of the 1896 presidential election. The United States had used both silver and gold as its monetary standard, but the Populists raised concerns about the limited use of silver. Populists supported an increase in silver to boost the money supply, in an attempt to help ease the credit burden on farmers. Their biggest push was for free silver coinage at a 16:1 ratio (16 ounces of silver for an ounce of gold, or bimetallism), because they believed that, with both gold and silver backing federal money, the money supply would increase along with mild inflation, helping farmers by making loans easier to pay off. They faced opposition from conservatives who protested unlimited silver coinage. Although Congress passed the Bland-Allison Act, authorizing the government to coin more silver, and the Sherman Silver Purchase Act, requiring the government to buy more silver, it made little difference.

In the 1896 campaign, the Republicans nominated William McKinley, and the Democrats chose William Jennings Bryan. Many wealthy businessmen donated to the Republican Party to keep the Democrats from winning the White House again. During the campaign, Bryan asked in his "Cross of Gold" speech whether the Democratic Party would stand on the side of the struggling masses or the idle holders of capital. To those in support of the gold standard, Bryan replied, "You shall not press down upon the brow of labor the crown of thorns or crucify mankind upon a cross of gold!"

Although Bryan ran on a free silver platform, McKinley won the election. During McKinley's presidency, prosperity began to return. This prosperity, combined with Bryan's defeat, killed the Populist Party and reduced the Democratic Party to its minority position in the South.

Lesson 4-4: Technology and Consumerism

Business and industrialization centered on the cities and transformed the nature of work and the urban growth of the country. By 1900, the population of the country had quadrupled to more than 92 million. More than 15 percent of the population was immigrant, and the population of cities grew sevenfold. In some of the major cities, 30 percent of the population was foreign-born. By 1910, the five biggest U.S. cities were New York City, Chicago, Philadelphia, St. Louis, and Boston.

The big cities were hubs of transportation, investment banking, mills, sweatshops, slaughterhouses, railroad yards, tenements and mansions, department stores, and skyscrapers. These urban areas experienced rapid development;

factory pollution; increases in crime, diseases, slums, poverty, and gang violence; and overcrowded and unsafe living and working conditions.

Cities in the West also began to expand as transportation improvements spawned growth in places including Denver, Los Angeles, San Francisco, and Seattle.

The ever-increasing number of factories created an intense need for labor, encouraging people in rural areas to move to the city and enticing European immigrants to the United States. Many of the new immigrants tended to cluster in certain areas of work in coal mines, steel mills, textile mills, and sweatshops.

America had an abundance of natural resources, a large labor pool, manufacturing opportunities, markets at home and abroad, and an expanding transportation system. As a result, the United States transformed from an agrarian nation to an urban nation, dramatically shifting the demographics of the country.

A Consumer Society Emerges

In the decades following the Civil War, the United States entered an extended period of rapid economic growth, with federal, state, and local government eager to promote the expansion. By the early 20th century, U.S. output equaled that of Great Britain, France, and Germany combined, making America the leading industrial nation in the world.

People across the country took advantage of the new innovations: typewriters, stock tickers, adding machines, Kodak cameras, processed foods from Quaker Oats, Campbell, Heinz, and General Mills, telephones, electric lighting, phonographs, Singer sewing machines, fresh meat from Armour and Swift, beverages from Coca-Cola, and products from the National Biscuit Company (Nabisco). **Alexander Graham Bell** (with his invention of the telephone and establishment of AT&T) and **Thomas Edison** (inventor of the lightbulb, innovator and establishment of General Electric) were two of the men behind the inventions that reshaped the country. Edison alone had nearly 1,100 personal patents on various inventions, and Bell's telephone use spread to more than 10 million phones after the turn of the century. In addition, AT&T and General Electric would see tremendous growth in the next few years.

Not only were products beginning to be aggressively marketed with brand names, but stores began promoting them as well. People shopped at cash-and-carry grocery chain stores such as A&P and Kroger; bought goods at the local Woolworth's; and shopped at Macy's, Bloomingdale, or Marshall Field's for clothing and other items; used the mail-order catalogs of Sears and Roebuck, JC Penney's, and Montgomery Ward to buy virtually anything. The consumer was a new force in American business, and business began to advertise and cater to the whims of the "always right" consumer.

The Development of Urban Life

The growth of U.S. cities helped create new features of urban life, such as **tenements**, narrow four- or five-story buildings with few windows, limited plumbing and electricity, and tiny rooms often packed with people, mostly blacks and immigrants. Tenements were the main housing available in slums and ghettos, the segregated communities into which blacks and immigrants were forced by poverty, prejudice, and even the law. These ghettos fostered disease, high infant mortality, and horrific levels of pollution, and they were often the site of interracial and ethnic strife.

The rise of big cities also created a unique urban culture. As transportation improvements and innovations developed (subways, steel-cable suspension bridges, cable cars, and trolleys), a growing number of workers became commuters, and a middle class of workers emerged. During the 1870s and 1880s, many of the cities' rich inhabitants moved outside the city center to escape the overcrowded conditions. When the more affluent workers began to move to the suburbs, they left behind the working class and the poorer districts of the city, resulting in segregation based on economic standing.

The cities' growth also gave rise to several social developments. The Religious Social Gospel promoted groups such as the YMCA, the YWCA, and the **Salvation Army**, which offered food, clothing, and housing in addition to a religious message to people in need. Beginning in the 1880s, *Ladies Home Journal* and *Good Housekeeping* magazines helped perpetuate the idea of the home as a woman's place, publishing articles and promoted advertising that told wives how to keep a clean, fresh, and orderly house; prepare meals; and perform other housekeeping tasks. Americans began to spend time on national pastimes at the growing number of civic clubs, churches, theaters, ragtime music concerts, dance halls, amusement parks, and sports competitions such as baseball, football, basketball, and boxing. Baseball was quickly becoming the "national pastime" sport.

Lesson 4-5: "Give Me Your Tired, Your Poor..."

Roughly 10 million European immigrants settled in the United States between 1860 and 1890. Nearly all of these **"old" immigrants** were from Northern and Western Europe, the traditional point of origin for European immigrants to the United States. Most of the immigrants in this group had some level of education, were hard-working, skilled laborers, and were mainly Protestants (except for the Irish Catholics who began coming to America after the potato famine in the mid-1840s). They easily assimilated into American society.

Beginning in the 1880s and continuing to 1914, millions of **"new" immigrants** came to the United States: Greeks, Poles, Czechs, Slavs, Armenians, and Jews from Southern and Eastern Europe. In fact, an estimated one-third of all European Jews fled to the United States during this wave of immigration. The immigration rate average around 800,00 annually at the turn of the century, as the decade of 1900–1910 ushered in the greatest number of immigrants (more than 9 million), which was by far the most for any single decade in the nation's history.

Economic problems, religious and political persecution, famine, and lack of jobs forced many people to immigrate to America. Between 1900 and 1914, nearly 9 million immigrants entered the United States, with 70 percent arriving on **Ellis Island**, welcomed by the **Statue of Liberty**. This statue, a gift of France symbolizing freedom and democracy, was formally dedicated on October 28, 1886. On the West Coast, immigrants landed at San Francisco Bay's **Angel Island**. As America adjusted to the influx of immigrants, these newcomers eventually helped transform political, economic, cultural, and social aspects of American life.

The "new" immigrants tended to be illiterate, were mostly Catholics and Jews, spoke a wide variety of different languages, generally lived in close-knit ethnic communities with fellow immigrants, and clung to "old world" traditions and culture. The first generation generally had difficulty assimilating into American society, but the second and third generations found it easier to do so. Most of the "new" European immigrants settled in ethnic communities in the Northeast, dominated by Irish and Italians, and the Midwest, dominated by Germans. The West also experienced an influx of European and Asian immigrants, mostly attracting workers from China and Japan.

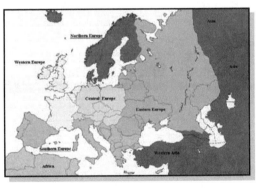

Lured by the prospect of earning money by working on the expanding Western railroad system, many Chinese immigrants settled in California.

Immigrants endured many hardships as they adjusted to their new language, jobs, education, and housing. Often, poor immigrants lived in dirty, crowded conditions and worked unskilled jobs in potentially dangerous factories. (More than 500,000 injuries to workers were reported each year from the 1880s to the 1890s.)

Immigrants, especially "new" immigrants, faced workplace discrimination from native workers who resented their willingness to accept lower wages and work in deplorable conditions. Many immigrants either adapted slowly or refused to adapt to new ways. Some assimilated into American society; others tried to preserve old country traditions by living with other immigrants in ethnic communities, maintaining similar religious practices, printing ethnic newspapers, and sending their children to private schools. However, as the immigrants' children grew up in America, they tended to become more Americanized. Despite the hardships, the immigrants were grateful for the seemingly endless opportunities for them in their new country and helped shape the "melting pot" culture of America.

The swelling wave of immigration engendered a rising nativist response. Many Americans showed their dislike of Chinese and Japanese immigrants, Catholics, Jews, and Southern and Eastern Europeans. In the 1880 presidential election, both major party platforms included anti-immigration measures, and in 1882 Congress passed the **Chinese Exclusion Act**, suspending Chinese laborers from immigrating to the United States, limiting their civil rights, and forbidding them to become naturalized citizens. The new law still allowed family members, students, teachers, tourists, and businessmen to enter the country. The act was renewed in 1892 for another 10 years, and in 1902 Chinese immigration was made permanently illegal.

In 1907, President Theodore Roosevelt negotiated a **Gentleman's Agreement** with the Japanese so that the government of Japan would stop issuing passports to laborers, slowing Japanese immigration to the United States. Nativist sentiment continued to put pressure on immigration, resulting in a 1924 law establishing strict immigration quotas based on countries of national origin aimed at stemming the tide of "new immigrants" from Eastern and Southern Europe. (The new figure allowed 2 percent of the number of immigrants from a particular country using 1880 data as a baseline.)

Review Exam

Multiple Choice

1. Although presidential elections were widely popular, presidents during this time period were generally characterized as _____.
   a) weak, as Congress took the lead in establishing policies
   b) pro-business, favoring a limited role of government regulating the economy
   c) mainly Republican, but working often with a Democratic Congress
   d) A, B, and C

2. Machine politics under the control of the Tweed Ring in New York _____.
   a) controlled Republican candidates on the ballots
   b) ran the city of New York with its form of corrupt politics
   c) made it illegal to "buy" votes
   d) had minimal influence with elected candidates

3. Department stores and chain stores were responsible for _____.
   a) using advertising to market name-brand items to consumers
   b) using their own names as a major selling point (Woolworth, Sears, Marshall Fields, and so on)
   c) increasing consumer loyalty by catering to the whims of the customer
   d) A, B, and C

4. Coxey's Army march in Washington, D.C., in 1893 proposed a government works program _____.
   a) for job assistance for unemployed during the depression
   b) that landed Jacob Coxey in jail for his actions
   c) that was met with armed resistance when the marchers reached Washington, D.C.
   d) A, B, and C

5. The _____ Party was aimed at representing the interests of farmers and other workers battling against big business interests.
   a) Republican   c) Democratic
   b) Populist   d) Know-Nothing

6. Right after winning the presidential election in 1892, President Cleveland _____.
   a) reached out for support from his opponents, especially the Populists
   b) switched political parties
   c) was faced with the economic challenges of a severe economic depression that would last for the remainder of his term in office
   d) pursued an agenda of compromise with the Republicans in Congress

7. After the Panic of 1893 began, _____.
   a) numerous business failed, as mines and banks were forced to close
   b) unemployment dramatically increased
   c) several railroads were forced into bankruptcy
   d) A, B, and C

8. The McKinley Tariff (1890) was significant for all of the following reasons EXCEPT that it _____.
   a) was a progressive tariff aimed at gradual increases in the tariff rate
   b) was a protective tariff that raised the price of imports by nearly 50 percent
   c) sought to protect American businesses from foreign competition
   d) sought to promote industrial growth that would stimulate unemployment and provide government revenue

9. The Sherman Antitrust Act of 1890 was signed into law by President _____.
   a) Arthur
   b) Garfield
   c) Harrison
   d) Cleveland

10. When the Populists and the Democrats pushed for their main platform of increased silver coinage to increase the money supply, _____.
    a) they faced opposition from conservatives who opposed this policy
    b) they appealed to the demands of the farmers and laborers
    c) the Republican Party capitalized on their opponents' goals by gaining support from business leaders who did not want the Democrats to win
    d) A, B, and C

11. All of the following are true of big cities and growth in the late 1800s EXCEPT that _____.
    a) they were hubs of transportation, slaughterhouses, sweatshops, and tenements
    b) pollution and overcrowding were not major concerns
    c) crime, disease, and poverty were becoming concerns
    d) New York, Chicago, Philadelphia, St. Louis, and Boston became the country's largest cities

12. A consumer society began to emerge during the Gilded Age with the development of _____.
    a) Kodak cameras
    b) processed foods from Quaker, Heinz, Campbell's, and General Mills
    c) stores and mail-order catalogs from Sears, Montgomery Ward, and JC Penney's
    d) A, B, and C

13. _____ was widely popular, becoming the "national pastime" sport, by the turn of the century.
    a) Baseball
    b) Football
    c) Boxing
    d) Basketball

14. Old immigrants tended to have all of the following characteristics EXCEPT that they tended to _____.
    a) immigrate primarily from Northern and Western Europe
    b) not assimilate easily into American society
    c) have a degree of education and some job skills
    d) be Protestant (except for the Irish Catholics, who began immigrating to America in the 1840s)

15. New immigrants tended to _____.
    a) migrate primarily from Southern and Eastern Europe in large numbers
    b) make up the largest segment of immigrants entering the United States from the 1890s until World War I
    c) have minimal education and job skills, and be of Catholic, Jewish, or Greek Orthodox religion
    d) A, B, and C

16. The Chinese Exclusion Act (1882) _____.
    a) also included Japanese immigrants
    b) limited immigration for a 10-year period
    c) was the first major legislation aimed at restricting immigration to a specific group of people attempting to immigrate to the United States
    d) allowed only Chinese immigrants to enter the country with guest labor permits

Matching

a. Tammany Hall
b. Alexander Graham Bell
c. Minor v. Happersett (1874)
d. Ellis Island
e. nativism
f. Salvation Army
g. Thomas Edison
h. Colored Farmer's Alliance
i. Statue of Liberty
j. Nabisco
k. Farmer's Alliance
l. Angel Island
m. tenements
n. Gentlemen's Agreement
o. "gilded"
p. Boss Tweed
q. quota
r. Omaha Platform
s. machine politics

_____17. symbolized political corruption in New York City with his control over the Democratic Party and elections in the city

_____18. the concept of Americans actually "born" in America, as opposed to immigrants who sought to become American citizens through naturalization

_____19. inventor of the light bulb and other innovations

_____20. a corporation known as the National Biscuit Company that produced processed foods

_____21. major destination and port of entry for the majority of new immigrants during this period

_____22. ruling that stated that the Constitution did not confer suffrage on women (and helped in the argument to deny them the vote)

_____23. one of the Social Gospel groups that offered food, clothing, and housing, and a religious message to people in need

____24. inventor of the telephone; helped establish AT&T

____25. the Democratic political machine in New York run by Boss Tweed

____26. adopted by the Populist Party in 1892 that included party platforms favoring government ownership of railroads, immigration restriction, a graduated income tax, an eight-hour workday, and the free coinage of silver

____27. major port of entry in San Francisco for immigrants entering the country on the West Coast

____28. largest organization of black farmers and agricultural laborers that aimed for self help, education, and economic concerns for black farmers

____29. the 1907 agreement limiting Japanese immigration into the U.S.

____30. the 1924 Immigration Act established this measure aimed at severely limiting immigrants from Southern and Eastern Europe

____31. replaced the Grange with its political alliances aimed at helping farmers and founded the Populist Party

____32. a system of control of city politics presided over by party bosses and characterized by corruption

____33. narrow four- or five-story apartment buildings with few windows, with limited plumbing and electricity, and often the place of overcrowded living conditions by poor inner-city immigrants

____34. gift from France symbolizing freedom and democracy

____35. a term that means marked by a thinly layered surface, often of gold; this thin covering often disguised things right below the surface and came to describe the era in U.S. history in the last three decades of the 19th century

Short Response

36. How was the political landscape of the country beginning to change from 1865 to 1900?

37. To what extent was America being changed by consumerism in the late 19th century?

38. How did immigration impact the social, political, and economic life of America from 1880 to 1914 with reference to the *dreams, opportunities, and roadblocks* that were evidenced during the Gilded Age?

Answers begin on page 284.

The Age of Imperialism: The United States on the World Stage

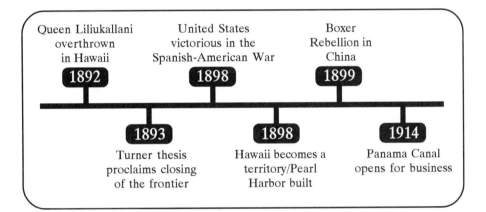

Queen Liliukallani overthrown in Hawaii — 1892

United States victorious in the Spanish-American War — 1898

Boxer Rebellion in China — 1899

1893 — Turner thesis proclaims closing of the frontier

1898 — Hawaii becomes a territory/Pearl Harbor built

1914 — Panama Canal opens for business

Trends and Themes of the Era

▶ American industrialization created a need for foreign markets in which to sell manufactured goods and from which to buy raw materials.

▶ Early efforts to find foreign markets involved economic expansionism, which focused on opening markets through investment rather than military involvement. Under President McKinley, near the end of the 19th century, the United States wanted to increase its exposure to foreign markets and shifted to a more militaristic and imperialist policy.

▶ Victory in the Spanish-American War not only gave the United States an empire, but it also marked the ascendance of the United States as a world power.

Expansion, growth, and power! In the late 19th century and beginning with the 20th century, the United States altered its focus on foreign affairs—not only restructuring its relationships with overseas nations, but insisting on its right to trade around the globe. Many Americans also wanted to reach beyond the U.S. borders and invest in other regions. Advances in communication and transportation helped inspire Americans to establish a dominant presence overseas. In September 1899, President McKinley stated, "We have become a world power." This transformation, however, was not without problems and questions about American involvement in foreign lands. Humanitarian efforts, national security, and economic competition were the driving forces behind overseas involvement. As America achieved greater wealth and power, it became increasingly entangled in world affairs that would have serious implications in the 20th century.

Lesson 5-1: Visions of Empire

In the 1860s through the 1880s, the United States focused primarily on domestic issues. Apart from acquiring Alaska from Russia in 1867, and gaining the uninhabited Midway Islands as a refueling station that same year, the United States paid little attention to foreign expansion.

But as the American factory system developed and industrial output soared, the nation began to look abroad with new interest. As a rising industrial power, the United States needed to find foreign markets where it could sell its manufactured products and farm produce, and acquire raw goods. Between 1870 and 1900, U.S. exports expanded, and businesses and owners such as Singer, Standard Oil, Kodak, Ford, McCormick, Edison, and Bell saw the advantages of foreign markets.

The initial U.S. policy was one of expansionism rather than **imperialism**. Instead of imposing a military presence and a colonial government, as many European countries were doing in Africa and throughout the globe, the United States tried to advance its interests through investments and business transactions. American businesses began opening up production sites and markets in Latin America and other regions. **Josiah Strong**'s theory of the White Man's Burden in Our Country argued that because the United States was the most economically advanced, most Christian nation in the world, it should play a providential role in imperialism abroad. Senator **Albert Beveridge** added that because America was a chosen country that should lead in the rest of the world's regeneration, it would be wrong to ignore that duty. It was up to the United States to establish trading posts and build its navy to greatness. Beveridge also proclaimed: "American law, American civilization, and the American flag will plant themselves on distant shores, and by doing so we would confer our immense benefits on the less fortunate around the world."

This new focus on foreign affairs had long-term implications throughout the 20th century. In the late 1890s God, gold, and glory justified an American empire, as European powers continued colonizing throughout the world.

In 1893, historian **Fredrick Jackson Turner** issued his infamous "Turner Thesis" stating that if the frontier were closed, where would America go from there? America had been built on rugged individualism, egalitarianism, and a democratic faith, and it needed more land to keep up with other countries.

In this new realm of manifest destiny, the United States struggled to reconcile imperialism with democracy. To help accomplish the goal of supremacy, **Alfred Mahan** urged the United States to rebuild its navy and establish a naval training school in Newport, Rhode Island. Later, President Teddy Roosevelt sent the "great white fleet" on a world tour in 1908. Mahan urged Americans to turn their "eyes outward instead of inward only, to seek the welfare of the country," and that "fate has written our policy for us—the trade of the world must and shall be ours as we establish trading posts throughout the world."

Lesson 5-2: Clash of Imperialists and Anti-Imperialists

McKinley was extremely pro-business and, instead of simply developing markets abroad, he supported military intervention and U.S. acquisition of foreign lands. Senator **Henry Cabot Lodge** and Assistant Secretary of the Navy Teddy Roosevelt ("I welcome any war; I want my medal") were among the most outspoken supporters of this aggressive foreign policy. They were nicknamed **"jingoes"** because of their willingness to fight at the drop of a hat.

Not all Americans, however, supported American imperialism. In November 1898, a group of Americans formed an organization known as the **Anti-Imperialist League**. The league had many well-known members, including Mark Twain, William Jennings Bryan, Andrew Carnegie, Samuel Gompers, and Grover Cleveland. The group opposed American expansion and foreign involvement on the grounds that the United States had no right to force its will on others, and also because such involvement would likely incite further conflict. They questioned the United States' right to acquire colonies in particular, arguing that America would end up behaving exactly as Great Britain had with its colonies. The group also criticized the subjugation of others, saying it violated principles of self-government. Still others questioned whether or not dark-skinned people were worthy of U.S. citizenship.

Lesson 5-3: The Spanish-American War

Nationalist rebels in Cuba had been resisting Spanish rule since 1895. The United States was now developing a vested economic interest in Cuba, especially in sugar plantations, and Spain was threatening those interests. America became increasingly sympathetic to the rebels' cause, primarily because of sensationalist news reports about Spanish brutality that portrayed Governor-General Weyler as a butcher. General Weyler was accused of cruel measures that resulted in the deaths of thousands of Cubans as they were placed in relocation areas without adequate food and shelter. New York newspapers, especially the *New York Journal*, owned by **William Randolph Hearst**, and the *New York World*,owned by **Joseph Pulitzer**, exaggerated the atrocities committed by the Spanish military against the rebels. These inflammatory journalistic practices, called **yellow journalism**, persuaded the public to side with the rebels and to call for government action against Spain.

On February 9, 1898, the *New York Journal* published the de Lome letter, in which the Spanish minister to Washington downplayed Spain's promise for reform in Cuba and then accused President McKinley of being a "would-be politician and a bidder for the admiration of the crowd!" The public was outraged by the comments and became further outraged by the report of the explosion rocking the hull and sinking the *USS Maine* in the Havana harbor on February 15, 1898. The cause of the explosion was unknown, but the Spaniards were blamed for the deaths of 266 Americans. The news was an instant media event, with the battle cry "Remember the Maine—to hell with Spain!"

McKinley sent a war message to Congress on April 11th asking Congress for a "forceful intervention" for events in Cuba by stating, "In the name of humanity, in the name of civilization, on behalf of endangered American interests...." Congress followed with its declaration on April 25th after debate and the addition of the **Teller Amendment**, which stated that the United States wasn't out to annex Cuba but instead to free the country from Spanish control.

At the outset of the war, the United States was ill prepared. Troop strength had shrunk from more than 200,000 at the end of the Civil War to just more than 28,000. Most of the new troops had outdated uniforms and weapons, and lacked adequate supplies. During the war, tropical diseases and rotten rations killed and sickened more troops than were actually injured in battle. The war lasted only 112 days but resulted in more than 5,500 deaths among soldiers (only 379 died in battle).

The Spanish-American War was short-lived. The United States easily crushed the Spanish forces. The war's naval battles included a May 1st conflict in the Philippines in which **Commodore George Dewey** crushed the Spanish fleet by destroying or capturing all 10 Spanish ships at anchor. On May 19th, the United States blockaded the remaining Spanish naval vessels in Cuba's Santiago Harbor. After five weeks, on July 3rd, Spain made a dash for the sea, and all seven Spanish ships were sunk. Spain's navy was now destroyed.

In early June, the Marines helped capture the harbor at Guantanamo Bay. The war's only major land battle was the U.S. capture of San Juan Hill in Cuba. Theodore Roosevelt, who headed the volunteer **Rough Riders** unit, led the attack. The makeup of eager men in this fighting unit included cowboys, clerks, NYC policemen, musicians, Texas Rangers, polo players, yachtsmen, and graduates of Harvard, Yale, and Princeton. On July 1st, more than 7,000 troops stormed up San Juan Hill and nearby Kettle Hill, assisted by the "smoked Yankees" (the nickname the Spanish troops gave to them) of the **Ninth** and **10th Cavalry** and the **24th** and **25th Colored Infantry** units. America's easy victory in the "splendid little war" ended with Spain's surrender on July 17th. The war established the United States as a significant presence on the world stage.

The **Treaty of Paris (1898)** formally ended the war in December, although Cuba and the Philippines weren't invited to the peace talks. Cuba achieved independence, and Spain ceded the Philippines, Guam, and Puerto Rico to the United States for a payment of $20 million. America's decisive war victory, coupled with the nation's economic prosperity, bolstered the popularity of the Republican Party and led to an overwhelming reelection win for McKinley in 1900. (Teddy Roosevelt was on the Republican ticket as vice president). The victory also encouraged the government to further demonstrate American strength abroad.

No one knew that anarchist Leon Czolgosz assassin's bullet would end McKinley's life in September 1901 and catapult Roosevelt into the presidency. Roosevelt would use his two terms in office to dramatically shape the office of the presidency in the 20th century.

Lesson 5-4: Sugar, Pineapples, and Pearl Harbor

U.S. missionaries had gone to Hawaii in the 1820s and, within a few short years, U.S. interests dominated the economy. By 1875, Hawaiian sugar cane entered the U.S. duty-free, making the islands' sugar cane industry dependent on the U.S. market for trade. In 1892, **Queen Liliuokalani** became the new leader in Hawaii and decided to eliminate American influence in her government. Within the next year, the U.S. minister to Hawaii, Sanford Dole, deployed marines to protect "American interests" and helped to overthrow the queen to create a government sympathetic to U.S. interests. Part of the acquisition of Ha-

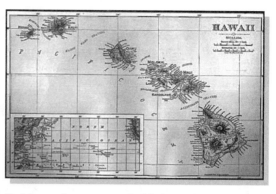

waii was seen as a way to get relief from the extremely high tariff rates of the recent McKinley Tariff of 1890.

President McKinley proclaimed in 1897, "We need Hawaii—it is manifest destiny," and that same year the United States built a coaling and repair station at **Pearl Harbor** on the island of Oahu. A year later, on August 12, 1898, Hawaii became an official U.S. territory (without the consent of the local Hawaiians). The United States built a naval base at Pearl Harbor.

Lesson 5-5: Legacy of Victory: Cuba and the Philippines

Victory in the Spanish-American War left the United States with new decisions to make. By the end of 1898, the country had acquired a number of new island territories: Guam, Puerto Rico, and the Philippines. In establishing U.S. governing policies abroad, Congress faced two pressing questions: how to grant Cuban independence in a way that would also protect American interests on the island, and whether to annex the Philippines or grant the small country independence.

Cuba

In 1901, the **Platt Amendment** listed the conditions for the U.S. Army's withdrawal from Cuban soil. After the withdrawal, Cuba wouldn't be allowed to sign any foreign treaties or limit its independence, and the United States reserved the right to intervene in Cuba when it saw fit. The United States also gained the right to maintain a naval base at **Guantanamo Bay**.

Unrest in the Philippines

Looming over the Senate was the question of what to do with the Philippines. Business interests claimed that the Philippines was a necessary stepping stone for increased trade with Asia. Booker T. Washington, however, stated that the United States needed to deal with racial problems at home before it took on social issues elsewhere.

The Senate ultimately voted to annex the country rather than give it independence. Filipino rebels resisted U.S. rule by attacking the U.S. base of operations and setting off a three-year guerrilla war that cost the lives of 5,000 Americans, 25,000 rebel soldiers, and 200,000 civilians. The fighting finally ended with a U.S. victory. In 1902, the agreement ending the conflict provided for Congress to appoint a Filipino governor general, and the Filipinos would elect an assembly. The eventual goal was a timetable for self-government by 1933. It finally became a reality when the United States granted the Philippines its independence on July 4, 1946.

Lesson 5-6: Opening Doors in China

The U.S. government also aimed to promote U.S. business and open trade markets in China. China's Manchu Dynasty was weak and particularly vulnerable to foreign intervention, as evidenced by the spheres of influence that other nations—Russia, Germany, France, England, and Japan—had succeeded in carving out. Each of these nations had secured exclusive trading rights to certain key ports in China so that entire regions, or spheres, were blocked to U.S. business.

In 1899, as a way to open up all "exclusive" ports to American business, Secretary of State **John Hay** proclaimed an **Open Door Policy** in China, which meant that no favoritism would be awarded at Chinese ports. The United States had most favored nation status but no sphere of influence; its policy was directed at the interests of American businessmen who wanted to be part of the lucrative trade with China. European countries, however, refused to endorse the U.S. policy. In the following years, Hay continued working to secure advantages for U.S. firms as part of his policy of economic expansionism, which sought not to control new territory but to open new markets for trade.

The heavy influence exerted in China by European nations and the United States angered many Chinese. That anger exploded in 1899 in the **Boxer Rebellion**. During the revolt, an anti-foreign secret society calling itself the Harmonious Righteous Fists, known as the Boxers to Westerners, promoted "death to the foreign devils" and killed thousands of foreigners and Chinese Christians. In 1900, the

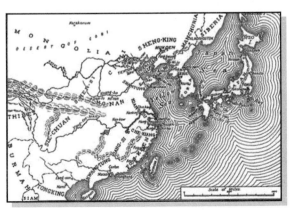

Boxers captured Beijing (Peking), and the United States then sent 2,500 troops as part of an international force that marched on Beijing and drove out the Boxers. By helping to dispel the Boxer threat, the United States gained bargaining power in the settlement that followed. Hay demanded that an Open Door Policy be implemented in all of China, and other powers agreed. The Boxer Rebellion further weakened the Chinese government. After the uprising ended, the U.S. government committed itself to propping up China's government in the interests of maintaining open markets for itself in Asia.

Lesson 5-7: The Big Ditch

The United States had been looking for a shortcut from the Atlantic to the Pacific, so it took notice in 1879 when the French got a 25-year concession from Colombia to build across the Isthmus of Panama (part of Colombia at the time). Corruption, mismanagement, yellow fever, and malaria halted the project after 10 years and more than $400 million in accumulated debt. The French then declared bankruptcy and offered to lease the project to the United States.

In 1902, Congress urged President Teddy Roosevelt to accept and to negotiate the deal with Colombia. Colombia's rejection of the U.S. offer in 1903 (holding out for an additional $25 million in cash) set off a string of events that drew the United States into the region.

Earlier in 1903, the Senate ratified the Hay Treaty. Columbia delayed its ratification of the treaty, hoping to get the United States to increase the price offered for the canal rights. Columbia rejected the treaty over dissatisfaction with the financial terms, the loss of national sovereignty, and a growing fear of "Yankee imperialism." When the staged Panamanian Revolution occurred on November 3, 1903, the *U.S.S. Nashville*, stationed off the coast of Panama, "urged" Columbia not to interfere. Philippe Varilla appointed himself U.S. ambassador, and two days later the United States recognized the "new" country.

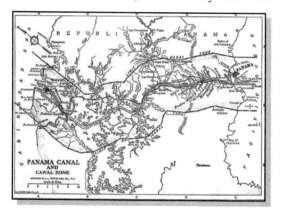

PANAMA CANAL AND CANAL ZONE

Within the next two weeks, the new Panamanian government signed the **Hay-Bunau-Varilla Treaty** (1903), which provided the United States with a 99-year lease for a 10-mile-wide strip of land for the canal in exchange for a one-time $10 million payment to Panama and an annual payment of $250,000.

The United States also agreed to guarantee the independence of Panama. Roosevelt boldly proclaimed, "I took the canal!" The final cost in building the canal exceeded $350 million and included a loss of more than 6,000 workers. When the canal was completed in 1914, it created a shortcut for trade and travel between the Atlantic and Pacific oceans.

In his annual message to Congress at the end of 1904, President Roosevelt proposed a new policy in the U.S. involvement in Latin America that became known as the **Roosevelt Corollary**. It was seen as an extension of the earlier policy of the Monroe Doctrine in 1823. The earlier policy aimed at keeping European nations from interfering in Latin American affairs. Now, the new policy stated the right of the United States to intervene in Latin America as a "policeman" of the region. The policy had public support and was a justification for further imperialistic measures. In the following years, as the United States intervened in Latin American affairs, those nations would view the United States with marked levels of suspicion and distrust.

Lesson 5-8: In Limbo

The last remaining question to be resolved from the Spanish-American War was what to do with Puerto Rico. Could the Puerto Ricans govern themselves after the acquisition from Spain? Although Luis Munoz led a campaign for Puerto Rican self-government, not all wanted independence. Some wanted statehood. The United States made no promises about independence after the war, but it did promise, "We are here to bring you protection to yourselves and your property, to promote prosperity, and to bestow upon you the blessings of our government."

Many in Congress saw Puerto Rico as essential to the U.S. strategy in the Caribbean. In 1900, Congress passed the **Foraker Act**, making Puerto Rico an unincorporated U.S. territory and initially denying U.S citizenship to Puerto Ricans. In addition, no promise of statehood was made. The United States appointed the governor and members of the legislature's upper house.

In a series of landmark decisions that became known as the *Insular Cases*, the Supreme Court ruled in 1901 "that the Constitution did not automatically apply to people in acquired territories" and upheld the right of Congress to establish an inferior status for Puerto Rico as an unincorporated territory without

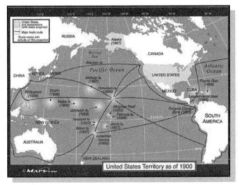

United States Territory as of 1900

promise of statehood. Congress retained the right to grant citizenship, which it did in 1917, along with allowing Puerto Rico the right to freely elect both legislative houses. Puerto Rico became a commonwealth in 1952.

Review Exam

Multiple Choice

1. Josiah Strong's work in *Our Country* promoted the idea of the "White Man's Burden" in all of the following EXCEPT _____.
   a) for religious reasons (to spread Christianity to other nations)
   b) for economic reasons (because of the economic strength of the United States)
   c) that the United States should pursue a limited role in world imperialism to let European nations continue to take the lead
   d) that the United states should take a leading role in world imperialism

2. _____ was not associated with the "jingoes," those wanting to go to war for imperialistic means.
   a) Teddy Roosevelt, Assistant Secretary to the Navy
   b) Senator Henry Cabot Lodge
   c) Andrew Carnegie
   d) President McKinley

3. All of the following EXCEPT _____ were called anti-imperialists who spoke out against U.S. foreign involvement on the grounds that the United States had no right to force its will on other countries.
   a) Mark Twain
   b) William Jennings Bryan
   c) Samuel Gompers
   d) Teddy Roosevelt (before becoming a Rough Rider)

4. "Yellow journalism" was a concept that came to describe _____.
   a) inflamatory news articles
   c) military news
   b) weak news stories
   d) truth in published reports

5. All of the following statements about the Spanish American War in 1898 are true EXCEPT that _____.
   a) more Americans died from diseases rather than bullet casualties
   b) "Buffalo Soldiers" served in a desegregated army for the first time
   c) public opinion greatly supported the war, according to media reports
   d) American troops were not adequately prepared or trained for battle

6. The _____ took place first in 1898.
   a) attack of the navy under Dewey's command in the Philippines
   b) attack on the *USS Maine*
   c) attack of the Rough Riders on San Juan Hill
   d) naval battle in Santiago, Cuba

7. As a result of the Treaty of Paris (1898) the United States acquired control over the following regions EXCEPT _____.
   a) Hawaii   c) Puerto Rico
   b) the Philippines   d) Guam

8. Hawaii became important for U.S. interests _____.
   a) because many Hawaiian favored the possibility of statehood
   b) for its location as a fueling and repair station for U.S. ships
   c) because it might put an end to anti-imperialist arguments in Congress
   d) when war with Cuba was imminent in 1898

9. Under the agreements stated in the Platt Amendment with Cuba in 1901 _____.
   a) the United States maintained the right to establish a naval base at Guantanamo Bay
   b) Cuba would not be allowed to sign any foreign treaties
   c) the United States would withdraw its troops from Cuba
   d) A, B, and C

10. The Open Door Policy with China negotiated by Secretary of State John Hay stated that _____.
   a) Chinese markets would be open to trade with the United States as a favored trading partner
   b) China could continue to show favoritism in opening ports to various countries interested in trade with China
   c) a five-year moratorium would be placed on opening new ports to European nations trading with China
   d) the United States sought to acquire territory for expansion in China

11. The Roosevelt Corollary was significant because it _____.
   a) provided low-interest loans and other economic support to developing nations
   b) attempted to make the United States the "policeman" of the Western Hemisphere

  c) attempted to prevent any foreign influences from exerting control in affairs of nations in the Western Hemisphere

  d) B and C only

12. All of the following were reasons for the United States to go to war against Spain in 1898 EXCEPT the _____.

  a) sinking of the *USS Maine* of the coast of Havana, Cuba, with the new battle cry "Remember the Maine—to hell with Spain!"

  b) attack by insurgents on San Juan Hill

  c) de Lome letter accusing President McKinley of being a "would-be politician"

  d) brutal policies of Wyler in Cuba

13. One of the main reasons business leaders and members of Congress sought to pursue a policy of expansionism in the latter years of the 19th century was _____.

  a) the U.S. need to seek new markets for its goods in order to expand businesses abroad

  b) the need to encourage immigration for a cheap labor source for businesses in the big cities

  c) America's need to catch up to the expansionist efforts of European nations

  d) businesses' need to compete against cheap imports

14. The construction of the Panama Canal was significant _____.

  a) in creating a shortcut for trade and travel between the two oceans

  b) because it gave the United States another "presence" in Latin America

  c) because it added to the image of Teddy Roosevelt with his claim of "I took the canal"

  d) A, B, and C

15. After the end of the civil war, an unrest in the Philippines in 1902 _____.

  a) set in process the procedure for the Philippines to apply for statehood

  b) set in process a timetable for self government over a period of 50 years

  c) set in process a timetable for self government by 1933 but did not actually happen until July 4, 1946

  d) made the Philippines a commonwealth

16. According to President McKinley in his war address to Congress, the main reason for the U.S. going to war against Spain was _____.

  a) on behalf of endangered American interests

b) purely revenge for the sinking of the *USS Maine*

c) to remove Weyler from power in Cuba

d) to gain more territory as an expansion of "Manifest Destiny"

17. The Supreme Court ruling in 1901 in the Insular Cases was significant in that it _____.

a) made people in acquired territory eligible for eventual citizenship

b) made the promise of statehood for newly acquired territories, including Puerto Rico, and limited immigration for a 10-year period

c) stated that the Constitution did not necessarily apply to people in acquired territories

d) allowed Puerto Rico but not the Philippines the right to apply for statehood

Matching

a. Rough Riders

b. Frederick Jackson Turner

c. Joseph Pulitzer

d. President McKinley

e. Alaska

f. Boxer Rebellion

g. Governor-General Weyler

h. Anti-Imperialist League

i. Alfred Mahan

j. 9th and 10th Calvary

k. imperialism

l. Commodore George Dewey

m. Teller Amendment

n. Hay Treaty (1903)

o. Philippe Varilla

p. Teddy Roosevelt

q. William Randolph Hearst

r. Queen Liliuokalani

s. Pearl Harbor

t. Foraker Act

u. Senator Albert Beveridge

_____18. land purchased from the Russians by the U.S. in 1867

_____19. owner of the newspaper *New York World* that published widely popular reports about the Spanish American War in 1898 and competed against the *New York Journal* for news and circulation

_____20. the army group of volunteers headed by Teddy Roosevelt who fought at the famous battle of San Juan Hill in the Spanish American War

_____21. the concept of imposing a military presence and a colonial government in a foreign country

_____22. Spanish leader in Cuba who was portrayed as a "butcher" in the American press

_____23. Buffalo soldier units that greatly aided Teddy Roosevelt and the Rough Riders in their victory on San Juan Hill

_____24. his thesis on the closing of the frontier spurred U.S. imperialistic efforts in the 1890s

_____25. a revolt in China in 1899 that attempted to get rid of foreign investors and Chinese Christians

_____26. promoted the concept of U.S. imperialism by stating that the United States should establish trading posts and build its navy to greatness in order to take the lead in world imperialism

_____27. leader of Hawaii who was overthrown by U.S. forces in 1893

_____28. owner of the newspaper the *New York Journal* that published widely popular reports about the Spanish American War in 1898 and competed against the *New York World* for news and circulation

_____29. opposed American expansion and foreign involvement on the grounds that it would illicit further conflict

_____30. played the role of Rough Rider, governor of New York, vice president, and president

_____31. location where a U.S. naval base in 1898

_____32. proposed that, in the Spanish American War in 1898, the United States was not out to annex Cuba but rather to free Cuba from Spanish control

_____33. urged the United Sates to rebuild its navy to aid in imperialism and the spread of democracy

_____34. led the Americans to victory in a naval battle in Manila Bay in the Philippines in May 1898

_____35. self-appointed U.S. ambassador from Panama after the "staged" Panama revolt in 1903

_____36. assassinated by anarchist Leon Czolgosz in 1901

_____37. provided the United States with a 99-year lease to construct a canal across Panama

_____38. made Puerto Rico an unincorporated U.S. territory with no promise of statehood

Short Response

39. What factors, old and new, shaped U.S. foreign policy in the late 19th century?

40. What were the major challenges faced by the United States as it became an imperialistic nation?

41. How did the concepts of **expansion, growth, and power** describe American foreign policy from the 1890s until 1914?

Answers begin on page 286.

The Progressive Era

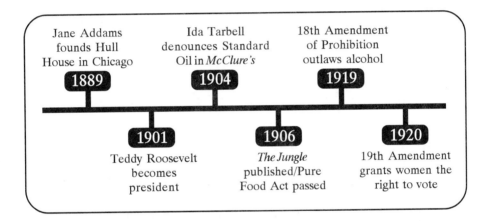

Jane Addams founds Hull House in Chicago	Ida Tarbell denounces Standard Oil in *McClure's*	18th Amendment of Prohibition outlaws alcohol
1889	**1904**	**1919**

1901	**1906**	**1920**
Teddy Roosevelt becomes president	*The Jungle* published/Pure Food Act passed	19th Amendment grants women the right to vote

Trends and Themes of the Era

▶ The backlash against the excesses and corruption of the Gilded Age led to a fervor for reform. Reform stretched across economic, environmental, social, and racial lines.

▶ Through the first half of the Progressive Era, the United States continued to assert its power internationally through military and economic means, especially in the Western Hemisphere. Wilson started to shift this aggressive interventionist policy to a more idealistic one.

▶ The outbreak of World War I interrupted the agenda of the progressive reformers.

Reform, remake, and revolutionize! "We've stumbled along for awhile, trying to run a new civilization in old ways, but we've got to start to make this world over," stated Thomas Edison. Americans were living in an era that had been preceded by great changes in transportation, communication, and business growth. Now, the challenge lay in adapting to the changes. Many Americans had come to believe that responsible citizens acting together, assisted by technical know-how and government power, could achieve social progress. Political agitators demanded changes and promoted new ideas: business regulation, moral revival, consumer protection, conservation of natural resources, educational improvement, and tax reform. Four amendments to the Constitution were adopted during this time, and the president assumed more of a political activist role. Reformers organized during this period to promote social change that would curb the ill effects of the urban industrialized society of the late 19th century. The period's optimism clouded over as the United States eventually became embroiled in a major world war that would change the country's focus.

Lesson 6-1: The Need for Change: Social, Political, and Economic

Teddy Roosevelt's assumption of the presidency in 1901 coincided with the beginning of the **Progressive Era**, which lasted roughly until the end of World War I. These years were marked by progressivism, a fervent reform impulse in America that promoted social justice and democracy. Progressives represented a diverse base: men and women; Republicans, Democrats, and Socialists; farmers, laborers, small-business owners, and many of America's elite, including esteemed authors, philosophers, and statesmen. Progressives saw themselves as enhancing the welfare of the entire nation. The movement arose partly in response to the down side of industrialization during the Gilded Age: urban poverty, ruthless business policies, exploitation of workers, and resource overuse. Progressives called for far-reaching reform in politics, business, poverty relief, and conservation with the assistance of local, state, and federal government actions.

Lesson 6-2: Urban Renewal

Reformers created more than 400 settlement houses that served as community centers in urban immigrant neighborhoods. In 1889, **Hull House**, founded in Chicago by **Jane Addams**, opened. Hull House not only served the immigrant families in the neighborhood, but also served as a model for other settlement houses. The settlement houses focused on organizing kindergartens and nurseries, teaching English classes, and offering lessons in cooking, hygiene, and other skills. It was all done with the goal of helping immigrant families adjust to life in America and rise above the poverty so prevalent in immigrant communities. Settlement workers also targeted city officials for housing reforms, improved public health, and promoted laws to protect women and children.

Also in 1889, *Scribner's Magazine* published a photographic essay with amazing eye-opening photography by **Jacob Riis** in which he documented the plight of the poor in New York City. The photographs required the use of flash powder to capture unique nighttime interior and exterior images. Riis, an immigrant from Denmark, expanded this photo journalistic work in 1890 by creating a larger work, *How the Other Half Lives*. His work helped to highlight the poor living in squalor in the slums of New York City and caught the attention of Teddy Roosevelt, Police Commissioner of New York City.

Lesson 6-3: Muckrakers and a Message for Change

Novelists and journalists helped spread the progressive spirit throughout the nation. Known as **muckrakers**, a term coined by Roosevelt to describe their journalistic tactic of "raking the filth" in search of wrongs, these authors and journalists wrote searing accounts of corporate and political evils. Their aim was to expose political corruption, corporate wrongdoing, and other offenses through investigative tactics, and to use media as an outlet for bringing about change. The muckrakers' numerous writings moved the public to demand reform.

Muckraker Chart

- **Ida Tarbell**'s *History of Standard Oil* (1904) exposed the ruthless and exploitative practices of Rockefeller's oil company in a four-part article in *McClure's* magazine. Her work ultimately led to the 1907 court case of *Standard Oil v. the United States* and the breakup of Rockefeller's Standard Oil Company in 1911.

- **Upton Sinclair**'s *The Jungle* (1906) exposed the inhumane working environment and unsanitary conditions in meatpacking plants. Although aimed at "the heart of the public" to promote socialism and the plight of immigrant workers, Sinclair's book hit "the public's stomach" with his portrayal of meatpacking practices in Packingtown. This led to the passage of the **Pure Food and Drug Act** (1906) and the **Meat Inspection Act** (1906).

- **Lincoln Steffen**'s *The Shame of the Cities* (1904) explored municipal corruption in a series of sensational articles.

- **Jacob Riis**'s *How the Other Half Lives* (1890) incorporated his photojournalism skills in documenting the plight of the urban poor. His work alerted the public to the need for reform.

Lesson 6-4: Prohibition

Many progressives saw it as their duty to clean up American society and morality. Early attempts at moral reform included censorship of movies and attempts to end prostitution. The Mann Act of 1910 prohibited the transportation of prostitutes across state lines.

Moral reform peaked with the Prohibition movement, which sought the legal abolition of alcohol. This movement, led by the **Anti-Saloon League** starting in 1893 under the leadership of **Howard Hyde Russell**, gained momentum during the Progressive Era, and in 1919, the group finally succeeded in pushing the **18th Amendment** through Congress. The amendment outlawed the manufacture, transport, and sale of alcoholic beverages.

During the push for Prohibition, **Carrie Nation**, a member of the **Women's Christian Temperance Union**, went from saloon to saloon in Kansas wielding a hatchet because she felt divinely ordained to forcefully promote temperance. She would enter a saloon with her Bible in one hand and a hatchet in the other and, while singing hymns, proceed to smash up bars. She endured multiple arrests and posted her bail with money from souvenir hatchets and tour fees.

Lesson 6-5: Dealing With Racism

During the Progressive Era, people fighting for the rights of black Americans were torn between two leaders with different strategies for achieving equality. **Booker T. Washington** argued that blacks must first acquire vocational skills and prove their economic worth before hoping to be treated equally. In 1881, Washington had founded **Tuskegee Institute** in an effort to implement his plan. In a famous speech that Washington gave to a mixed audience in Atlanta in 1895, "The Atlanta Compromise," Washington urged blacks to focus on economic advancement as the main way to gain acceptance in society. In 1901, President Roosevelt invited Booker T. Washington to a White House dinner to discuss racial issues.

Many Northern blacks, however, rejected Washington's philosophy in favor of the more radical ideas presented by **W. E. B. DuBois**, who demanded immediate equal treatment for blacks and equal access to all intellectual opportunities, not just vocational training. DuBois was the first black to graduate with a doctorate from Harvard, and he began to campaign against all forms of racial segregation. DuBois and several black activists met in Niagara Falls, Canada, in 1905 to outline their plans for political and economic equality. The **Niagara Movement** joined with a group of white reformers in 1910 to form the **National Association for the Advancement of Colored People (NAACP)**, which called for an end to racial discrimination. DuBois became the editor of a publication titled *The Crisis*, in which he helped shape public opinion on the need to end segregation. The NAACP, along with groups such as the National Urban League, attacked Jim Crow laws in the South and the 1896 *Plessy v. Ferguson* Supreme Court decision. Although these organized efforts led to few political or social gains at the time, they did begin laying the foundation for the future of the civil rights movement in the 1950s and 1960s.

Ida B. Wells became an outspoken proponent for anti-lynching legislation. Despite efforts to curb the violence, lynchings continued to increase. Between 1900 and World War I more than 1,100 lynchings took place, mostly in the South and Midwest. Between 1880 and 1930, nearly 5,000 blacks were lynched in this country. Very few state or local lynching laws were enforced, and very few perpetrators were ever brought to justice.

Examples of this violence could be seen throughout parts of the South and Midwest. A race riot broke out in Springfield, Illinois, in the summer of 1908, resulting in 84-year-old William Donnegan, a black barber, being lynched. On May 31, 1921, **Tulsa**, **Oklahoma**, became the site of yet another riot and lynching. The Greenwood district, known as the "Black Wall Street" section of town, was burned, resulting in the destruction of 35 city blocks and more than 300 deaths.

In 1922, the **Dyer Anti-Lynching Bill** came up for a vote in the House of Representatives. After 16 attempts to pass anti-lynching legislation in the previous 20 years, this time many black women within the NAACP worked tirelessly with the male leaders of the organization to see this bill make it to a vote. After passing the House, it went for a vote in the Senate but failed to make it out of committee. Pressure from Southern Democrats and passive Republicans kept the attempted bills from becoming federal law. This crusade would continue until the mid-1930s.

The small town of Rosewood, Florida, was the site of a massacre in January 1923, when a black man was accused of raping a white woman. The reaction to the accusations resulted in a white mob murdering and lynching several blacks and burning the entire community of Rosewood to the ground. A grand jury investigation found "insufficient evidence" to prosecute those involved with this incident.

Lesson 6-6: Women's Issues

Female suffrage, granting women the right to vote, was the primary feminist cause of the Progressive Era. In its early stages, the movement had been led by Susan B. Anthony, who retired as president of the National American Woman Suffrage Association (NAWSA) in 1900. She was succeeded by **Carrie Chapman Catt**. During the early 1900s, NAWSA served as the point of central control for nationwide grassroots groups that lobbied legislators, held rallies, and distributed literature. Other suffragists staged demonstrations and picketed the White House. Despite their continued efforts, women would have to wait until after World War I for ratification of the **19th Amendment**, which finally granted them suffrage in 1920. As acknowledgement for their valiant efforts shown during World War I, and the efforts of women's groups pressing for suffrage, President Wilson urged the passage of an amendment granting women the right to vote. Women participated in their first presidential election in 1920.

Women supported campaigns for building playgrounds and nurseries, improving conditions for women workers, equalizing women's wages with those of men, and banning child labor. The women's movement was also affected by a new Supreme Court ruling by Louis Brandeis in *Muller v. Oregon* (1908). The ruling approved the constitutionality of limiting working women's hours on the grounds that women were in general "weaker than men in muscular strength and in nervous energy" and "needed special protection because of their social roles as mothers." As a result of the ruling, by 1917 all but nine states had laws restricting women's working hours. This would set up workplace segregation based on gender for most of the first half of the 20th century.

Another issue facing the women's movement was brought to the forefront in 1916 by **Margaret Sanger**, when she opened the first birth control clinic in Brooklyn, New York. Her support of birth control for women not only challenged the **Comstock Laws** and societal standards, but helped more information get out to women in need. The 1873 law forbade anyone from using the mail to send any material deemed "obscene, lewd, or lascivious." Its goal was to limit the spread of pornography and birth control material. Sanger worked to create the American Birth Control League in 1921. In addition, the **Sheppard-Towner Act** (1921) resulted in Congress passing the first federal social welfare law providing federal funds for infant and maternity health care.

Lesson 6-7: Labor Strife

Many reformers focused on labor problems during the Progressive Era, especially after several key incidents involving labor struggles, unions, and business leaders.

Child labor was already a serious problem in the country. By the turn of the 20th century, nearly 20 percent of children ages 5 to 15 worked at jobs. **Florence Kelley** campaigned tirelessly against child labor and other issues: protective legislation for working women, minimum wage laws, and maternal and child health services.

In 1903, longtime labor activist **Mother Jones** led a children's march from Kensington, Pennsylvania, to the Long Island, New York, home of President Roosevelt, protesting child labor. Along the way, several maimed and young children walked from town to town to show people the child laborers' plight. In 1904, the **National Child Labor Committee** was organized to curtail child labor. Within 10 years, all but one state had laws establishing a minimum age for working.

By 1912, Congress had created a children's bureau of the Department of Labor. Local, state, and federal legislation were difficult to pass, yet reformers such as Kelley weren't deterred.

A tragic fire at the **Triangle Shirtwaist Company** in New York City on March 25, 1911, illustrated the growing problem of industrial accidents. At that time, the United States had the highest rate of industrial accidents in the world. The tragedy at the Triangle Company in the Asch Building occurred when a fire broke out on the eighth floor, trapping several young women workers. The company employed mainly immigrant girls who worked more than 60 hours per week for very low wages. The fire claimed the lives of 146 women. Locked exits, doors that opened inward, and a faulty fire escape left few escape routes. Several people leaped out windows and met their deaths on the streets below, their falls not broken by the safety nets.

Rose Schneiderman drew national attention to the incident when she spoke at a funeral march days later in New York City in which 80,000 people marched. Schneiderman accused the city leaders of not doing enough, and she said they were "found wanting" for failing to prevent such tragedies. Soon, cities began enacting stricter building and fire codes. New labor codes began being enacted in the workplace. The owners of the Triangle Shirtwaist Company were brought to trial but were acquitted of any negligence.

Easter Sunday, April 20, 1914, brought workplace fatalities of a different kind during the **Ludlow Massacre** in the mining community of Ludlow (in southern Colorado near Trinidad). At the mining camp at the Rockefeller-owned Colorado Fuel and Iron Company, the state militia and company guards were breaking a strike that had lingered for several months, after miners' efforts to join the UMWA (United Mine Workers Association) had been thwarted. The Baldwin Felts Detective Agency had been brought in to suppress the Colorado miners, and on the day of the attack the militia and guards used torches, kerosene, and machine guns to attack a tent colony, killing 20 people there (mostly women and children). By the end of the strike, 66 strikers and supporters were dead.

Lesson 6-8: Local Government Reform

In the late 1890s, local political reform began to spread through American cities. Municipal and state governments passed a slew of progressive laws, including labor laws that established the eight-hour workday and workers' compensation that restricted child labor. Local governments also attacked private monopolies in gas, water, and electricity by regulating rates and weakening the companies' political power. Some states, including Wisconsin and California, reformed their statewide election systems by developing the **direct primary**, in which party members rather than the party leadership selected candidates for office. Other efforts at political reform included: **recall elections**, special elections to remove elected officials from office; **initiatives**, which allowed groups of individuals to propose a law by gathering signatures to place the proposed law on the ballot; **referendums**, which permitted voters to approve or reject legislative measures; and **term limits**, which specified the number of terms an elected official could serve. Some cities even began adopting city commission or city manager forms of government, where professionals ran the city.

Robert LaFollette, governor of Wisconsin and a U.S. senator, championed many of these causes and others by establishing sweeping reform measures across the state. His broad reform agenda became known as "the Wisconsin Idea" and would be copied by several other progressive governors and political leaders.

Lesson 6-9: "Square Deal": Roosevelt in the White House

Theodore Roosevelt became president in September 1901 after William McKinley's assassination. Although he had been vice president under McKinley, Roosevelt didn't share McKinley's conservative, pro-business policies. Instead, President Roosevelt pushed aggressive political reforms, including heavy business regulation. Known as the "trust-buster," Roosevelt was the first president to successfully invoke the Sherman Antitrust Act against monopolies, and he continued to restrict businesses throughout his presidency.

Roosevelt's reforms reached far beyond business as well. He greatly influenced economic, environmental, and international affairs. His platform became known as the **Square Deal** because he vowed not to favor any one group of Americans but to be fair to all.

Relations With Labor and Corporations

Roosevelt was committed to addressing the problems of labor and corporate activity. He defended labor's right to organize, and he resorted to the use of federal troops to put down strikes. In 1902, he intervened in a United Mine Workers strike and helped labor get management to agree to binding arbitration. The arbitrators awarded the miners a wage increase and a shortened workday.

Roosevelt also worked to restrict the power of big business by attacking monopolies. In his administration's first trust-busting case, his attorney general filed suit against the Northern Securities Company for violating the Sherman Antitrust Act, which had not been successfully used against monopolies since its passage in 1890. In 1904, the Supreme Court ordered that the Northern Securities Company be dissolved, a decision that launched a series of antitrust suits. After this, the Sherman Antitrust Act became an extremely important tool for government regulation of corporations.

In all, the Roosevelt administration filed 43 trust-busting suits. After winning reelection in 1904, Roosevelt focused on more permanent regulations and successfully negotiated the passage of the **Hepburn Act** in 1906. It empowered the Interstate Commerce Commission (ICC), previously a weak agency, to set maximum railroad rates and to inspect railroad companies' financial records.

Protecting Consumers and Conserving the Environment

Responding to the muckrakers' exposés of unsanitary conditions in food plants and dangerous ingredients in foods and medicines, Roosevelt endorsed the **Pure Food and Drug Act** (1906) and the **Meat Inspection Act** (1906). The first act prohibited the sale of adulterated or inaccurately labeled foods and medicines; the second established federal regulations for meatpackers and a system of inspection.

The early 20th century also saw a rise in concern for the wilderness. Those who supported conservation and protection of wilderness sites were called preservationists. Preservationists were often in conflict with business interests, who saw the wilderness in terms of resources and space for commercial and residential development. At heart, Roosevelt was a preservationist, but he understood the need for compromise. Roosevelt achieved compromise through his conservation program, which provided for regulated use of the nation's wilderness. Roosevelt designated 200 million acres as national forests, mineral reserves, and potential waterpower sites, and added five national parks and eighteen national monuments to the list of protected lands.

Gifford Pinchot, head of the Bureau of Forestry, also promoted conservation as a movement for preservation and wise use of natural resources. Pinchot was ultimately dismissed in 1910 by President Taft after he publicly criticized Secretary of Interior Richard A. Ballinger's actions in coal lands in Alaska.

Aggressive Foreign Policy: "Big Stick" Diplomacy

Roosevelt summed up his approach to foreign policy in a single sentence: "Speak softly and carry a big stick." Having become president shortly after the American victory in the Spanish-American War, Roosevelt was confident in America's status as a major power, so he adopted an aggressive diplomatic approach.

Roosevelt's most notable achievement in foreign policy was the building of the Panama Canal. His intervention in Panama exemplified his attitude toward Latin America, evidenced in his addition of the Roosevelt Corollary to the Monroe Doctrine (see Chapter 5). In 1904, with several European nations poised to invade the Dominican Republic, Roosevelt declared that the United States, not Europe, should dominate Latin America. Although the United States had no expansionist intentions, any "chronic wrongdoing" by a Latin American nation would justify the U.S. intervention as a "global policeman," Roosevelt said. During Roosevelt's presidency, the United States repeatedly invoked the Roosevelt Corollary as justification for its involvement in the affairs of the Dominican Republic, Haiti, Venezuela, Nicaragua, and Cuba.

Roosevelt also involved himself in Asian affairs after the Russo-Japanese War broke out in 1904. Concerned about maintaining the balance of power between nations, Roosevelt invited delegates from Russia and Japan to the United States in 1905 for a peace conference, which resulted in the signing of a treaty. Roosevelt received the Nobel Peace Prize for his actions.

Lesson 6-10: "Dollar Diplomacy": Taft in the White House

In the 1908 election, William Howard Taft won by a large margin on a conservative platform. Nevertheless, Taft couldn't match Roosevelt's popularity or legislative success. Although he continued Roosevelt's progressive reform programs, his pace was more gradual, and he even lent his support to some conservative pro-business policies. Taft's policies divided the Republican Party into progressive and conservative factions.

Taft supported corporate regulation and even strengthened the Interstate Commerce Commission's powers and extended its authority to the telephone and telegraph industries. He surpassed the Roosevelt administration in trust-busting, prosecuting 90 cases to Roosevelt's 43.

Additional reform under Taft centered on two amendments to the Constitution, both ratified after he left office. In 1913, the **16th Amendment** granted Congress the authority to tax income. After the amendment passed, Congress quickly established a graduated income tax with a maximum tax rate of 7 percent. The **17th Amendment**, also ratified in 1913, provided for direct election of U.S. senators by the people rather than selection by state legislatures. The amendment was one part of a general movement for government reform to give the public an increasingly powerful and direct role in electing officials.

Foreign Policy

In foreign affairs, Taft moved away from Roosevelt's "big stick" policies toward **"dollar diplomacy."** Aiming to avoid military intervention, Taft argued that the growth of American investment abroad, as well as the advancement of American economic interests, would promote stability. Dollar diplomacy failed in China, where European and Japanese economic interests squeezed out American businesses, and it proved only marginally more successful elsewhere. In 1912, Taft resorted to "big stick" policies in Nicaragua when Marines were sent in to suppress a revolt.

Republicans Divided

Taft alienated the progressive members of his party by supporting the Payne-Aldrich Act to raise protective tariff rates, a move supported by conservative pro-business interests. He further outraged progressives by supporting ultraconservative Speaker of the House Joseph Cannon and ultra-conservative Secretary of the Interior Richard A. Ballinger, who reversed Roosevelt's conservation efforts by selling off several million acres of public land in Alaska to bankers interested in mining the land for coal.

3rd-Party Political Challengers

During the Progressive Era, candidates from third-party political groups continued to challenge the status quo. **Eugene Debs** became one of the most widely known politicians in the **Socialist Party**, formed in 1901. Debs was a prominent player in American politics and ran for the presidency five times. (His last campaign was conducted in 1920 from jail while he served time for World War I charges related to the Sedition Act.)

The other political party challenge came from the **Progressive Party** in 1912. Teddy Roosevelt had failed to secure the Republican Party presidential nomination when Taft supporters blocked Roosevelt's nomination at the Republican Convention. Instead, the party re-nominated Taft. Roosevelt and his supporters then broke with the Republican Party and formed the **Progressive Party**, nicknamed the "Bull Moose" Party, after Roosevelt commented upon returning from an African safari that he felt as strong as a bull moose.

Roosevelt and Taft entered the election against Socialist Eugene Debs and Democrat Woodrow Wilson. Although Roosevelt campaigned passionately, he couldn't defeat Woodrow Wilson, the progressive Democratic candidate. But the Bull Moose party still proved to be the most successful third party in American history, coming in second with Roosevelt winning more than 27 percent of the popular vote to Taft's 23 percent. With the Republican Party divided, Democrat Wilson was able to capture the presidency, winning 42 percent of the vote.

Lesson 6-11: "New Freedom": Wilson in the White House

Once in office, Wilson pushed a more aggressive progressive agenda than either of his two predecessors had. He lowered tariffs, and championed corporate regulation and banking reform, among other policies. Wilson's first legislative action was to lower the tariff. In 1913, he sponsored the Underwood Tariff, which cut tariffs substantially. It was the nation's first tariff reduction since before the Civil War. In 1913, Wilson additionally helped launch an investigation into the possibly corrupt relations between pro-tariff lobbyists and certain senators.

The Federal Reserve System

Wilson and his supporters sought to create a centralized bank system under public control that would be able to stabilize the economy in times of panic. After months of bargaining, Congress passed the Federal Reserve Act (1913). The act established a network of regional Federal Reserve banks under partially private and partially public control. The Federal Reserve Board was created to oversee the entire network along with national fiscal policy, and it would become a powerful force in American economics.

Business Regulation

Wilson pushed two important regulatory measures through Congress in 1914. First, the **Federal Trade Commission Act** created a five-member agency to investigate suspected violations of interstate trade regulations and to issue cease-and-desist orders when it found corporations guilty of unfair practices.

Second, the **Clayton Antitrust Act** improved on the vague Sherman Antitrust Act by enumerating a series of illegal business practices. The Wilson administration initiated antitrust suits against almost one hundred corporations.

Wilson also strongly supported workers' rights. Under his administration, Congress passed a series of labor laws designed to ban child labor, shorten workdays, and, through the Workmen's Compensation Act, provide injury protection to federal employees. Wilson also supported reforms benefiting farmers, such as low-interest loan programs.

"New Freedom" in Foreign Policy

Wilson rejected both the "big stick" and the "dollar diplomacy" approaches to foreign policy in favor of **"new freedom,"** an idealistic foreign policy aimed at morality in international affairs. He pledged never to seek territorial expansion by conquest, and instead focused on advancing capitalism and democracy throughout the world.

In 1914, war erupted across Europe. In line with the peaceful foreign policy he had followed since 1912, Wilson was determined not to get involved in the conflict. In 1914, soon after the war's outbreak, Wilson issued a statement of neutrality designed to keep the United States out of the conflict. In 1916, Wilson was reelected in large part on the slogan: "He kept us out of war."

Wilson would soon face new challenges as he urged America's entry into World War I in April 1917. He continued his progressive agenda during the war with his Fourteen Points plan that stressed the formation of a League of Nations to work to prevent any further wars. Following the end of the war, he traveled to Europe to work with world leaders on drafting the Treaty of Versailles in 1919 and promoted his plan for the League of Nations. He then came back to this country and traveled by train visiting communities across the nation to urge ratification and support for the treaty. Wilson suffered a stroke after his collapse in Pueblo, Colorado on September 25th. As a result, his work on the treaty ended, and, after a fierce debate in the Senate, the treaty was never ratified. The political climate was beginning to change in the country following the end of World War I and progressive reforms were slowed.

Review Exam

Multiple Choice

1. The Progressive Era was generally a time period in which _____.
    a) socialist ideas were promoted and adopted
    b) the major reform measures were proposed and enacted by Republicans

c) major reform measures promoted social justice and democracy, and sought government support

d) broad support was never achieved as different groups promoted their own agendas

2. Hull House, founded by Jane Addams, was part of a settlement house movement that was established in order to _____.

a) serve immigrant families

b) provide social services such as education, lessons in cooking and hygiene, English classes

c) promote reforms in housing and public health to city officials

d) A, B, and C

3. All of the following were true of Ida Tarbell's exposes for *McClure's* magazine EXCEPT that _____.

a) her magazine articles exposed the ruthless exploitation of Rockefeller's Standard Oil Company

b) the work led to the 1907 Supreme Court case against Standard Oil

c) the work was attacked by Rockefeller's rebuttals in several articles in the *Petroleum Journal*

d) the work led to the Supreme Court ruling in 1911 to break up the monopoly of Standard Oil

4. Booker T. Washington was associated with all of the following EXCEPT _____.

a) proposing a gradual approach to civil rights for blacks in his speech "The Atlanta compromise"

b) stating that blacks should first acquire vocational skills thereby proving their economic worth to society

c) urging President Roosevelt to move quickly in adopting new legislation for civil rights for blacks

d) founding the Tuskegee Institute as a school to provide education and training to blacks

5. The women's movement succeeded in _____.

a) securing the right to suffrage with the passage of the 19th Amendment

b) participating in strikes and union activities to begin to bring about changes in the work place

c) seeing large numbers of women from a cross-section of social and political arenas become involved in reform efforts

d) A, B, and C

6. Margaret Sanger is best known for her campaigns and work with_____.
    a) birth control
    b) child labor laws
    c) tenements in the slums
    d) civil rights

7. W. E. B. DuBois became _____.
    a) the first black to graduate with a doctorate degree from Harvard
    b) the most outspoken critic of segregation and a proponent of immediate equal treatment and equal access for programs for blacks
    c) one of the organizers behind the formation of the NAACP in 1910
    d) A, B, and C

8. In addition to her work with unions, Mother Jones worked tirelessly to advocate for _____.
    a) improvements to slums in the inner city
    b) safety codes for businesses
    c) child labor laws which was highlighted in a children's march in 1903
    d) women's suffrage

9. Ludlow, Colorado, was the scene of _____.
    a) a violent railroad strike resulting in the deaths of 15 strikers and the arrest of its leader
    b) a tragic scene at a coal mining community in which a tent colony was attacked, resulting in the deaths of 13 people
    c) an attempt by the coal operators, led by the Colorado Fuel and Iron Company, to thwart the attempts of workers to join the union (UNWA)
    d) B and C only

10. As a result of the tragedy of the Triangle Shirtwaist Factory fire in 1911 in New York City, _____.
    a) new labor codes began to be enacted
    b) new building and safety codes began being enacted
    c) 146 women were killed in the fire, but the resulting trial of the owners of the building ended with their acquittal for negligence
    d) A, B, and C

11. Teddy Roosevelt's platform on issues that became known as the Square Deal sought to focus _____.
    a) squarely on foreign affairs issues
    b) a balanced approach in dealing with economic, environmental, and foreign issues

   c) attacks on monopolies

   d) solely on domestic issues

12. All of the following examples are true about Roosevelt in his dealings with labor EXCEPT that _____.

   a) he intervened in the United Mine Workers strike in 1902 and urged management to agree to arbitration

   b) he attacked the Northern Securities Company for its violation of the Sherman Anti-Trust Act

   c) his administration was seen as weak in dealing with illegal business practices, as only a handful of trust-busting suits were filed against businesses

   d) he encouraged the passage of the Hepburn Act to strengthen the Interstate Commerce Commission and its role in regulating railroad rates

13. The Pure Food and Drug Act in 1906 _____.

   a) was a direct result of Upton Sinclair's muckraking work on *The Jungle* that highlighted unsafe meatpacking practices

   b) was legislation aimed at reforming the meatpacking industry

   c) aimed at gradual government intervention to protect the rights of the business owners

   d) A and B only

14. Taft's concept of "dollar diplomacy" _____.

   a) aimed at securing more American investments in overseas markets as a means to ensure political stability in various regions

   b) aimed at using both economic and military measures to ensure political stability in regions in conflict

   c) targeted offering financial aid to businesses

   d) targeted financial aid to underdeveloped nations to ensure political stability

15. When the Republican Party split in 1912 it produced a new political party, the Progressive Party, nicknamed the "Bull Moose" Party, led by _____.

   a) Eugene Debs   c) Teddy Roosevelt

   b) Mother Jones   d) President Taft

16. Progressive reformers tended to _____.

   a) not favor the use of federal laws to bring about changes

   b) believe in the use of local, state and federal government agencies and regulations to bring about reform measures

c) favor the old policies of "laissez-faire"

d) be primarily men from the middle and upper class and members of the Republican Party

17. Wilson's New Freedom agenda _____.

a) aimed at regulating business practices with the creation of the Federal Trade Commission and the Clayton Antitrust Act

b) pursued a "moralistic" path with foreign policy initiatives

c) had Wilson pursuing the League of Nations at the end of WWI as a means of preventing future wars from breaking out

d) A, B, and C

Matching

a. NAACP

b. recall

c. 18th Amendment

d. Sheppard-Towner Act

e. Mann Act

f. Robert LaFollette

g. initiatives

h. Carrie Nation

i. Tulsa, Oklahoma

j. Comstock Laws

k. Howard Hyde Russell

l. 16th Amendment

m. Dyer Anti-Lynching bill

n. referendum

o. 17th Amendment

p. Gifford Pinchot

q. muckrakers

r. Jacob Riis

s. Payne-Aldrich Act

t. term limits

u. direct primary

v. 19th Amendment

w. Federal Reserve Act

x. Ida B. Wells

_____18. a member of the Women's Christian Temperance Union who forcefully promoted temperance with her hatchet, hymns, and Bible

_____19. legislation that attempted to prevent lynchings by making it a crime; Congress failed to pass this bill

_____20. his photographic work in *How the Other Half Lives* exposed the living conditions of the poor in New York City

_____21. worked with the Anti-Saloon League to abolish alcohol (and succeeded with the passage of the 18th Amendment)

_____22. allowed for the direct election of senators

_____23. a censorship attempt to curb prostitution by banning transportation of prostitutes across state lines

_____24. 1873 law that forbade anyone from using the mail to send any materials that were deemed to be "obscene, lewd, or lascivious"

_____25. organization that was formed in 1910 out of the work of the Niagara Movement and aimed at ending racial discrimination

_____26. journalists earned this nickname, as it referred to the tactic of journalists using the media to expose corruption, wrongdoing, and "filth" in society

_____27. party members rather than the party leadership would choose candidates running for office

_____28. outlawed the manufacture, sale, and transportation of alcohol

_____29. the site of a race riot in 1921 in which lynchings and mob violence took place resulting in the destruction of an area of 35 city blocks and the deaths of more than 300 blacks

_____30. special election that could be used to remove a public official from office

_____31. allowed for a graduated income tax on income

_____32. outspoken proponent for anti-lynching legislation

_____33. voters could approve or reject legislative measures with the use of this

_____34. granted suffrage to women in 1920

_____35. specified the number of terms an elected official could serve

_____36. head of the bureau of forestry and promoted conservation measures and setting aside land for national parks

_____37. the first federal social welfare law that provided federal funds for infant and maternity healthcare

_____38. governor of Wisconsin and a U.S. senator who championed many of the political reforms being adopted; his work became known as the "Wisconsin idea"

_____39. established a network of regional Federal Reserve Banks under partially private and partially public control

_____40. a measure supported by President Taft to raise protective tariffs

_____41. groups of individuals could propose laws by gathering a specified number of signatures and getting the measure on the ballot

Short Response

42. What were the strengths and weaknesses of the Progressive movement?

43. What was the role of the presidents during the Progressive Era?

44. How did the concepts of *reform, remake, and revolutionize* describe what is known as the Progressive Era in America?

Answers begin on page 288.

World War I

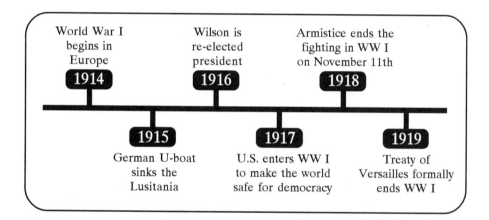

World War I begins in Europe
1914

Wilson is re-elected president
1916

Armistice ends the fighting in WW I on November 11th
1918

1915
German U-boat sinks the Lusitania

1917
U.S. enters WW I to make the world safe for democracy

1919
Treaty of Versailles formally ends WW I

Trends and Themes of the Era

▶ Although the United States wanted to stay neutral , it eventually became involved and helped turn the tide in favor of the Allies. World War I established the United States as a dominant world power.

▶ President Wilson saw the conflict as an opportunity to end all future wars with the adoption of his proposed 14 Points in the Treaty of Versailles.

▶ The war effort brought blacks and women into the workforce in record numbers. It also prompted the migration of nearly 500,000 blacks from the South to the North. Women's efforts in the war had a direct result: They were granted the right to vote.

▶ Isolationism would take hold in the United States after the end of World War I. The country wasn't ready to take an active role in foreign affairs to help secure the future peace of the world.

Over there, over there…! In 1914, the Yanks weren't quite ready to join in the conflict on the continent of Europe. Americans were enjoying peace on their side of the Atlantic, and President Wilson was continuing the work of progressive reform. Yet, loyalties remained divided as war ravaged the European continent. As the Germans continued their quest for dominance on land and at sea, Wilson urged the United States to remain neutral. Even with political neutrality, the United States dramatically boosted its economic trade with the Allies and did much less business with the Central Powers. As propaganda and submarine attacks increased, America was drawn into the conflict on the premise of "making the world safe for democracy." This idealism would continue into the peace settlements in Versailles in 1919, with the formation of the League of Nations. Following America's involvement in the ravages of war, the post-war mood was one of retreat as reforms were curtailed, the peace treaty failed to be ratified, and the country retreated into isolationism.

Lesson 7-1: The Great War: The War to End All Wars

World War I pitted the **Allies** (Great Britain, Russia, France, and later Italy) against the **Central Powers** (Germany and Austria-Hungary). In August 1914, Wilson proclaimed U.S. neutrality and urged the public to be "impartial in thought and deed." The American public, however, was partial to the Allies: Though most Americans were glad to be remote from the war, Allied propaganda helped sway public opinion in favor of the war against the Germans.

American sources provided weapons, food, and funding to the Allies equal to nearly 100 times that provided to the Central Powers. Wilson himself seemed to favor an Allied victory, but clung to neutrality.

A crisis in the Balkan Peninsula soon embroiled Europe in open conflict. On June 28, 1914, Austrian Archduke Franz Ferdinand and his wife, Sophie, visited **Sarajevo**, the capital of Bosnia, on a mission of goodwill. **Gavrilo Princip**, a member of a Serbian terrorist group, the Black Hand, fired two shots into the motorcade, killing Sophie and the archduke. Austria delivered an ultimatum to Serbia on July 23, 1914, and five days later Austria declared war on Serbia for noncompliance. By August 6th, all the members of the Triple Alliance (Allies) and the Triple Entente (Central Powers) were engaged in conflict.

Most people felt jubilant at the outset, thinking it would be a short war and that "the boys would be home by Christmas." Instead, the war lasted four long years and forever changed Europe and the rest of the world. World War I became the most destructive war up to that time. Within the first two and one-half years of conflict more than five million deaths had occurred. During the war, 30 nations fought in bloody battles that resulted in 26 million deaths by the war's end in 1918.

After the flawed **Schlieffen Plan** by the Germans in northern France in August 1914, the war soon became entrenched in a two-front war. The Germans planned a quick attack against France and then to regroup and send its troops to the east to defeat the Russians. This failed miserably. The French fought back, and the war soon became a two-front war, causing Germany to divide its troops and resources.

Leading Causes of World War I

- **Nationalism:** national groups of people uniting under governments controlled by their own people (land = power)

- **Imperialism:** one country's domination of the political, economic, and social life of another country; empires built in quest for power (new natural resources and markets for goods)

- **Militarism:** the glorification of armed strength; only the use of force could solve conflicts; buildup of navies and armies, mobilization of armies at a moment's notice, and development of new weapons as the way to defend national boundaries

- **Alliances:** friendships between countries that would aid each other in time of conflict; Germany viewed as a threat to the balance of power in Europe; Germany in Triple Alliance with Austria-Hungary and Italy; France, Russia, and Great Britain in Triple Entente; alliances threat to peace in Europe because any hostile act could start war

World War I in Europe

Following the **Battle of the Marne** in 1914, the **Western Front** became the site of more than 600 miles of trenches. By November, the war had reached a stalemate, and it remained that way for most of the war. One side would succeed in taking over a piece of territory only to lose it later in retreat. Between the two sides of the trenches lay a stretch of land known simply as "no man's land" filled with barbed wire and land mines. The trenches were generally 6–8 feet deep and wide enough for two people. The conditions were inhumane and characterized by rats, moisture, cold, disease, and a new weapon: poison gas.

Germany's other war front was along the **Eastern Front**, with its border with Russia. At the Battle of Tannenburg in August 1914, Germany beat

Russia and prevented the Russians from gaining substantial momentum for the remainder of the war. At the Battle of Gallipoli in 1915 (along the Dardanelles Black Sea to Mediterranean route), the Germans defeated the Allies. This forced difficulties in the Allies getting supplies to the Russian army.

As the war continued to go badly for the Russians, a political move was afoot in Moscow with the November 1917 **Bolshevik Revolution** in which the

New Weapons in World War I

- Machine Guns: provided quick, rapid fire, and combined with long-range rifles and hand grenades to add to the war's casualty rate
- Tanks: armed with guns and steel protection; first used in the Battle of the Somme
- Airplanes: used in dogfights in the air
- Submarines: U-boats designed by Germany to subvert the blockades and destroy the enemy
- Poison Gas: mustard gas, nerve gas used in the trenches; gas masks invented to combat the new chemical weapon
- Trucks, Cars: used to transport troops
- Propaganda: widely used as a tool of war on both sides to influence public opinion

---

Communist Party, under the leadership of Lenin, Trotsky, and Stalin, established itself in power. Four months later, in March 1918, Russia signed a secret pact with Germany at **Brest-Litovsk** and left the war without telling the other Allies. This angered the Allies so much that Russia was not invited to the peace negotiation talks in Versailles in 1919. Not only did the Allies not trust the new Communist Party, but Russia became involved in a fierce civil war between the Reds (Bolsheviks) and the Whites (the opposition) that lasted from 1918 to 1920. The war ended with the deaths of nearly 20 million Russians and with the Bolsheviks firmly in control.

After 1914, Americans found neutrality increasingly difficult to maintain. In 1915, Germany announced a **U-boat** blockade of the Allies' ports and, in the ensuing months, killed a number of people in torpedo attacks on British vessels and one U.S. tanker. On May 7, 1915, a U-boat sank the British ocean liner *Lusitania*, killing close to 1,200 people, including 128 Americans. The sinking provoked an anti-German backlash in American public opinion. In 1916, Congress passed the National Defense Act, authorizing a military buildup in anticipation of war.

After the *Lusitania* incident, Germany stopped attacking passenger ships for a few months. But in August 1915, Germany resumed attacks, sinking both British and French vessels. In 1916, when Wilson threatened to break diplomatic relations after one such incident, Germany responded with the **Sussex Pledge**, promising not to attack merchant ships without warning. The pledge eased the strain on U.S. neutrality for the rest of 1916.

In 1916, Wilson was reelected on the slogan of "he kept us out of war," a tribute to his maintaining American neutrality. Wilson and the Democrats portrayed the Republican Party as one of war and uncertainty. He later stated that it would be an "irony of fate if my administration had to deal chiefly with foreign affairs."

Lesson 7-2: "To Make the World Safe for Democracy..."

The United States remained neutral in World War I until April 1917. Many Americans felt that Europe's problems didn't directly affect the United States. In 1910, Andrew Carnegie started the **Peace Fund** with a $10 million donation to try to avert U.S. involvement in foreign conflicts.

Wilson and many others also felt that war was justified only in self-defense. Despite the fact that the United States continued to trade food, raw materials, weapons, and munitions with Europe, the goal was to keep the country out of the war in Europe.

Meanwhile, problems cropped up closer to home as Wilson became involved in conflicts in Central America and Mexico. In 1915, Wilson continued to push his pro-American policies in the Dominican Republic, Haiti, and Nicaragua to protect American interests. These actions met with mixed results among the local populations.

The United States was concerned about the Mexican Revolution in 1911 because of the $2 billion in various U.S. business interests in Mexico (railroads, mining, rubber, and oil). Porfirio Diaz was overthrown and replaced by General Victorian Huerta. On April 22, 1914, American forces bombarded and occupied Veracruz and forced Huerta out of power. A civil war then began between the forces of Pancho Villa and Venustiano Carranza. In January 1916, **Pancho Villa** turned against the United States, and, in March 1916, he raided and burned the tiny town of Columbus, New Mexico. President Wilson ordered 12,000 troops and several National Guard units to the border. Villa was pursued 300 miles into Mexico, but the army couldn't capture him. Wilson's policies with Mexico contributed to future difficulties in Latin America.

On January 31, 1917, German minister Alfred Zimmerman sent a telegram to Mexico, urging the country to get involved in the war with Germany. If Germany won the war, Mexico was promised the part of the Southwestern United States that it had lost in 1848 in the Mexican-American War; the telegram also hinted at Japan attacking U.S. bases in the Pacific. Great Britain intercepted the **Zimmerman Telegram** and sent it to the United States, where the contents were made public on March 1st. Germany then resumed unrestricted submarine warfare in the Atlantic and sank seven U.S. merchant ships. In response, Wilson cut diplomatic relations with Germany. On April 2, 1917, he asked for a declaration of war in order to "make the world safe for democracy." Congress voted on April 6th, and the United States began to prepare for war.

Raising an Army

When the United States passed the war declaration, the U.S. Army included 120,000 enlisted men and 80,000 National Guardsmen. In 1917, Congress passed the **Selective Service Act**, requiring all men ages 21 to 30 register for military duty. By November 1918, some 2.8 million men had been drafted. More than 250,000 black Americans served in the war, but racism was strong in the military. Black troops were segregated, given menial positions, and excluded altogether by the marines.

More than four million copies of James Montgomery Flagg's famous Uncle Sam war poster was used to help recruit soldiers and promote patriotism during the war.

About 11,000 women served in the navy, and a few hundred more joined the marines. Women were invaluable in non-combat positions as nurses, clerks, and operators during the war; served in the Red Cross; and entered the work force to replace men in all kinds of jobs.

During the war, the War Labor Policies Board was firm in its demand that women in war industries receive the same amount of pay as a man. High wages encouraged many women to get involved in the labor force, and they became accustomed to working outside the home and enjoying economic independence. After the fighting soldiers returned, women were expected to give up their jobs and return home.

Concerned by the anti-war campaigns, Wilson's administration enlisted the help of movie stars urging Americans to aid the war effort and conducted government bond drives to finance the war. Music also played a key role in songs including "Over There," "The Star-Spangled Banner," and "America the Beautiful." In 1917, the federal government established the **Committee on Public Information**, a propaganda agency that discredited government critics and set up guidelines for self-censorship. The committee also enlisted the help of artists, journalists, and authors to publicize the war through speeches, posters, articles, and films. There were sporadic outbreaks of violence against citizens for not displaying the flag, not buying war bonds, objecting to the draft, and criticizing the war. These pro-war efforts helped intensify the public's mistrust, even hatred, of Germany and the Central Powers.

The **Espionage Act** in June 1917 became the government's key tool for suppressing anti-war sentiment, allowing for 20 years' imprisonment and a $10,000 fine for "aiding the enemy, obstructing recruitment, or causing insubordination in the armed forces." The postmaster general had the power to exclude certain items from the mail if they were thought to be treasonous. In May 1918, the **Sedition Act** outlawed any "disloyal, profane, querulous or abusive language intended to cause contempt, scorn, or disrespect for the government, Constitution, or flag."

Government officials invoked these measures to suppress dissent and justify nearly 6,000 arrests and 1,500 convictions during the war. The laws were used primarily against socialists. **Eugene Debs**, a prominent socialist and five-time presidential candidate, was imprisoned in 1918 for denouncing the government's aggressive tactics under the Sedition Act. He was pardoned by President Harding in 1921.

In the Supreme Court case *Schenck v. the U.S.* (1919), Charles Schenck, general secretary of the Socialist Party, was arrested for mailing pamphlets to army inductees that urged them to resist the draft. Justice Oliver Holmes ruled that "Congress could restrict free speech when the words are used in such circumstances and are such a nature as to create a clear and present danger."

Fighting the War

American involvement in World War I lasted from the summer of 1917 until the armistice in November 1918. With Russia out of the war, Germany moved its remaining troops to the Western Front, where American troops overran heavily fortified German trenches and reinvigorated the British and French war efforts.

The last major offensive of the war was another battle of the Marne in France. The Allied strength finally weakened the Germans so that on November 9, 1918, Emperor William II abdicated and fled the country; Germany surrendered two days later.

The **Armistice** agreed to on November 11, 1918 (at the 11th hour of the 11th day of the 11th month), forced Germany to surrender in a railcar outside the city of Paris. In the agreement, Germany canceled its secret treaty with Russia, surrendered its submarines, reduced its fleet, gave up all munitions, and submitted to occupation by the Allies.

At the war's end, the American death toll exceeded 110,000. As soldiers began returning from Europe, the **Spanish Influenza** spread across the country, claiming more than 600,000 lives in 1918, the single worst U.S. epidemic in history. Worldwide, the epidemic resulted in 20 to 40 million deaths. The global disaster was one of the most devastating epidemics in recorded world history.

Lesson 7-3: Treaty of Versailles Negotiations

Even before the armistice in November 1918, complex negotiations for peace had begun. Achieving international peace was a complicated process, and many Americans feared further involvement in world affairs.

Wilson led the all-Democratic American peace delegation to Paris. The most notable Republican absence was **Senator Henry Cabot Lodge**, chairman of the Foreign Relations Committee. In January 1919, representatives from 27 nations (excluding the Central Powers and Russia) gathered in Paris to work on the treaty.

Wilson's 14 Points

From the beginning of World War I, Wilson had hoped for a peace settlement promoting America's democratic ideals. He saw the Allied win as an opportunity to advance democracy and liberalism worldwide. In a 1918 speech to Congress, Wilson summarized American goals for the terms of peace after the war in the **14 Points**.

Summary of 14 Points

• No secret treaties—no secret diplomacy.

• Freedom of the seas for all nations in peace and war.

• Removal of tariffs and trade barriers.

• Reduction in armaments.

• An end to imperialism.

• Readjust borders along lines of nationalities (self-determination).

• Proposed the creation of a general association of nations to guarantee political independence (the League of Nations).

Republicans in Congress opposed the plan, and no Allies fully endorsed it. Many Americans, however, supported Wilson's plans, and the 14 Points became a rallying issue for the U.S. war effort and a key point of negotiations in the peace process at Versailles.

The Treaty of Versailles

The U.S. delegation and those of other countries arrived at Versailles in 1919 full of optimism, but it quickly faded. The delegates from the Allied powers fiercely resisted Wilson's attempts at a liberal settlement. President Woodrow Wilson, Prime Minister Georges Clemenceau (France), Prime Min-

ister Lloyd George (UK), and Vittorio Orlando (Italy), the **"Big Four,"** represented bitter, war-torn nations bent on destroying the Central Powers, and the Allies sought to firmly dictate the terms of peace. Britain and France aimed to impose penalties and made vindictive demands.

The **Treaty of Versailles,** signed in June 1919, was harsh toward the Germans. Germany was disarmed, forced to admit to a "total war guilt clause," and required to pay massive reparations (more than $33 billion) to the Allies. Numerous territorial adjustments meant Germany would lose territory; Alsace-Lorraine would be given back to France, and the coal-rich Saar region would be occupied by France for 15 years. Germany would face Allied occupation for 15 years in the Rhineland, along the German/French border. The new nation of Poland was carved out of German territory, and Poland received the Polish corridor between East Prussia and Germany, dividing Germany into two parts. Germany also lost all of its overseas territories.

Other parts of the agreement stated that Germany would reduce its army, that it not be allowed to manufacture major weapons of aggression, and that its navy have no submarines, large battleships, or airplanes. Wilson succeeded in achieving autonomy for the Baltic states, Czechoslovakia, and Yugoslavia, but overall did little to salvage his liberal aims. The harsh measures instilled in the German people a spirit of resentment that would resurface in the 1930s and play a part in World War II.

Wilson's one clear victory at Versailles was the acceptance of his plan for a **League of Nations**. It was formed with five large nations (the United States, Britain, France, Italy, and Japan) serving as permanent members of a security council and with a General Assembly of more than 42 other nations; Germany and Russia were denied membership. The League of Nations embodied Wilson's dream of an organization whose purpose was to preserve peace and resolve conflicts. Article X of the League Covenant called for member nations to respect and preserve the integrity of other member nations against external aggressors.

Battle Over the League of Nations

In 1919, Wilson presented the **Treaty of Versailles** to the Senate for ratification in what became an uphill battle. Wilson had already alienated most Republicans in the Senate, and many senators were against American participation in any treaty.

Thirty-nine senators signed a letter rejecting the League of Nations, primarily because of the requirement in **Article X** that members protect the "territorial integrity" and "political independence" of other member states. This meant that the United States could become involved in a foreign conflict without the express approval of Congress and that the role of American sovereignty and independence in foreign affairs would be called into question. Ten to 15 senators, known as "irreconcilables," refused to consider joining the League altogether, and a group of about 35 "reservationists," led by **Senator Henry Cabot Lodge**, pledged to ratify the treaty only with major revisions. Wilson went on an 8,000-mile speaking tour in support of the treaty and collapsed in Pueblo, Colorado, on September 25, 1919, and later suffered a stroke on his return to Washington. He refused to compromise, however, and the treaty was rejected. The United States never joined the League of Nations and retreated into a period of isolationism in which it attempted to distance itself from involvement in foreign affairs.

Lesson 7-4: Post-War America

British, French, and Americans alike were greatly disillusioned by the war. The resulting "Lost Generation" had to deal with the reality of having its brightest and best killed by the war, leaving fewer men to carry on in leadership. German resentment about the war began to grow, and national problems arose in newly formed nations. Great Britain, France, and the United States retreated into **isolationism** during the 1920s and 1930s, leaving Europe ripe for new political leaders and new regimes that would create unique challenges for Europe in the 1930s.

World War I stimulated growth in the U.S. economy. Women and blacks entering the workforce added more people to the ranks of working Americans, and factory output, along with agricultural production, increased tremendously. After the war, the boom continued, in part because there was great demand for American goods from war-torn European countries.

Racism

The war also affected the demographics of the United States. An estimated 500,000 Southern blacks moved north during the war, most of them settling in cities to work at industrial jobs. But as urban black populations increased, so did racial strife. In 1917, a white mob in Illinois lit black homes on fire and shot the fleeing inhabitants, killing nearly 40 people. Weeks later, the NAACP organized a silent march down Fifth Avenue in New York to protest racial violence. In 1919, 83 blacks were victims of lynchings. That same year, race riots erupted in several cities.

More than 350,000 black solders served in World War I. They served in segregated units, mostly as support troops in cavalry, infantry, engineer, and artillery units. Some of the combat troops served with the French Army. They

served their country with honor and distinction, and several were awarded French medals of honor for their service. The Germans nicknamed soldiers of the black **369th Regiment** from New York the "Harlem Hellfighters" because of their dogged determination in fighting. They were one of the first groups to arrive in Europe for battle, and were one of the most widely decorated units upon their return from the war. Following the end of the war in 1918, many black soldiers expected to be treated as "war heroes" as the white soldiers they served with in war were, but, upon arriving back home, they were awakened to a new wave of racism and racial tension. Many feared a push by blacks to attain equality by challenging a segregated society. As the troops returned in 1919, several anti-black race riots erupted in cities across the country. Black war veterans became victims of lynchings and other acts of violence. Despite the conditions and treatment of veterans of World War I, black soldiers went on to serve with honor and distinction in World War II and served in an integrated army in the Korean War.

Red Scare

After World War I, anti-German hysteria turned into anti-Russian hysteria in response to the **Bolshevik Revolution** of 1917, which brought a communist regime to power. Although fewer than 100,000 Americans were members of the nation's communist parties, many Americans feared that communist influence went deeper and had infiltrated the working class, immigrant communities, and labor unions. They were afraid of communism, and socialism was increasingly suspect in labor problems.

In January 1919, a five-day strike by trade unions paralyzed Seattle. Mayor Hanson blamed radicals, and Congress began to suspect Bolshevist activity. Later in April, Mayor Hanson received a mail bomb at his office, and on May 1, 1919, **Attorney General Palmer** received a letter bomb, along with J. D. Rockefeller, Supreme Court Justice Holmes, and the postmaster general.

Palmer then began raids on radicals. The FBI was created, with J. Edgar Hoover as its first director. The bureau's directive was to root out subversives, and Hoover arrested hundreds of suspected radicals and deported many "undesirable" aliens, especially those with Eastern European backgrounds. In 1920, in a coordinated operation, police and federal marshals raided the homes of suspected radicals and the headquarters of radical organizations in 32 cities. These Palmer Raids resulted in more than 4,000 arrests, 550 deportations, and numerous challenges of civil rights violations.

Immigrant Fears

The 1920 **Sacco-Vanzetti case** aroused immigrant concerns when Sacco, an Italian shoemaker, and Vanzetti, a fish peddler, were arrested for the robbery and murder of a shoe company paymaster and a security guard in Massachusetts. At the time of their arrest, Sacco and Vanzetti were armed, self-proclaimed anarchists and Italian immigrants. They were convicted in 1921, and, after six years on death row, they were electrocuted in 1927. This incident, along with other strong anti-immigrant fears, would help inspire the passage of stricter immigration laws in the 1920s.

Review Exam

Multiple Choice

1. At the outset of World War I in 1914, Wilson _____.
   a) was determined to get the United States actively engaged in the conflict
   b) sought negotiations with the warring countries
   c) proclaimed a commitment to American neutrality
   d) imposed a military draft and an increase in military spending for weapons

2. In addition to secret alliances made before the war, all of the following are generally regarded as leading causes to World War I EXCEPT _____.
   a) an increase in militarism with the development of new weapons of warfare
   b) a decrease in nationalism
   c) an increase in imperialism
   d) the formation of the Triple Entente and Triple Alliance

3. The Zimmerman Telegram in 1917 was significant in that _____.
    a) Britain had intercepted the message from the German minister and passed it on to the United States
    b) it greatly outraged the United States against Germany and would lead to a formal declaration of war within weeks of its disclosure
    c) it made the promise to Mexico of awarding it territory it lost in 1848 when the United States seized the territory of the Mexican Cession after the Mexican American War in 1848
    d) A, B, and C

4. Former Ally _____ was not a member of the "Big Four" at the peace talks in Versailles, France in 1919.
    a) Lenin (USSR)   c) Lloyd George (Britain)
    b) Clemenceau (France)   d) Wilson (United States)

5. Republican Senator Henry Cabot Lodge on the Senate Foreign Relations committee _____.
    a) supported Wilson's 14 Points
    b) supported ratification of the Treaty of Versailles only with major revisions
    c) failed to support any of the provisions in the Treaty of Versailles
    d) held a series of debates in several places across the country to discuss the merits and problems of the treaty

6. Key components of Wilson's 14 Points included _____.
    a) freedom of the seas
    b) the formation of a League of Nations to promote peace
    c) national self-determination (the redrawing of boundary lines for countries in Europe)
    d) A, B, and C

7. Wilson's idealism in foreign affairs is best seen in his _____.
    a) declaration of war message to Congress on April 11, 1917, when he stressed the need to go to war was that of "making the world safe for democracy"
    b) dogged determination to see the formation of a League of Nations with the United States becoming a member in the new organization
    c) personal work in Europe and back at home with the Treaty of Versailles
    d) A, B, and C

8. The Bolshevik Revolution in Russia in 1917 was significant for all of the following EXCEPT that it _____.
   a) led to a nearly 74-year rule of the communists in Russia
   b) triggered a "Red Scare" of anti-communism in the United States in the early 1920s
   c) was a short-lived regime that came to an end with the Russian civil war that soon followed the takeover in 1917
   d) created animosity and distrust among the Allies in World War I that led them to not invite Russia to Versailles for peace negotiations

9. The sinking of the *Lusitania* in 1915 was significant in that it _____.
   a) was a surprise U-boat attack by the Germans
   b) resulted in the deaths of 128 Americans onboard the ship
   c) promoted an immediate declaration of war by the United States
   d) A and B only

10. The Committee on Public Information had the role of _____.
    a) using propaganda as a means of bolstering the war effort
    b) enlisting the help of artists, musicians, journalists, and authors to publicize events about the war in order to gain public support
    c) using the government's Espionage Act to suppress antiwar sentiment
    d) A, B, and C

11. *Schenck v. the U.S.* (1919) ruled _____.
    a) that Congress could restrict free speech when it might create a "clear and present danger," especially during a time of war
    b) for a balanced approach in dealing with economic, environmental, and foreign issues
    c) against attacks on monopolies
    d) solely on domestic issues

12. Most of the major fighting in World War I was centered in the _____ region.
    a) Western Front
    b) Eastern Front
    c) the waters of the English Channel, North Sea, and north Atlantic
    d) Southeastern Europe in the Balkan Peninsula

13. New weapons of warfare that were used in World War included _____.
    a) poison gas and gas masks   c) machine guns
    b) submarines (U-boats)   d) A, B, and C

14. The involvement in the war changed America in all of the following ways EXCEPT that _____.
    a) women were still viewed as the protectors of the home and were discouraged from assisting in the war effort
    b) propaganda was used to shape and unify public opinion
    c) famous movie stars were used to promote the sale of war bonds
    d) the pro-war efforts helped generate the public's mistrust, even hated, of Germany and the Central Powers

15. The Treaty of Versailles included many of the provisions of Wilson's proposed 14 Points as well as establishing all of the following EXCEPT _____.
    a) a total "war guilt" clause to punish Germany and make it libel for war reparations
    b) the new country of Poland as a buffer nation between Germany and Russia
    c) the League of Nations, which allowed for Germany and Russia to be participants
    d) President Taft

16. Article X of the League of Nations proposal in the Treaty of Versailles angered some in Congress when the treaty came up for ratification because _____.
    a) this meant that the United States could become involved in a foreign conflict without the express approval of Congress
    b) the role of American sovereignty and independence in foreign affairs would be called into question
    c) the proposed treaty already had enough votes for ratification and they feared that their concerns would not be addressed
    d) A and B only

17. The end of the conflict in Europe in World War I and the rise of communism in Russia led the United States to _____.
    a) move toward isolationism and withdrawing for involvement in foreign affairs
    b) fear a communist infiltration here at home
    c) become disillusioned about war
    d) A, B, and C

Matching

a. Eugene Debs
b. isolationism
c. Spanish Influenza
d. Allies
e. Armistice
f. Espionage Act
g. Gavrilo Princip

h. 369th Regiment
i. Sussex Pledge
j. Sedition Act
k. Central Powers
l. Brest-Litovsk
m. Alsace-Lorraine
n. 14 Points

o. Selective Service Act
p. Sacco-Vanzetti case
q. Palmer Raids
r. Big Four
s. Attorney General Palmer
t. Peace Fund
u. Pancho Villa

____18. Wilson's plan to resolve the conflict in Europe

____19. Great Britain, France and Russia (later to include Italy and the Untied States) in WWI

____20. started with Andrew Carnegie's donation in 1910 to form a group that would try to avert U.S. involvement in foreign conflicts

____21. draft bill that Congress passed in 1917 authorizing men ages 21 to 30 years old to register for military duty

____22. agreement that was signed on November 11, 1918, at 11 a.m. formally ending the conflict in WWI

____23. the United States, Great Britain, France, and Italy were known as this at the peace negotiations in 1919

____24. Germany and Austria-Hungary in WWI

____25. action that resulted in more than 4,000 arrests and deportations of more than 500 for suspected communist activity in 1920

____26. Germany issued this agreement promising not to attack any further merchant ships with U-boats without a formal warning

____27. Serbian terrorist responsible for the assassination of Archduke Ferdinand in 1914 that led directly to the outbreak of WWI

____28. place where Russia signed a secret treaty with Germany and withdrew from the war in 1918

____29. the government's main tool for suppression of antiwar sentiment during WWI

____30. he and three other prominent Americans received letter bombs in the mail during the "Red Scare" following the end of WWI

____31. leader in Mexico who in 1916 who mounted a raid on a small town in New Mexico; in retaliation, President Wilson ordered more than 12,000 troops to the border to pursue him

____32. prominent Socialist and presidential candidate who was jailed for his anti-war activities

____33. law that outlawed any "disloyal, profane, querulous or abusive language intended to cause contempt, scorn, or disrespect for the government, Constitution, or flag"

____34. massive flu outbreak that spread worldwide near the end of WWI and was responsible for more than 600,000 deaths in the United States

____35. disputed territory between France and Germany that was returned to France following the end of WWI and the peace negotiations

____36. following the end of WWI and the treaty negotiations the United States retreated into this, choosing to limit its involvement in foreign affairs

____37. known as the "Harlem Hellfighters"; one of most determined group of black soldiers that served with distinction in WWI

____38. case involving anarchist immigrants who were sentenced to death for their crimes of robbery and murder

Short Response

39. How did the United States move from its stance on neutrality to involvement in World War I **"over there"**?

40. How did Americans react to dissent and suspicion during the war and in the period immediately following the war?

41. To what extent was the United States ready to assume a role on the world stage after World War I ended?

Answers begin on page 290.

The Roaring '20s

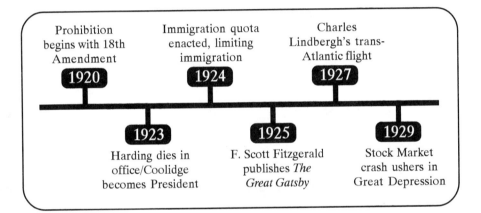

Prohibition begins with 18th Amendment
1920

Immigration quota enacted, limiting immigration
1924

Charles Lindbergh's trans-Atlantic flight
1927

1923
Harding dies in office/Coolidge becomes President

1925
F. Scott Fitzgerald publishes *The Great Gatsby*

1929
Stock Market crash ushers in Great Depression

Trends and Themes of the Era

▶ America turned away from the ideals of progressivism. Republicans regained the presidency and ushered in an era of pro-business policies.

▶ Government policies, technological progress, and a new consumer society produced a booming economy, and a mass popular culture developed that was largely based on the consumption of luxury items and "making it rich."

▶ Tired and disillusioned from the war, America entered a period of isolationism. The United States aimed to stay out of European affairs and to make life at home as "normal" as possible.

▶ The younger generation rebelled against traditional morals. Women became more forward in dress and behavior. The two symbols of this new, looser social behavior were jazz and the "flapper."

Fords, flappers, and fanatics! World War I drastically changed how people viewed themselves and the world during the decade of the 1920s. Many people were disgusted with death and destruction, and became almost frantic in their pursuit of pleasure. Although the economy prospered and consumer goods boomed after the war, underlying problems became evident throughout the decade. Traditional values came under attack as Americans defied conventional morality, and many people felt a loss of security. Hollywood and Harlem, along with radio, newspapers, and magazines, helped define this new era. It was also the era of jazz music, bootleggers, gangsters, Babe Ruth, radio shows, and "talkies." The dark side of the decade was evidenced by the Red Scare, strikes, social tensions, lynchings, walkouts, and general lawlessness during Prohibition. The basic weakness in the '20s economy lay in the unequal shares of corporate and individual wealth. The extension of easy credit and speculation of the stock market added to the growing problems in the economy. The cry of a "return to normalcy" began the 1920s, but the decade ended with the disastrous stock market crash of 1929, which led to hard times and the worst economic depression in U.S. history.

Lesson 8-1: "A Return to Normalcy"

In the early 1920s, weary from fighting a world war, Americans sought stability. Popular support for Republicans grew, because the Republican platform promised a "return to **normalcy.**" Republicans stopped promising progressive reforms and instead aimed to settle into traditional patterns of government.

Domestic Policies

In 1920, after eight years under a progressive Democrat, Americans elected a conservative Republican as president. Big business and isolationism advocates reaped the benefits of Republican rule. The Republican presidents of the 1920s—Harding, Coolidge, and Hoover—reversed the Progressive Era trend of regulating big business and lowering tariffs. Instead, their policies generally gave corporations free rein, raised protective tariffs, and cut taxes for the wealthy.

The Supreme Court overturned a number of measures designed to regulate business activities. The Court declared boycotts by labor unconstitutional and authorized the use of antitrust laws against unions. The **Fordney-McCumber Tariff** (1922) and the **Hawley-Smoot Tariff** (1930), along with other tariffs, hiked rates to all-time highs to protect American companies from international competition. In addition, Andrew Mellon, treasury secretary from 1921 to 1932, persuaded Congress to lower income tax rates for the wealthy.

Warren G. Harding won the 1920 election by a landslide on the promise of a "return to normalcy." Harding was relatively unknown nationally, but he gained a reputation for "enjoying good liquor, good stories, and a good game of poker." In addition to its pro-business stance, however, the Harding administration's legacy was one of corruption, exposed fully after Harding's death from a heart attack in 1923. Many officials were forced from office, and some narrowly escaped prison time.

The most prominent affair, the **Teapot Dome Scandal**, involved Secretary of the Interior **Albert B. Fall** secretly leasing government oil reserves in Wyoming and California in 1922 to two businessmen and accepting about $400,000 in return. Accusations of an illicit affair resulting the birth of a daughter also surfaced from the president's mistress, **Nan Britton**. Attorney General Henry Daughtery accepted bribes from Prohibition violators and failed to investigate problems within the Veterans' Bureau. Charles Forbes, who headed the bureau, pocketed large chunks of $250 million earmarked for veterans' hospitals and supplies; he fled the country to avoid prosecution.

Herbert Hoover, secretary of commerce, proposed a pro-business policy based on the assumption that when encouraged and informed by the government, businesses would act in the public interest, essentially a return to the laissez-faire politics of the Gilded Age. **Andrew Mellon**, secretary of treasury, proposed in his economic plan to trim the federal budget and cut taxes on income, corporate profits, and inheritances. He claimed that tax cuts would free up capital for new investment and economic growth. Mellon's policies benefiting business and the rich would be one of many factors leading to the Great Depression in late 1929.

Foreign Affairs

After World War I, the United States retreated into **isolationism**, and the foreign policy focus reflected the philosophy of non-aggression and retreating from global affairs. The United States refused to join either the League of Nations or the World Court established by the League.

However, despite its isolationism, the United States did become involved in international affairs over the issue of war debts and reparations. The Allies had borrowed substantially from the United States during World War I and couldn't pay back the debt. Meanwhile, Germany owed reparations to the Allies but also couldn't pay. The **Dawes Plan**, devised by American banker Charles G. Dawes in 1924, scaled back U.S. demands for debt payments and reparations and established a cycle of U.S. loans that provided Germany with money to pay reparations to the Allies, thus funding Allied debt payments to America.

Harding's secretary of state, Charles Hughes, worked at drawing up the **Five-Power Treaty** in 1922, which served as a plan for the most powerful naval powers to disarm to a set level and to delay future large naval construction for 10 years. The United States, Great Britain, Japan, France, and Italy signed the agreement. Coolidge's secretary of state, Frank Kellogg, negotiated the **Kellogg-Briand Pact** in 1928 with France and 13 other nations. This agreement outlawed war as a means of resolving international conflicts, relying on peaceful negotiations instead.

Presidential Successors

Harding's vice president, Calvin Coolidge, became president upon Harding's death from a heart attack in 1923, and then ran for office himself in 1924. In contrast to his predecessor, the "Keep Cool with Coolidge" presidency ran a relatively scandal-free White House. Coolidge believed that government should interfere as little as possible in the affairs of businesses. He was anti-union and staunchly pro-business; Coolidge opposed government regulating or interfering with the economy. In 1926, the Revenue Act was passed to reduce high income and estate taxes, a form of trickle-down economics intended to boost the economy.

Herbert Hoover, the third Republican president of the decade, rode the tide of economic prosperity to victory in 1928. Shortly after the election, he proclaimed, "We in America are nearer to the final triumph over poverty." Yet, within a year, America would be rocked by the worst depression in its history.

Hoover took a slightly different tack toward big business than had his predecessors. He thought that capitalism produced social obligations, but he believed in voluntarism rather than government coercion as the best way to fulfill those obligations. Hoover urged industry reform but refused to mandate it with laws. This reliance on voluntarism would hurt him as prosperity began to fade.

Lesson 8-2: A Decade of Prosperity: Economic and Political Challenges

Following a postwar recession from mid-1920 to the end of 1921, the economy picked up again and remained strong until the end of the decade. This prosperity, combined with tax cuts for the rich, led to a booming consumer culture.

The very nature of consumerism changed during this period, as new products poured into the market. The automobile first became popular outside wealthy circles in the 1920s. Electrical appliances, such as refrigerators, washing machines, and vacuum cleaners, were consumer favorites. The incredible speed and the vast reach of the newly invented radio created a national market and spurred advertising to unprecedented levels.

One effect of prosperity was the consolidation of big business and banks. By 1929, more than 1,000 companies a year were being swallowed up by mergers. A few corporations dominated major industries, such as Ford and Chrysler in automobiles and General Electric in electricity and electric appliances.

Rising Productivity

New technologies allowed corporations to meet public demand by boosting productivity. By 1913, Henry Ford began to apply the **assembly line** process in his automobile plants to maximize output by having workers stay in one place and master one repeated task. This process greatly increased the production of automobiles. Sales of the car were so brisk that by the mid-1920s the price for a new Model T Ford was advertised at $298—well within reach of most Americans (even on an installment plan). Buyers could purchase the Model T "in any color as long as it was black." Ford also revolutionized the industry by paying his workers a $5/day working wage. This was the highest in any industry. Ford was able to build a large and reliable workforce that built his cars, but it also gave his workers money to keep them happy at work so that they could afford to buy the things they needed for their families, including a car from Ford!

Ford also faced increased competition from automobile manufacturers such as Chevrolet, which used the concept of planned obsolescence, and color and interior upgrade options to keep consumers coming back for more. New developments in management methods improved efficiency by departmentalizing various business concerns and creating a class of professional managers. Installment buying and credit programs allowed consumers to buy expensive goods they couldn't afford to purchase with one payment. Consumer debt increased along with consumer spending during the 1920s.

Labor and Agriculture

The 1920s ushered in a new era for workers. To increase productivity, some employers raised the wages of skilled workers without the urging of labor unions. Manufacturers' associations praised the nonunion workplace, and companies made concessions to workers in attempts to stave off unionization. Union membership declined during the 1920s.

This industrial boom largely left agriculture behind. Crop prices fell rapidly between 1919 and 1921, and remained low throughout the 1920s. Although crop yields continued to increase, farmers were hard-pressed to make a profit. Many farmers also saw their family-owned farms consolidated into larger farms run by corporations. The Republican policy of noninterference in the economy meant there would be little help for the struggling farmers.

Immigration

Immigration restriction emerged as a part of American isolationism. Not only did isolationists oppose U.S. involvement in European affairs, but they also opposed the flood of European immigrants coming to the United States. Between 1900 and 1915, more than 13 million immigrants arrived in America, many of them from Eastern and Southern Europe, and many either Catholic or Jewish, to the general dismay of the Protestant American public. Many Americans viewed these immigrants as a threat to traditional religious and social values, as well as to economic opportunities because many felt that immigrants took jobs away from Americans.

In 1921, Congress set a quota of 350,000 for annual immigration. In 1924, the **National Origins Act** (1924) cut that number to 164,000 and restricted immigration from any one nation to 2 percent of the number of people of that national origin in the United States in 1890. The new standard greatly curtailed immigration from southern and Eastern Europe, and excluded Asians entirely. The quotas would remain in place until 1965.

Lesson 8-3: Social and Racial Tensions

The prosperity and leisure of the 1920s masked serious social tensions. In the political realm, these tensions were exposed in isolationism and anti-immigration policies. Elsewhere in American society, social tensions centered on questions of race, religion, and religious fundamentalism.

Marcus Garvey

Many blacks, unhappy with the continued slow pace of social advancement, turned to **Marcus Garvey** and the United Negro Improvement Association (UNIA), which Garvey had moved from Jamaica to the United States in 1916. Garvey glorified black culture and founded a chain of UNIA businesses to promote black economic cooperation. His separatist philosophy claimed that white people's racial bias made it impossible to appeal to their sense of justice. Garvey urged American blacks to return to Africa and establish an independent nation.

The Garvey movement attracted many followers with its message of racial pride and self-reliance. The UNIA claimed more than half a million members, though Garvey himself said membership was around six million, but the group was sharply criticized by the NAACP for being too radical. W. E. B. DuBois labeled Garvey "the most dangerous enemy of the Negro race." In 1923, Marcus Garvey was found guilty of mail fraud, and in 1927 he was deported to Jamaica. The UNIA couldn't survive without Garvey's leadership, but the group left an important legacy as a prominent African American mass movement.

The NAACP was a more conservative force for social reform. Led by W. E. B. DuBois, the NAACP called for integration and equal treatment for blacks. In part because of the black migration northward during World War I, membership in the NAACP grew markedly during the early 1920s. Still, lynchings continued in the South, and racist Americans gained influence through organizations such as the KKK. In 1922, an anti-lynching bill was passed in the House, only to be defeated by a filibuster by Southern senators. Although the bill died in Congress, lynchings began to decline, due in large part to the efforts of the NAACP. The NAACP also continued to fight vigorously for the enforcement of the 14th and 15th Amendments.

The Ku Klux Klan

Nativism, the concept of distinguishing "native" or natural-born Americans from those people who were foreigners who immigrated to this country, and intolerance were the driving forces in the resurgence of the Ku Klux Klan (KKK) in 1915. Thanks in large part to D. W. Griffith's 1915 movie, *Birth of a Nation*, which glorified the KKK as the heroes of Reconstruction, the Klan organized a wildly successful membership drive in 1920. By the mid-1920s, the number of new recruits was estimated as high as 5 million.

Instead of targeting just blacks for attack, as the earlier Klan had done, the new Klan expanded its targets to include feminists, Jews, and Catholics. By calling for "100 percent Americanism," the Klan capitalized on middle-class Protestant dismay at changing social and economic conditions in America. The group continued to be portrayed as a patriotic organization dedicated to preserving the values of liberty, duty, justice, and honor.

The Klan took root throughout the South, where it mostly targeted blacks, and in parts of the West and Midwest, where Catholics and Jews bore the brunt of Klan intimidation and murder. In some states, the Klan even exerted dominant political and social power. The Klan collapsed in 1925 after widespread corruption among Klan leadership was exposed. Membership faded quickly, but the Klan would return after World War II as a significant force.

The Scopes Monkey Trial

During the late 19th and early 10th centuries, science challenged the infallibility of religious doctrine. Liberal Protestants accepted the majority of scientific findings and tried to integrate these findings into their religion, but more conservative Protestants refused to do this. That refusal was part of **fundamentalism**, a philosophy that insisted on the divine inspiration and literal truth of every word in the Bible.

In the early 1920s, one of fundamentalism's main goals was refuting the theory of evolution. Articulated by Charles Darwin in 1895, evolution contradicted strictly literal biblical accounts of man's creation. **William Jennings Bryan**, former presidential candidate and secretary of state, led a movement to ban schools from teaching evolution. In 1925, the Tennessee legislature did just that, prompting the American Civil Liberties Union (ACLU) to offer to defend any teacher willing to challenge the law. John T. Scopes accepted the offer, broke the law, and was arrested, bringing the issue to court.

In the famed **Scopes Monkey Trial**, Bryan aided the prosecution, and Chicago lawyer **Clarence Darrow** defended Scopes. The judge wouldn't allow expert testimony, leaving the matter basically up to debate between Darrow and Bryan. In cross-examination, Darrow made a fool of Bryan, exposing Bryan's lack of scientific knowledge. Although Scopes was found guilty, the nation generally considered the antifundamentalist forces to have won the argument.

Lesson 8-4: The Jazz Age: Culture in the 1920s

According to one journalist in 1920, Americans were "weary of being noble" after a decade of intense progressive reform, morality, and self-righteousness. The 1920s saw a restless culture, with rebellious youth openly challenging the moral restrictions of past generations.

"The Flapper"

During the decades, many youth challenged traditional notions of proper behavior. Buoyed by the decade's prosperity, young people threw wild parties, drank illegal liquor, and danced new, sexually suggestive steps at jazz clubs. One of the symbols of this decade was the **flapper**, a name given to the fashionable, pleasure-seeking young women of the time. The flapper look was tomboyish and flamboyant: short, bobbed hair; knee-length, fringed skirts; long, draping necklaces; rolled stockings and makeup. **Clara Bow** became known as the "It Girl," promoting the flapper image on the big screen. Although few women actually fit this image, it was widely used in media and movies to represent the rebelliousness of the period.

With new social thinking and activities came new social conventions. Among the youth of the 1920s, sex became far less taboo. It was more openly discussed, and premarital sex became more common. Such activity led to the promotion of birth control, even though it was still widely illegal. The sexual revolution also brought changing ideas about women. New women's fashion trends of higher hemlines, bobbed hair, and makeup illustrated more of these changes.

Margaret Sanger and other activists began promoting specific ideas about sex including birth control, limiting family size, and the woman's role in sex. In 1923, the National Woman's Party proposed an Equal Rights Amendment (ERA) stating that "men and women shall have equal rights throughout the U.S. and in every place subject to its jurisdiction." Many women continued to push for full legal and civil rights.

It's important to note that although Roaring '20s characters and events came to symbolize the decade, these stereotypes fit only a small segment of society. Outside the cities, traditional values were never discarded completely, or even much changed. As movies, radio, and advertising spread across the country, Americans began to adopt the media's ideal and to share the sense of a national culture.

Prohibition

The **18th Amendment**, which made it illegal to manufacture, sell, or transport alcoholic beverages, was ratified in January 1919 and went into effect in 1920. It also provided a measure that allowed U.S. federal agents to investigate and prosecute violators. Enforcement of Prohibition, however, was sporadic and under-funded. For most of the decade, U.S. Marshals were used as the principal enforcers of Prohibition laws. Prohibition faced opposition in a number of states and cities, especially Northern cities, where many Prohibition laws were repealed. By the end of the decade, alcohol consumption was 70 percent of pre-1920 levels. Prohibition fueled much debate until its repeal in 1933 with the **21st Amendment**.

Given this lax enforcement, many Americans viewed Prohibition as a passing fad. Bootleggers smuggled liquor from the West Indies and Canada, and **speakeasies** in many cities provided alcohol illegally. Organized crime controlled alcohol distribution in major American cities, and gangsters such as **Al Capone** made a fortune as law enforcement officials often looked the other way. Capone's income in 1927 reportedly exceeded $1 million at a time when the average American's income was less than $2,500. In 1929, he ordered the massacres of bootlegger "Bugs" Moran and some of his men in what became known as the **St. Valentine's Day Massacre**. Two of Capone's men disguised themselves as policemen and during the raid; they easily killed Moran's men.

Moran escaped the gunfire by staying across the street when Capone's men arrived. Capone's alibi in this assault was simple: He was in Florida during the massacre. Two years later, he was tried and convicted for tax evasion in 1931, and was given an 11-year sentence. He was released in 1939 after spending eight years at Alcatraz.

The Harlem Renaissance

During World War I, Southern blacks migrated from tenement share-cropping farms to Northern cities including Detroit, Chicago, and New York. They sought better jobs and living conditions as they migrated northward. The harsh realities of violence, segregation, and few job opportunities left them with few options.

The 1920s saw a flowering of African-American artistic culture. Black musicians expressed themselves through jazz, an improvisational and sponta-neous musical form derived in part from slave songs and African spirituals. Jazz first emerged in the early 1900s in New Orleans, then spread to Chicago, New York City, and elsewhere. The 1920s is often called the **Jazz Age** because jazz flourished and gained widespread appeal during the decade. The music was associated with the "loose" morals and relaxed social codes of the time. Among the famous jazz performers of the period were Louis Armstrong, Josephine Baker, Bessie Smith, and Duke Ellington. Harlem became "the place" to be for jazz, as performers played in venues such as the **Cotton Club**. At this nightclub, and others like it, black jazz musicians and dancers per-formed to all-white audiences because blacks often were not allowed to at-tend the clubs. Harlem was the site of social as well as intellectual activity, where prominent and wealthy blacks hosted extravagant gatherings for Harlem Renaissance figures.

The blossoming of black literature in the Northeast, especially in New York City's Harlem, was known as the **Harlem Renaissance**. Black artists ex-plored the African-American story through poetry and novels. Three of the most famous authors of the time were Langston Hughes, who published "The Weary Blues" and "Let America be America Again"; Claude McKay who published several works, including *Home to Harlem*; and Zora Neale Hurston, who wrote *Their Eyes Were Watching God*. These works dealt with portrayals of black life and struggles during this time.

Lesson 8-5: The "Lost Generation"

Authors continued to emphasize 1920s stereotypes in their works, espe-cially F. Scott Fitzgerald. Fitzgerald wrote extensively about the rebellious youth of the Jazz Age in stories and novels such as *This Side of Paradise* (1920) and *The Great Gatsby* (1925). In *The Great Gatsby*, his most famous novel, Fitzgerald criticized the superficiality and material excess of post-war culture. Other literary figures questioned American post-war society as well. Sinclair Lewis attacked America's Protestant, middle-class, conformist morality in his 1922 work, *Babbitt*.

Disgusted with an American lifestyle that they saw as overly materialistic and spiritually void, many writers of the period fled to Europe and spent time in Paris with other expatriates, including Ezra Pound, Gertrude Stein, and Ernest Hemingway. The most famous expatriate, Hemingway, produced *The Sun Also Rises* (1926) and *A Farewell to Arms* (1929), both reflecting the horror and futility of World War I. Their self-imposed exile gave them the nickname the **"lost generation."**

Lesson 8-6: Popular Culture and Entertainment

Hollywood and Harlem both rose to become centers of culture in the 1920s. Popular recreation grew by leaps and bounds during the decade, in part because of high wages and increased leisure time. Just as automobiles were mass-produced during the 1920s, so was recreation. Mass-circulation magazines such as *Reader's Digest* and *Time* (established in 1922 and 1923, respectively) enjoyed enormous success. Radio also rose to prominence as a source of news and entertainment during the 1920s: NBC was founded in 1926 and CBS a year later.

Hollywood movie studios such as Paramount, Fox, MGM, Universal, and Warner Brothers made a dramatic impact on the culture. Movies were the most popular leisure attraction of the times, making stars out of Charlie Chaplin, Rudolph Valentino, Gloria Swanson, and Mary Pickford. In 1927, the "talkies" (movies with sound) debuted with Al Jolson's *The Jazz Singer,* and 1928 saw the first animated sound film, *Steamboat Willy*. Its main character's name, Mortimor Mouse, was later changed to Mickey Mouse.

Professional sports gained new popularity as well. The decade started with the infamous **Black Sox baseball scandal** in the 1919 World Series when eight players, including Shoeless Joe Jackson, from the Chicago Black Sox, were accused of gambling and throwing the World Series to the Cincinnati Reds. News of this event swept the nation and, although acquitted of charges, the eight players were banned from professional baseball for life.

Soon, new baseball stars such as New York Yankee **Babe Ruth** restored the country's passion for the game, and fans flocked to stadiums to cheer on their new heroes. When Yankee Stadium was opened in 1923, it became known as "The House that Ruth Built" in large part due to the huge crowds that Ruth and the Yankees drew out to games. When Babe Ruth retired from baseball in 1935, his homerun record stood at 714.

Other sports figures helped add popularity to spectator sports during the 1920s and well into the 1930s. Boxing had many heroes that included **Jack Dempsey**, heavyweight champion from 1919 to 1926, and **James J. Braddock**, who made a great comeback after losing the fight for the light heavyweight title in 1929. In 1935, after being an underdog and nearly forgotten by the public, he won the heavyweight championship by beating Max Baer. College sports, especially football, also captured the attention of sports enthusiasts across the nation during this time.

Non-sporting national heroes also emerged, such as **Charles Lindbergh**, who made the first solo nonstop flight across the Atlantic in May 1927. The idolization of silver-screen heroes as well as other famous people and sports figures dominated the headlines. The broad appeal of these role models helped expand the developing national culture.

Lesson 8-7: From Boom to Bust

Several economic factors of the 1920s assisted in ushering in the worst depression in American history. What began as a decade of self-identity, and a bull market with stock values that continued to rise promising prosperity, ended with the loss of nearly everything. Five days before the crash of the stock market in October 1929, President Hoover stated, "The fundamental business of the country is on a sound and prosperous basis." In an interview for *Ladies Home Journal* in August 1929 entitled "Everybody Ought to Be Rich," **John Raskob**, vice president of General Motors, stressed the need to invest at least $15 a month in investment stock in order to retire in a "comfortable manner." During the amazing bull market of the mid- to late 1920s, people would buy stock on margin, with as little as 10 percent down, because prices were continuing to rise along with profits. With the profits from the stock investments, they would be able to pay back the loan and continue to invest in the stock market by purchasing more stock.

What began on **Black Thursday**, October 24, 1929, continued on **Black Tuesday**, October 29, 1929. The inflated and overextended stock market crashed, resulting in a one-day loss of $14 billion worth of the value of stock. Rampant speculation, installment credit policies, and overpriced stock during the latter part of the decade led to the problems on Wall

Street. The minor fluctuations in the market in 1929 set off a downward spiral that would not bottom out until 1932. By the end of 1929, stock prices had fallen by 50 percent, and they were down by another 30 percent by 1932. Many stocks on the exchange either were wiped out or suffered dramatic price declines. Within three years, $74 billion of wealth had vanished from the economy.

The Crash of '29 had a catastrophic effect on the economy and on the lives of nearly every American in the following decade. Throughout the first year of the depression, President Hoover refused to use the word *depression* and encouraged the general public that things would soon turn around and that "hope was just around the corner." That corner never came. Within three years, industrial production dropped more than 50 percent; the Gross National Product declined by nearly 50 percent; business, farm, and personal bankruptcies were prevalent; and unemployment reached 25 percent. The crash started a 12-year downturn in the American economy, making it the most devastating economic event in the history of the United States. It would become one of the major defining points of the 20th century.

Review Exam

Multiple Choice

1. Although he campaigned on the slogan of promising a return to "normalcy," Harding's presidency was _____.
   a) marked by scandal
   b) seen as a reaction to the end of World War I and wanting to forget the harsh realities of war and return to "normal"
   c) a return of the Republicans in power and a focus on "pro-business" measures
   d) A, B, and C

2. Despite the policy of isolationism following the end of World War I, the United States sought a very limited role in foreign affairs, as evidenced by the _____.
   a) Dawes Plan that proposed a scale-back in demands for Germany war reparations
   b) Five-Power treaty that was a naval disarmament plan between the United States, Great Britain, France, Italy, and Japan
   c) Kellogg-Briand Pact, which was an agreement outlawing the use of war as a means of resolving international conflicts
   d) A, B, and C

3. All of the following are true about Henry Ford's impact on the country with his model T automobiles EXCEPT that _____.

a) the assembly line of production was a slow process that meant that it took more time to build automobiles

b) sales of the Model T were so brisk that the price dropped to $298 for a new car

c) the model T could be purchased in any color as long as it was black

d) his workers were paid a $5 a day wage (the highest of any industry)

4. The National Origins Act of 1924 was significant in that it _____.

a) aimed at curtailing immigrants from coming into this country, especially those from Southern and Eastern Europe

b) dramatically reduced immigration rates

c) totally excluded all Asian immigrants

d) A, B, and C

5. The Scopes Monkey Trial _____.

a) involved the teaching of evolution in a Tennessee science classroom

b) sought to promote both creationism and evolution

c) saw both Clarence Darrow and William Jennings Bryan make impassioned arguments in court for or against the teaching of evolution

d) A and C only

6. The flapper _____.

a) was a symbol of the modern woman of the 1920s

b) was the new fashion look that involved a bobbed hairstyle; knee-length, fringed skirts; and long, draping necklaces

c) symbolized a "rebellious" spirit

d) A, B, and C

7. All of the following are true about the era of Prohibition EXCEPT that _____.

a) the newly ratified 18th Amendment banned the manufacture, sale, and transportation of alcohol

b) crime was vigorously enforced in the 1920s and actually declined during the decade

c) repealed with the 21st Amendment in 1933

d) organized crime increased in the decade of the 1920s

8. The Jazz Age _____.
   a) was a time of the enforcement of conservative values
   b) was short-lived due to the enforcement of Prohibition
   c) is the name given to the period of the 1920s because of the growth and popularity of jazz music
   d) was a phenomenon that soon ended by the stock market crash of 1929

9. All of the following are true about the Harlem Renaissance EXCEPT that it was _____.
   a) a black literary and artistic movement popular only with blacks
   b) the time when Harlem was "the place to be" for jazz performers such as Duke Ellington and others
   c) a time of the blossoming of black literature by authors such as Langston Hughes, Claude McKay, and Zora Neale Hurston
   d) popular with a cross-section of society

10. All of the following are true about media and entertainment in the in the 1920s EXCEPT that _____.
    a) *Reader's Digest* and *Time* magazines began to be published
    b) radio was finding limited success with their news, music, and entertainment shows
    c) silent movies were the rage of the decade with actors including Charlie Chaplin, Rudolph Valentino, and Mary Pickford
    d) *The Jazz Singer* and *Steamboat Willie* were two of the first "talkies" that revolutionized the movie industry

11. The decade of the 1920s was a time for "heroes"—sports figures and other individuals—whose feats encouraged widespread public admiration. This is true for all of the following EXCEPT _____.
    a) Jack Dempsey, heavyweight boxing champion
    b) Shoeless Joe Jackson of the Chicago Black Sox
    c) Babe Ruth of the New York Yankees
    d) Charles Lindbergh with his trans-Atlantic flight in 1927

12. The Stock Market Crash of 1929 was significant in that it had a catastrophic effect on the economy so that _____.
    a) by the end of 1929 stock prices had plummeted by nearly 50 percent
    b) the inflated and overextended stock that had grown due to rampant speculation was losing value
    c) within three years more than $74 billion of wealth had been wiped out
    d) A, B, and C

13. Consumer spending was encouraged during the 1920s with _____.
   a) increased advertising and marketing of goods
   b) consumers' ability to buy on credit with an installment plan
   c) a wide range of new products, including automobiles
   d) A, B, and C

14. _____ was not a Republican president during the 1920s.
   a) Warren G. Harding   c) Charles Forbes
   b) Herbert Hoover   d) Calvin Coolidge

15. All of the following helped create a "national culture" during the 1920s EXCEPT _____.
   a) radio programs
   b) ragtime music
   c) silent movies and the new "talkies" (movies with sound)
   d) the automobile

16. _____, written in 1925 by F. Scott Fitzgerald, is often used as a symbol of life during the Jazz Age of the 1920s.
   a) *A Farwell to Arms*   c) *The Great Gatsby*
   b) *The Sun Also Rises*   d) *Their Eyes Were Watching God*

17. During the 1920s, _____ affected or symbolized the decade.
   a) jazz music
   b) the automobile
   c) Prohibition, speakeasies, and gang violence
   d) A, B, and C

Matching

a. Herbert Hoover

b. John Raskob

c. Equal Rights Amendment

d. NAACP

e. Cotton Club

f. fundamentalism

g. Andrew Mellon

h. KKK

i. Black Sox

j. Fordney-McCumber and Hawley-Smoot Tariffs

k. Lost Generation

l. William Jennings Bryan

m. "normalcy"

n. St. Valentine's day Massacre

o. Marcus Garvey

p. Clarence Darrow

q. Al Capone

r. nativism

s. speakeasies

t. trickle down economics

u. Teapot Dome Scandal

_____18. served as Harding's secretary of the treasury and proposed big tax cuts to benefit the rich

_____19. Harding's campaign slogan in 1920

_____20. team involved in the infamous baseball scandal in 1919 and was accused of gambling and throwing the World Series to the Cincinnati Reds

_____21. organization whose membership peaked at nearly 5 million by the middle of the 1920s

_____22. raised tariffs to all-time highs during the 1920s in an attempt to protect American companies for foreign competition

_____23. secret places that provided illegal alcohol during the 1920s

_____24. the concept of distinguishing "native" or natural-born Americans from those people who were foreigners who immigrated to this country

_____25. served as secretary of commerce during the Harding administration and ran for president in 1928

_____26. defended John T. Scopes when the biology teacher was on trial for violating Tennessee law by teaching evolution in his classroom

_____27. a philosophy that insisted on divine interpretation and literal truth of every word in the Bible

_____28. the symbol of organized gangster crime in the 1920s, who was eventually arrested and convicted of tax evasion in 1931

_____29. leader of the United Negro Improvement Association that glorified black culture and promoted the concept of blacks returning to Africa to establish an independent nation there

_____30. Fitzgerald, Pound, Stein, and Hemingway were famous Americans who were disgusted and disillusioned with the American lifestyle of the post-war era of the 1920s and came to symbolize this group

_____31. led a movement to ban the teaching of evolution in schools and debated this issue during the famous Scopes Trial

_____32. an attempt by Capone to kill bootlegger "Bugs" Moran and some of his men in 1929

_____33. opposed Garvey's UNIA and denounced Garvey as "the most dangerous enemy of the Negro race"

_____34. promoted the concept of "everybody ought to be rich" in a 1929 article in *Ladies Home Journal*

_____35. a proposed amendment in 1923 that advocated equal rights for women

_____36. this involved the secret leasing of government oil reserves in 1922 by Albert Fall, Secretary of the Interior

_____37. a Republican Party policy that favored tax breaks for the rich and a reduction in estate taxes intended to boost the economy

_____38. the site in Harlem where jazz performers such as Duke Ellington and Louis Armstrong could be heard

Short Response

39. To what extent did isolationism shape American foreign policy in the 1920s?

40. What effect did Republican policies have on the economy of the 1920s? What comparisons can be made between the economic policies of the 1920s and those of the Gilded Age?

41. What influences did Harlem and Hollywood exert on the national culture during the 1920s?

42. How did the concepts of *Fords, flappers, and fanatics* describe American lifestyle in the 1920s?

Answers begin on page 291

The Great Depression and the New Deal

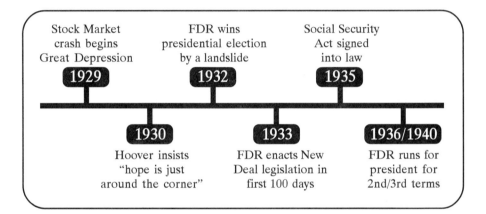

Stock Market crash begins Great Depression
1929

FDR wins presidential election by a landslide
1932

Social Security Act signed into law
1935

1930
Hoover insists "hope is just around the corner"

1933
FDR enacts New Deal legislation in first 100 days

1936/1940
FDR runs for president for 2nd/3rd terms

Trends and Themes of the Era

❯ The frenzied speculation and mergers of the booming 1920s economy led to the dire depression of the 1930s.

❯ Under President Franklin Roosevelt, the government committed itself to unprecedented levels of regulation and control over the national economy. These New Deal policies made FDR and the Democrats extremely popular and expanded the role of American government.

❯ FDR's support for blacks, the poor, and labor unions won him and the Democrats support from those groups, a support base that remains today.

❯ The Depression, a worldwide phenomenon, created circumstances that culminated in World War II, as the rise of totalitarian dictatorships in Germany, Italy, and Japan challenged the status quo. Britain, France, and eventually the United States were forced to challenge these new regimes.

Hardship, hunger, and hope! No one could have predicted that the events of Black Tuesday would plunge the United States into a decade-long depression. The U.S. economy and millions of Americans were hit especially hard as local, state, and federal leaders and agencies grappled with the effects of the Depression. Relief agencies weren't able to meet the mounting needs of the homeless and unemployed. Bread lines and soup kitchens sprang up as local communities began reacting to the Great Depression's effects. The events of the 1930s dramatically transformed the federal government's role, establishing the principle of government responsibility for providing citizens with a level of economic security. FDR's first order of business was restoring not only faith in the economy, but hope too. He would transform the federal government by establishing the principle of government responsibility in providing a level of economic security for its citizens. The New Deal became FDR's tool to ease the harsh consequences of the Great Depression. FDR expanded the president's role by taking the initiative in defining public policy, lobbying for change, and communicating his message to the American public. The leadership FDR exhibited in the Great Depression would be tested and expanded as the country responded to a surprise attack at Pearl Harbor on December 7, 1941. World War II would not only involve the United States in a global conflict, but it would also bring an end to the 12 years of the Great Depression in the United States.

Lesson 9-1: The Crash: From Bulls to Bears

During the 1920s, the United States enjoyed unprecedented prosperity. Levels of investment, often speculative investment, hit new heights. The economy couldn't support such unchecked growth. On Thursday, October 24, 1929, **Black Thursday**, the stock market suffered a huge decline, resulting in the Dow Jones Industrial Average posting a 9 percent trading loss after the close of trading that day.

Despite the loss, though, reports remained optimistic. New York banks united to buy $30 million worth of stock in efforts to stabilize the market, and President Herbert Hoover announced that recovery was expected. But the situation only became bleaker during the next week. Yet another drop in the market on **Black Tuesday**, October 29th, saw the Dow drop more than 17 percent in panic selling, beginning a continued downward cycle in the stock market and confirming the permanency of the crash. By mid-November, market losses topped $30 billion.

No single factor caused the crash and the resulting depression, but several underlying causes during the 1920s had been largely ignored. Stock market trading ran rampant, with businesses promoting stock buying and the notion that everybody ought to be rich. During the 1920s, stock prices rose at twice the rate of industrial production. More than 75 percent of stocks were bought on margin (credit). The stock market crash undermined confidence, investments, and spending and the prosperity of the 1920s gave way to the harsh economic realities of the '30s.

Labor productivity increased during the 1920s, but wages and salaries failed to keep pace. Consumer consumption wasn't keeping up with the rate of overproduction by many industries. Agricultural woes also continued throughout the decade, and wealth was distributed unequally in the country: 80 percent of Americans had no savings, and the top 0.1 percent of American families (24,000) had wealth that equaled the worth of the bottom 42 percent of society (11.5 million families). Most consumers lacked enough money to buy goods, so many bought on credit, adding to the rise in consumer debt.

Other economic problems illustrated fundamental weaknesses in the economy: Mining and textile industries were depressed, auto production had slowed, construction had declined, international economic instability was growing, and there was a general lack of economic expertise in dealing with the crisis.

Adding to the problems at home were international economic difficulties. High tariffs kept European investors from trading with the United States. As European nations curtailed U.S. imports and defaulted on war repayments, U.S. exports declined dramatically.

After the Crash

As a result of the crash, the national economy fell into the worst depression in its history. At first, Americans believed that this depression was similar to others since the 1870s. The October crash began a 12-year downward cycle in the United States, and many people failed to grasp the seriousness of the situation early on. Banks closed in record numbers, more than 30,000 businesses failed in 1932 alone, and average personal income dropped by one-third from 1929 to 1932. By 1933, the money from 9 million savings accounts had vanished from the 5,500 banks that failed. Unemployment reached 25 percent by 1932. Manufacturing output declined by 46 percent by 1932.

Few groups were able to escape the suffering brought on by the depression. Blacks were hit hard by rising unemployment, as they were often the first to be laid off from factory jobs in the North, illegal Mexican migrant workers were deported, and small towns and villages were hit the hardest, as were unskilled workers and minorities. Poverty spread as children suffered from inadequate nutrition and healthcare, and starvation became an everyday occurrence. Middle-class families struggled with having to accept government

assistance or other forms of charity. Some men, unable to cope with joblessness and a lack of money, simply abandoned their families by either committing suicide, or by riding the rails and joining a growing group of homeless hoboes and living in shacks. The refrain of a popular song during the period—"Brother, can you spare a dime?"—became a sign of the times. Government photographer **Dorothea Lange** helped record images of this period that displayed the stark realities of life. Her image of a California migrant worker came to symbolize the despair of the period.

Lesson 9-2: From Hope to a New Deal

During the first few months of the Depression, Hoover was optimistic about recovery. The Depression presented an enormous challenge to the Republican leadership, and their inability to effectively deal with the problems brought on by the Depression would allow the Democrats to regain control in the next presidential election. Hoover believed the economy would rebound by itself without federal government intervention. The year after the crash, Hoover stated, "We have passed the worst," and he didn't even use the word *depression*, relying instead on the phrase "hope is just around the corner."

Hoover's actions, however, were largely ineffective at countering the Depression. At the outset of the crisis, Hoover met with bankers and business leaders in an attempt to ease credit and spur construction projects. Despite Hoover's attempts, the situation continued to worsen.

Two years earlier, in 1930, Hoover signed a bill appropriating federal money for a massive public works project to construct the **Boulder Dam** on the Colorado River at the border of Arizona and Nevada. Work began on this project in 1931 and was completed in 1936. Even the name of the project was changed to "Hoover Dam" in 1931 in honor of President Hoover in an effort to gain public opinion support that the president was indeed taking charge in providing jobs to aid in relief efforts of the Depression.

As the Depression continued into 1930 and and took another downturn, Hoover was forced to take action. At first, he relied on relief agencies and local and state governments for assistance rather than the federal government. Hoover believed in using the federal government to help businesses but not to aid individuals. He felt that offering federal assistance to the unemployed would only demoralize them. Hoover tried to restore confidence in the business sector of the economy and spur economic growth, but he failed to realize that no one had money to spend to invest into the economy.

Hoover's most notable foray into trade regulation was his advocacy of the **Hawley-Smoot Tariff** (1930). The tariff was designed to protect the nation's farmers, but it hurt more than it helped. Hoover also tried to help farmers by overseeing the activity of the **Federal Farm Board**, which administered loans to farmers, and by creating the Grain Stabilization Corporation, which bought wheat at high prices in attempts to drive up prices.

To help businesses, Hoover created the **Reconstruction Finance Corporation (RFC)**, formed to loan money to large, stable institutions such as banks, railroads, and insurance firms, with almost $2 billion in loans available for 1932. In July 1932, Hoover authorized the RFC to spend an additional $2 billion on state and local public works projects.

Hoover's biggest failure was not using the federal government to offer relief to the unemployed and jobless. The onset of the Great Depression left many without jobs, without homes, and without hope. In an effort to address these problems, Hoover established the Emergency Committee for Employment in 1930. It coordinated the efforts of private agencies to provide unemployment relief, but it had limited resources because Hoover remained opposed to using federal funds for public works programs, preferring private charity.

Hoover's efforts did little to spur the economy or redress unemployment. Rising unemployment also upset the psychological balance in many families as men, traditionally the breadwinners and heads of households, lost their jobs. The symbols of Hoover's failure were the "Hoover flag," an empty pocket waving; the "Hoover blanket," a newspaper to huddle under; and **"Hoovervilles,"** communities of homeless Americans living in shanties and makeshift shacks that sprang up around many U.S. cities, including the Hooverville in Seattle, Washington.

The 1932 Election

As the Depression worsened, public calls for aggressive government intervention intensified. People wanted their president to be a hero and a representative of the people.

The 1930 congressional elections of 1930 returned control of both houses of Congress to the Democratic Party. The Republicans also faced another problem, a result of the **Bonus Army March** in Washington, D.C., in July 1932. Several thousand World War I veterans and their families had protested and lobbied for an early payment of their veteran's benefits due in 1945, but Hoover refused to meet with them. While waiting, they erected a shantytown on the outskirts of town in Anacostia Flats along the Potomac River. At the end of the congressional session, many ended up leaving the area empty-handed. **General Douglas MacArthur** was in charge of driving out the protesters, and ordered the use of more than 1,000 troops, tear gas, tanks, and machine guns. The scene of federal troops assaulting war veterans would not be forgotten in the upcoming November election.

Franklin Delano Roosevelt promised to answer Americans' call for action. In 1932, FDR won the presidential election against Hoover, taking 89 percent of the Electoral College votes and 57 percent of the popular vote. Hoover, who had done too little, too late, many believed, had lost public support, and now Democrats controlled Congress and the presidency. FDR's first action was to declare war on the real enemy: the Great Depression itself.

Lesson 9-3: A New Deal: Recovery, Reform, Relief

FDR came to office convinced of the soundness of **John Maynard Keynes**'s economic theories, which argued that government spending could revive a faltering economy. Part of this theory of "priming the economic pump" claimed that for every dollar the government spent, two to three dollars would be pumped into the gross national product (GNP). FDR's New Deal embodied this strategy. He began tackling the immense problem immediately after the election, up until his inauguration in March. During this time of planning, the effects of the Depression worsened across the nation. FDR reassured the public by stating, "I pledge myself for a New Deal for the American people."

The 1st 100 Days and the 1st New Deal

In his inauguration speech in 1933, FDR pledged to devote his presidency to helping the poor and promoting recovery, claiming, "The only thing we have to fear is fear itself." During the first 100 days of his presidency, FDR set forth his **New Deal** recovery plan. It would usher in an unprecedented era of government intervention in the economy.

The first problem FDR faced during the early months of 1933 was a rash of bank closures in 38 states. In response, he called for not only a special session of Congress but also for a bank holiday, during which he met with the heads of many suffering banks and developed the **Emergency Banking Relief Act,** passed on March 9th. This act provided a framework under which banks could reopen with federal support. FDR used a radio message that became known as a **"fireside chat"** to speak directly to and reassure the American public. FDR put a personal touch on reform by reaching out to the public by radio, and he used this outlet repeatedly during his presidency. He spoke

Reforms of the 1st 100 Days

March 31st: Congress passed the Unemployment Relief Act, which created the **Civilian Conservation Corps (CCC)**, a program to employ young men ages 18 to 25 in conservation and other productive work. Payment was $30 per month, $25 of which was sent home.

May 12th: The passage of the Agricultural Adjustment Act created the **Agricultural Adjustment Administration (AAA)** to manage federal aid to farmers and regulate production. The AAA controlled the production of crops, and thus prices, by offering subsidies to farmers who produced under set quotas. The same day, the **Federal Emergency Relief Act (FERA)** was passed, appropriating $500 million to support state and local treasuries that had run dry.

May 18th: A bill was passed creating the **Tennessee Valley Authority (TVA)**, a plan to develop dams and hydroelectricity along the Tennessee River and conserve resources in the Tennessee Valley.

May 27th: The Federal Securities Act was passed to foster corporate honesty by regulating trading practices for stocks and other securities, prefacing the creation of the **Securities Exchange Commission (SEC)** in 1934.

June 16th: The National Industrial Recovery Act was passed, creating the **National Recovery Administration (NRA)** to manage the recovery of industry and finance. The NRA established regulations for fair competition by managing productrion, prices, labor relations, and trade practices among leading business. The National Industrial Recovery Act also created the **Public Works Administration (PWA)**, which spent more than $6 million on projects designed to employ the jobless and infuse the economy with money.

June 16th: The passage of the Banking Act of 1933 created the **Federal Deposit Insurance Corporation (FDIC)** to back individuals' bank depostits with federal guarantees of funds up to $5,000.

---

candidly to the public, presenting his plans of actions directly to them. Because of the rise in FDR's popularity, it took a staff of 50 to handle his correspondence from Americans.

Results from some of the programs could begin to be seen quickly. The goal was to provide jobs and relief for people. **Henry Hopkins** was put in charge of directing the relief programs for FDR. FDR developed the **Civilian Conservation Corps (CCC)** with the goal of putting young men to work on conservation projects across the nation building roads and trails, planting trees, building bridges on public lands, including massive projects at many of the nation's National Parks. By the end of the project in 1941, more than 2 million youth had worked in this program, which was deemed one of the great successes of New Deal legislation.

FDR created the **Public Works Administration (PWA)** as part of the NIRA in 1933 and the **Works Progress Administration (WPA)** in 1935. The intent of these two agencies was simply to put people to work. It meant large amounts of money to be spent on numerous big and small projects across the country. The programs employed people in a variety of construction and conservation jobs. Many of the projects strengthened the country's infrastructure. Nearly 75 percent of the budget was spent on public projects such as highways, bridges, dams, parks, libraries, airports, and other buildings. Some of the more famous projects built by these two programs include the Golden Gate Bridge in San Francisco, the Lincoln Tunnel in New York City, the Grand Coulee Dam in Washington, the Key West Highway in Florida, and the Tacoma Narrows Bridge, "Galloping Gertie," in Tacoma, Washington.

In addition, WPA projects employed artists, actors, and writers to display and preserve their crafts. Although not a direct WPA project, John Steinbeck conducted a series of interviews and research of the plight of Oakies near Weedpatch, California; their story, in the form of the Joad family, was depicted in his 1936 novel *The Grapes of Wrath*.

Challenges to the New Deal

After June 16th, Congress recessed, officially ending the first 100 days of reform that created the framework for heavy government involvement to help bring the United States out of the Depression. Continued economic distress and mounting opposition to FDR's programs cast doubt on the New Deal.

The first sign that the New Deal was in danger was trouble with the **National Industrial Recovery Act (NIRA)** and the **National Recovery Administration (NRA)** in particular. This agency aided in cooperation between government, labor, and business. Opposition to the NRA finally came in 1935, when the Supreme Court declared the agency unconstitutional, claiming the NRA gave the executive branch regulatory powers that belonged exclusively to Congress. This decision kicked off a series of court rulings that overturned key elements of the New Deal. The 1935 case *Schechter Poultry Corporation v. the United States* questioned the use of price and wage fixing, and shipping requirements within a state. The NIRA had attempted to control shipping at all levels and involve itself with local business codes. The Supreme Court ruled that the federal government could not get involved in intrastate trade—only interstate trade. Even though there was a charge of selling unfit chickens, the federal government could not intervene.

The efforts of the **Agricultural Adjustment Administration (AAA)**, combined with a severe drought in the American heartland, affected a drop in farm production, prompting a rise in farm prices. The AAA did much to help large landowners and commercial farmers, but it did little for landless laborers and tenant farmers who populated the rural Midwest. This large group of dispossessed farmers, **"Oakies,"** made up the majority of those who participated in the western migration from the **Dust Bowl** (Oklahoma, Texas, New Mexico, Colorado, and Kansas) to California along the famed **Route 66** in search of land and employment. The situation was so bad in

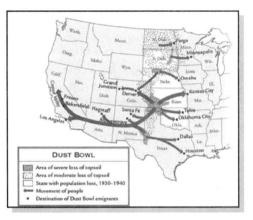

the dust bowl region that, at its heart, more than 6 feet of topsoil were literally blown away. Black clouds of dust across the region turned daylight to night, and families hung wet sheets and towels over windows and doorways to keep out the fine dust.

As the plight of the dust bowl poor became more widely recognized, questions arose about the effectiveness of the AAA. In 1936, the Supreme Court ruled the AAA unconstitutional, claiming that it enforced illegal taxation. The organization was reworked after the ruling.

Other challenges to the New Deal came from those appealing to the discontented lower and middle classes. In 1934, socialist Upton Sinclair ran for governor of California and lost. He campaigned for a 50-dollar **pension (EPIC [End Poverty in California])** for everyone over the age of 60 and proposed using higher income taxes and inheritance taxes to pay for the program.

Father Charles Coughlin, **Francis Townsend**, and **Huey Long** also argued that the New Deal wasn't going far enough in alleviating poverty. At first, Father Coughlin used his Sunday radio program to support FDR's New Deal. Soon, that support turned to attacks against FDR and his entire New Deal. Father Coughlin claimed that not enough was being done to help the common man, and he began to advocate a redistribution of wealth in the country. Meanwhile, Francis Townsend became a spokesman for the poor and elderly who advocated a federal old-age pension plan and a national sales tax to finance programs.

The most famous political opposition movement of the Great Depression years was Senator and Louisiana governor Huey Long's Share the Wealth program. It pressed for far greater income redistribution and benefits for the poor. Long promoted his program by stating, "Every man ought to be a king," by proposing an annual check for $2,000, a home, a car, a radio, and a college education for all. This would all be financed by increasing taxes on the rich.

Many people feared that Long might join forces with other sympathizers, form a third party, and make a run for the presidency in 1936. Long's assassination in 1935 ended this prospect.

These challenges passed, at least in part, with the 1934 midterm elections. Despite a vocal minority of dissenters, FDR remained a popular president because of his efforts at relief, his charismatic leadership, and his connection with citizens, symbolized by his frequent fireside chats. This resulted in a resounding approval of the Democratic program in the 1934 elections as Democrats gained seats in both the House and Senate.

Lesson 9-4: The 2nd New Deal

Reassured by the overwhelming Democratic victory in the 1934 midterm elections, FDR laid out his plans for the Second New Deal in his January 1935 state of the union address.

The 3 R's: Relief, Recover, and Reform

FDR had seen success in providing much-needed immediate relief for citizens in the form of money and jobs. He outlined six ways in which the administration would renew and intensify the efforts begun under the First New Deal. These plans included an enlarged unemployment relief program, assistance to the rural poor, support for organized labor, social welfare benefits for the elderly and disadvantaged, strict regulation of business and finance, and heavier taxes on the wealthy. This plan represented a shift from just relief and recovery to also embrace reform.

A major part of this reform came from the 1935 **Social Security Act**, intended to be a welfare program to aid the elderly and disabled. The project was to be funded by a payroll tax from workers and employers. The first part of the program provided old-age pensions to workers over the age of 65. The next part of the program established unemployment compensation payments. The last part of the program set up welfare payments for the blind, handicapped, needy elderly, and dependent children. It was signed into law on August 14, 1935.

Under the government's favorable treatment of labor, unions gained membership, power, and political influence, and they often lent their support to the Democratic Party, an alliance that remains in place today. Strikes were common throughout the 1930s, and workers increasingly won concessions. In 1935, the Committee for Industrial Organization formed within the American Federation of Labor (AFL), eventually becoming the independent Congress of Industrial Organizations (CIO) in 1938. In less than two years, the CIO claimed more than 4 million members. The AFL and CIO were the nation's most dominant and successful unions throughout the late 1930s and 1940s; in 1955, they merged to form the AFL-CIO.

The 2nd New Deal

- In April 1935, Congress passed the Emergencey Relief Appropriation Act. This act granted FDR $5 billion to use on whatever programs he chose. The majority of that funding went to the **Works Progress Administration (WPA)**. Over eight years, the WPA pumped $11 billion into the economy and supported the unemployed of all backgrounds, from industrial engineers to authors and artists. Unemployment fell more that 5 percent from 1935 to 1937, partially due to the WPA's efforts.

- To regulate the economy, FDR empowered the Federal Reserve Board to exert tighter control over the money supply and called for strict enforcement of the **Securities Exchange Act** of 1934, which required that detailed and truthful information be publicized for each company issuing stock in the U.S. market.

- One of the most lasting achievements of the Second New Deal was the creation of Social Security benefits for the elderly through the **Social Security Act** of 1935. This act, passed largely in response to the elderly rights movement, exemplified the New Deal focus on social services. It provided not only old-age pensions, but also aid for dependent mothers and children, assistance for the blind, and compensation for the unemployed.

- The government supported unionization and collective bargaining with the 1935 National Labor Relations Act, popularly known as the **Wagner Act**, which provided a framework for collective bargaining. The Wagner Act granted workers the right to join unions and engage in bargaining, and forbid employers to interfere with union rights.

- The **National Youth Administration (NYA)** was a WPA program that provided part-time jobs to high school and college students, allowing them to stay in school while earning money. It also established programs for young people who weren't in school.

The New Deal Changes Party Alignments

FDR's landslide victory in the 1936 election confirmed his party's success in becoming the representatives of the downtrodden and disadvantaged. Farmers appreciated FDR's consistent efforts to forge an effective agricultural plan. Urban voters and organized labor, a great source of FDR's campaign funding, valued his support of union rights and his plans to cope with rampant unemployment. Many women recognized that FDR's programs attacked the concept of inequality, and they appreciated that he had appointed the first female cabinet member, **Frances Perkins**, as secretary of labor.

Black Americans, the group most devastated by unemployment, had benefited extensively from New Deal measures. Black support gradually shifted toward FDR and the Democratic Party and away from the Republican Party, which had traditionally won the black vote since the end of the Civil War. By 1936, more than 75 percent of blacks were registered Democrats.

The 1936 election ushered in a new Democratic coalition that included farmers, urban workers, women, and blacks. This coalition not only helped FDR win the 1936 election by a landslide, but it remains an important part of the party's membership to this day. FDR's presidency and the New Deal thus brought about a realignment of the Democratic and Republican parties. As Democrats won the support of blacks, urban workers, and farmers, they lost the support of the white South, a traditional Democratic stronghold. The Republican Party, meanwhile, lost its long-held black votes, but it gained voter support from white Southerners who had grown disenchanted with FDR's policies.

Lesson 9-5: Popular Culture of the 1930s

The 1930s saw the marked growth of mass culture as citizens sought diversion from their troubles. Most popular culture centered on escapist themes and humor. Hollywood produced movies in the '30s that appealed to a wide range of audiences. The Marx Brothers, Shirley Temple, Clark Gable, Cary Grant, Greta Garbo, and Mae West became huge stars, appearing in a wide range of productions that let movie-goers escape the realities of the Depression for a short time. In 1937, Disney's *Snow White and the Seven Dwarfs* was released as the first full-length color animated movie. Also made into hit movies were popular novels *The Grapes of Wrath* and *Gone with the Wind*. They showed pain and suffering coupled with belief in the possibility of overcoming disaster, because, as Scarlet O'Hara said at the end of *Gone with the Wind* as Rhett Buttler walked away, "After all, tomorrow is another day."

Radio shows also became immensely popular during this period; in fact, the 1930s is often called the golden age of radio. By the end of the 1930s, 90 percent of Americans owned a radio and tuned in for news, music, and entertainment, often on the NBC or CBS stations. Radio was so popular that the October 31, 1938, broadcast of Orson Wells's "War of the Worlds" frightened many listeners into believing that Martians really were attacking the earth.

Magazines provided similar popular diversions. *Life* magazine began publication during the 1930s, filling its pages with pictures of spectacular scenes and glorified personalities. Parker Brothers also tapped into the need for entertainment and escapism with its new board game, Monopoly, a fantasy of real-estate speculation at a time when many people were facing foreclosures and bankruptcies.

Lesson 9-6: Legacies and Limitations of the New Deal

One of the lasting legacies of FDR and the New Deal was **Eleanor Roosevelt**, who greatly transformed the role of first lady by actively campaigning in support of certain policies. She quite literally became the "legs" for FDR, who had been crippled by polio, traveling and reaching out to people as she promoted FDR's New Deal policies and representing him. She also wrote a newspaper column, made radio broadcasts, gave speeches, listened to the concerns of women, and helped push the president toward social reform. Although attacked by critics, she took stands on social issues and civil rights by promoting anti-lynching legislation and proposing more work be done for black civil rights. In fact, Eleanor Roosevelt quit her membership in the Daughters of the American Revolution (DAR) when the group refused to hear African-American contralto Marian Anderson sing in Constitution Hall; instead, Eleanor Roosevelt arranged for Anderson to sing on the steps of the Lincoln Memorial on April 9, 1939, in front of a crowd of more than 75,000.

The stage seemed set for FDR's continued success in pushing through the New Deal, but he faced a host of political challenges. The first sign of downturn was his involvement in the Court Packing scheme. Early in 1937, FDR proposed a court-reform bill that would allow the president to appoint an additional Supreme Court justice for each current justice over the age of 70; it also would expand the Supreme Court from nine to 15 members. FDR claimed that the bill addressed concerns about the justices' workload, but it was clear that the proposal was meant to dilute the power of the conservative justices of the Supreme Court, who had been hostile to New Deal legislation. The Senate vetoed the scheme in July 1937, and several justices retired shortly after or announced their intention to do so. The Supreme Court presented less resistance during the final years of the Second New Deal than it had during earlier years, but the Court Packing scheme was a blemish on Roosevelt's record. By the time of his death in 1945, FDR had been able to appoint eight of the nine justices on the Court.

A more direct cause of the Second New Deal's decline was the inability of FDR's programs to revive the economy. In August 1937, the nation plunged into a recession. By early 1938, unemployment had again risen above 20 percent. The final obstacle to the Second New Deal's extension came from within Congress, where FDR's critics were growing in power. A conservative coalition legislated cuts in relief programs and blocked further legislation by New Deal supporters. As a result, FDR proposed few new reform measures during his second term in office.

Although bold attempts were made to deal with the effects of the Great Depression, various problems still plagued the nation at the end of the decade. FDR made great attempts to deal with the social, economic, and political aspects of the Depression during the 1930s, but it would take U.S. involvement in World War II to effectively end the longest depression in history and help make the United States an economic and political superpower.

Review Exam

Multiple Choice

1. All of the following are generally thought of as leading causes of the Great Depression EXCEPT _____.
   a) the moderate rise of stock prices in the 1920s
   b) the crash of the stock market in 1929 that undermined consumer confidence
   c) over-extension of credit in the 1920s
   d) speculation on the stock market during the bull market years of the 1920s

2. Hoover's main plan for dealing with the Depression within its first two years was to _____.
   a) simply not call it a depression for the first year by telling people that "hope is just around the corner"
   b) allowing people to rely on local and state governments for assistance
   c) sponsoring a series of federal programs to assist business and workers
   d) A and B only

3. The Bonus Army March in August 1932 resulted in _____.
   a) World War I veterans receiving their pension after a successful march on Washington, D.C.
   b) General Douglas MacArthur being in charge of the army troop, driving out the protesters with tear gas, tanks, and machine guns
   c) an example of the lack of concern by the federal government and the Republican president (Hoover)
   d) B and C only

4. FDR instilled hope in Americans by _____.
   a) proclaiming in his inaugural address in 1933, "The only thing we have to fear is fear itself!"
   b) using the radio to deliver fireside chats in which he spoke directly to the American public
   c) promising a "New Deal" to the American public
   d) A, B, and C

5. The purpose of the Emergency Banking Act was to do all of the following EXCEPT _____.
   a) close all banks for four days to allow them to reorganize with new federal regulations
   b) aim to restore consumer confidence in the banking system
   c) allow banks to operate in the same manner once they had more money from the federal government
   d) provide government insurance for bank deposits under the FDIC program

6. The AAA had a goal of _____.
   a) bringing an end to the practice of sharecropping
   b) providing low-interest loans to farmers
   c) stabilizing produce prices by controlling production
   d) B and C only

7. _____ was the major component of the NIRA.
   a) State and federal cooperation on business practices
   b) Federal guidelines for all levels of business practices
   c) A gradual increase in federal regulations for businesses
   d) Broad support from the Supreme Court in challenges to the regulations

8. _____ was NOT an outspoken critic of FDR and his New Deal policies, claiming that they failed to fully address the needs of poverty in America.
   a) Father Charles Coughlin   c) Francis Perkins
   b) Huey Long   d) Francis Townsend

9. The purpose of the CCC was to create a series of conservation jobs for _____.
   a) young adult males ages 18–25   c) migrant farmers in California
   b) hoboes   d) minorities

10. The dust bowl region _____.
    a) was the site of a severe drought and dust storms in Oklahoma, Texas, New Mexico, Colorado, and Kansas
    b) turned day into night with the onset of severe dust storms that blew away 6 feet of topsoil in the most affected areas
    c) had families either leaving the region or being forced to resort to various methods to combat the dust and drought if they remained
    d) A, B, and C

11. The Tennessee Valley Authority (TVA) is one of the great legacies of the New Deal in that it _____.
   a) planned to construct a series of dams along the Tennessee River to protect farmland and create hydroelectric power in a seven state area
   b) was a program financed mainly by the states with minimal government funding
   c) revitalized one of the regions hardest hit by the Great Depression
   d) A and C only

12. The PWA and WPA programs were intended to _____.
   a) employ people to work on massive construction projects to benefit the infrastructure of the nation (roads, bridges, hospitals, libraries, schools, and so on)
   b) employ artists, actors, and writers to help them preserve their craft
   c) employ people in conservation jobs
   d) A, B, and C

13. _____ was not a component of FDR's Second New Deal plan.
   a) Relief   c) Remake
   b) Recovery   d) Reform

14. The Social Security program passed in 1935 was a program that intended to do all of the following EXCEPT _____.
   a) provide old-age pensions for those over the age of 65
   b) provide benefits to farm workers
   c) provide welfare payments for the blind, needy elderly, and dependent children
   d) establish unemployment benefits

15. Blacks began voting as a group by switching their allegiance to the _____ Party in the 1936 election.
   a) Democratic   c) Socialist
   b) Republican   d) Progressive

16. The role of First Lady Eleanor Roosevelt _____.
   a) increased as she became the "legs" for FDR in visiting people and promoting programs
   b) decreased as she was not involved in promoting New Deal programs
   c) increased as she wrote a newspaper column, made radio broadcasts, and simply listened to the plight of women, minorities, and poor people all affected by the Great Depression
   d) A and C only

17. _____ finally succeeded in bringing an end to the Great Depression.
    a) FDR's Second New Deal programs
    b) FDR's original New Deal program
    c) America's involvement in World War II
    d) The resurgence of the stock market by the mid-1930s

Matching

a. EPIC
b. Frances Perkins
c. Oakies
d. Black Thursday
e. Hoovervilles
f. Share the Wealth program
g. Dorothea Lange
h. John Maynard Keynes
i. Black Tuesday
j. *Schechter Poultry Corporation v. the United States*
k. Hawley-Smoot

l. AFL-CIO
m. Marion Anderson
n. New Deal
o. Hoover Flags and Hoover Blankets
p. Reconstruction Finance Corporation
q. Federal Farm Board
r. Henry Hopkins
s. Route 66
t. *The Grapes of Wrath*
u. Hoover Dam
v. Dust Bowl

_____18. communities of homeless Americans who were forced to live in shanties and makeshift shacks on the outskirts of many U.S. cities

_____19. FDR's campaign promise in the 1932 election to deal with the effects of the Great Depression

_____20. FDR's secretary of labor

_____21. October 24, 1929, the stock market suffered a huge decline of more than 9 percent

_____22. people who fled the hardest hit area of the dust bowl in Oklahoma and migrated to California in hopes of finding new jobs and homes

_____23. a photographer hired by the federal government who documented the effects of the Great Depression in photographs

_____24. Upton Sinclair's plan to end poverty in California if elected governor

_____25. tariff that was imposed in 1930 and raised the tariff on imports to protect American businesses; it actually hurt trade dramatically

_____26. this was mainly a five-state area affected by severe climate conditions of drought and dust storms during the 1930s

_____27. highway that was made famous by the Oakies traveling west to California during the Great Depression era

_____28. October 29, 1929, the stock market suffered its worst one day loss in history and this continued a downward cycle resulting in the Great Depression

_____29. according to Louisiana Governor Huey Long wealth should be redistributed so that "every man could be a king"

_____30. a Hoover program aimed at providing loans to certain stable businesses and institutions such as banks, railroads, and insurance firms

_____31. his economic theories dealt with the need to increase government spending in order to revive a faltering economy known as "priming the pump"

_____32. an attempt by Hoover to provide assistance to farmers in the form of government loans

_____33. John Steinbeck's classic Depression-era novel that not only depicted the Joad family, but presented a picture of the harsh reality of the effects of the Great Depression on people's lives

_____34. the combination of the American Federation and the Congress of International Organizations into one union

_____35. Eleanor Roosevelt arranged for this black opera singer to perform on the steps of the Lincoln memorial when the DAR refused to hear her perform in the Constitution Hall

_____36. an empty pocket and an old newspaper

_____37. financing for this massive public works project on the Colorado River began in 1931 and was completed in 1936

_____38. placed in charge of directing the New Deal relief programs for FDR

_____39. the "sick chicken case" that helped overturn the actions of the NIRA

Short Response

40. How did the role of the federal government change as a result of the Great Depression?

41. To what extent were the solutions offered by Hoover and FDR in dealing with the Depression effective in relationship to *hardship, hunger, and hope*?

42. What were the expectations for relief programs offered by the New Deal? To what extent did they provide recovery, reform, or relief?

43. How did people begin to respond to the effects of the Great Depression?

Answers begin on page 293.

World War II

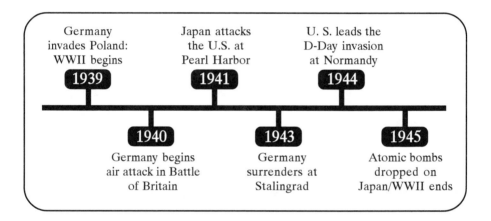

Trends and Themes of the Era

▶ The Treaty of Versailles and the 1930s Depression created conditions that encouraged nationalism in Germany, Italy, Japan, and the USSR. The expansionist plans of these fascist regimes led to World War II.

▶ The United States attempted to maintain its isolationist policies, but, as the war continued, American sympathies moved toward the Allies. American isolationism shifted first to indirect involvement and then to full involvement after Japan bombed Pearl Harbor on December 7, 1941.

▶ Discussions about how to divide and rebuild Europe after the fall of Germany became an occasion for the United States and the USSR to vie for power and control; this signaled the beginning of the Cold War.

▶ When the United States dropped atomic bombs on Japan, it changed the nature of war and escalated the U.S.—USSR arms race.

Apathy, appeasement, and aggression! World War I left many Americans disillusioned about war, and the United States retreated into isolationism. Britain and France began to acquiesce to the demands of a new aggressor: Adolf Hitler. Indifference about the changing nation-states in Europe and appeasement of aggressors had ultimately led to global violence. By the late 1930s, 70 percent of Americans felt that the role the country had played in World War I was a mistake. The United States passed Neutrality Acts allowing it to deny the sale or shipment of munitions to warring nations, opting instead for a cash-and-carry policy. The country needed the income, but it was unwilling to commit to another war. The rumblings of conflict frightened many as totalitarian leaders across the globe flexed their muscles. These leaders posed a threat to security, and the United States couldn't ignore the possibility of involvement in yet another global conflict. The deaths of 50 million people, along with the horrors and destruction of war, provided a stark conclusion to the conflict of World War II. The devastating loss of population and property in Europe and Japan, the Holocaust that killed six million Jews, the development and use of the atomic bomb, the Soviet domination of Eastern Europe, a divided Germany, Japanese internment camps, and the founding of the United Nations made this war far different from any other in history. Isolationism was no longer possible. In the United States, World War II highlighted racial inequalities, gave women new opportunities, and fostered growth in the South and West. By devastating the nation's commercial rivals, World War II left the United States dominant in the world economy. It also increased the scope of the federal government and built an alliance among the armed forces, big business, and science that helped shape post-war America.

Lesson 10-1: The Road to War

In the 1920s and 1930s, many people referred to World War I as the "war to end all wars." Nevertheless, the vindictive terms of the peace agreement that ended World War I, along with the international crisis of the depression of the 1930s, directly led to the circumstances that started World War II. In Germany, the Treaty of Versailles provoked intense resentment. This paved the way for a charismatic dictator, Adolf Hitler, to rise to power and install the Nazi regime in 1933. Eleven years earlier, a fascist regime had taken hold in Italy under Benito Mussolini. Both fascist governments combined extreme nationalist rhetoric with an aggressive desire to expand.

In the USSR, Trotsky and Stalin fought for control after Lenin's death in 1924 and, by 1929, Stalin was in charge. Stalin dedicated himself to the idea of a world revolution and began a series of five-year plans to make the USSR a leading industrial country. In August 1939, Stalin and Hitler signed a non-aggression pact, which would stall Germany's army from fighting a two-front war until the invasion of Russia in June 1941.

In Asia, Japan invaded Manchuria in 1931 and dominated it within five months; its acts of aggression were condemned by the United States and the League of Nations. Hoover's secretary of state, Henry L. Stimson, regarded the Japanese invasion as a violation of international law. After Japan failed to cease hostilities in China, in January 1932 Stimson declared that the U.S. government wouldn't recognize any territorial changes imposed on China by the Japanese, a declaration that became known as the **Stimson Doctrine**.

Japan began building up its navy in 1934 and set its sights on expanding its empire in the Pacific. By 1939, Japan controlled one-fourth of China and was continuing its expansionist actions in the Pacific. Japan then signed the Tripartite Axis Pact with Hitler and Mussolini in September 1940.

The failure of the League of Nations became evident in a series of events. Germany was admitted in 1926 but withdrew its membership in 1933. Japan left the league to pursue its empire in the Pacific in 1933, and Italy exited the league over sanctions following the invasion of Ethiopia in 1935. The United States, meanwhile, had never joined the league. Clearly, the League of Nations was powerless over these actions and could not prevent another war.

In 1935, Hitler announced plans for German troops to reoccupy the Rhineland, which had been demilitarized by the Treaty of Versailles. Troops marched into the Rhineland unopposed in March 1936. Germany and Italy then formed an alliance, the **Rome-Berlin Axis**, in October 1936. In March 1938, Austria joined this alliance when Hitler announced the Anschluss, a union between Germany and Austria, and German forces marched into Vienna. After Hitler declared his intention to take the Czech Sudetenland by force if necessary, British and French leaders agreed to his demands by signing the Munich Pact in September 1938, granting the Sudetenland to Germany. Britain and France declared "this is peace in our time," using the policy of **appeasement** with Hitler in making concessions to him in an attempt to avoid war.

Germany continued by invading Czechoslovakia in March 1939, and on September 1, 1939, Hitler used his **blitzkrieg**, "lightning warfare," plan to invade Poland. Two days after the invasion, Britain and France declared war on Germany, honoring their treaty with Poland. World War II had begun.

Lesson 10-2: The Challenge to Isolationism

American public opinion began to turn against the fascist powers, mostly in response to the publicized brutality of Hitler's Nazis toward German Jews and other groups. Though alarmed, 85 percent of Americans agreed that the nation should fight only if directly attacked. Many Americans continued to push for neutrality and for immigration restriction, in part because roughly 60,000 Jewish refugees fled to the United States between 1933 and 1938. In 1939, the *St. Louis,* a German luxury liner filled with Jewish refugees, sailed to Miami, Florida. Although most of the passengers had landing permits, they were denied permission to leave the vessel and were sent back to Europe. They were later taken to a concentration camp.

In early 1939, FDR asked Congress to appropriate funds for a military buildup and increased production of military material. In September 1939, FDR succeeded in pushing Congress to revise the **Neutrality Acts** to allow warring nations to purchase arms from the United States as long as they paid in cash and carried the arms away on their own ships. This cash-and-carry provision appealed to a nation that was increasingly committed to aiding the Allied war effort but didn't want to get directly involved in the war.

In this atmosphere of growing alarm, FDR decided to run for an unprecedented third term in office. During his 1940 campaign, Roosevelt created a Council of National Defense to oversee defense production, appointed Republican Henry Stimson as secretary of war, and approved the first peacetime draft by signing the Selective Service and Training Act. Although he approved the draft, FDR pledged to never "send an American boy to fight in a European war." Isolationists opposed to FDR's reelection sponsored the Committee to Defend America First, urging neutrality and claiming that the United States could stand alone regardless of Hitler's advances in Europe. FDR won reelection.

After winning the presidency again, FDR pushed for passage of the **Lend-Lease Act** in March 1941, which allowed the president to lend or lease supplies to any nation deemed "vital to the defense of the United States," such as Britain. FDR extended lend-lease aid to the Soviet Union after Germany invaded it in June 1941. The United States also helped the Allies by tracking German submarines and warning the British about their locations, and by convoying British ships carrying lend-lease supplies (that is, surrounding British ships with U.S. Navy vessels ordered to attack any menacing ships).

In August 1941, FDR met with British Prime Minister Winston Churchill to discuss military strategy and issued the **Atlantic Charter,** outlining their ideal post-war world. Among other provisions, it called for disarmament and freedom of the seas. It worked out common principles between Britain and the United States, promised a "better future for the world," proposed the concepts of self-government and free trade for all nations, and ended territorial seizures. In response to a German attack against a U.S. destroyer, Roosevelt issued a shoot-on-sight order in September 1941, which authorized American naval patrols to fire on all Axis ships found between the United States and

Iceland. While escorting a convoy of ships, in October 1941, the *USS Rueben James* was attacked by a German U-boat and sunk with the loss of more than 100 crewmen. It was the first naval ship lost in World War II. It was largely ignored by the public at the time. After American destroyers were twice attacked in October, Congress authorized the arming of merchant ships.

Lesson 10-3: Hitler and Western Europe (1939–41)

In April 1940, Great Britain blockaded Germany. Hitler then followed with the invasion of Norway. Denmark surrendered before an invasion by accepting Hitler's protection, and Hitler invaded the Netherlands, Luxembourg, and Belgium on May 10, 1940. France prepared for a German invasion along the Maginot Line, but by May 26, 1940, German troops had pushed the Allies back to Dunkirk along the English Channel, forcing the evacuation of more than 340,000 troops to Britain. On June 16th, France surrendered and five days later signed an armistice with Germany.

The Battle of Britain, Operation Sea Lion, got under way in the summer of 1940, with Britain the only country in Europe still fighting against Hitler. Britain was greatly outnumbered, but its secret use of radar, along with the inspiring encouragement of the new Prime Minister, Winston Churchill, helped the country withstand Germany's assaults. After months of attacks, Germany abandoned its efforts and, in June 1941, Hitler began the invasion of Russia, opening a two-front war in Europe. By November, German troops were within sight of the capital of Moscow, more than 600 miles inside the border of Russia.

World War II, European Theater, 1940-1945

Lesson 10-4: The Attack at Pearl Harbor

In September 1940, Japanese forces continued to pursue their goal of Pacific domination by invading French Indochina. The United States responded as it had to past invasions: It added more items to the lengthy list of embargoed Japanese goods, and eventually it froze all trade with Japan.

In 1941, U.S. intelligence became aware of plans for a Japanese attack and sent out warnings to commanders of U.S. bases in the Pacific, but most American officials didn't believe the threat was immediate. By October, General Hideki Tojo had assumed control in Tokyo, and the United States had placed an embargo on Japanese goods. In November 1941, Japan prepared for an attack on the United States by secretly moving 31 ships to Hawaii. After cracking the Japanese code, the United States suspected an attack but remained unsure of its location. On December 7, 1941, Japanese planes bombed the U.S. base at **Pearl Harbor** on the Hawaiian island of Oahu. The two-hour, early-morning attack by Japanese planes in two unopposed bombing strikes sunk or damaged 19 ships, destroyed nearly 200 aircraft, wounded more than 1,100, and killed 2,403 Americans.

In his request for a declaration of war on Japan on December 8th, FDR reminded Americans that December 7th would be "a day that will live forever in infamy." The Senate voted unanimously in favor of FDR's request. The House had only one dissenting vote. On December 11th, Germany and Italy joined Japan in war against the United States.

Four months later, on April 18, 1942, American spirits got a boost. Lieutenant Colonel James Doolittle of the U.S. Army Air Corps led 16 planes on a bombing raid over Japan nicknamed **"Doolittle's Raid."** Four cities, including the capital city of Tokyo, were bombed. Not only did it excite the American public, but it also served as a warning to the Japanese that they were vulnerable.

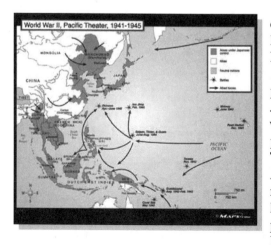

General MacArthur, U.S. commander in the Pacific, launched a surprise attack in the **Battle of Midway** on June 3, 1942, destroying 322 Japanese planes and four aircraft carriers. Japan was forced to retreat in what proved to be the turning point of the war in the Pacific. The **Battle of Guadalcanal** in August 1942 was the first in a series of U.S. victories using the leapfrog method of "island hopping," or claiming islands in the Pacific with the ultimate goal of closing in on Japan. The United States used Navajo Indians as **"code talkers"** in radio transmissions during the war in the Pacific to confuse the Japanese.

One of the most infamous events of the Pacific war took place in 1942, after the Japanese captured more than 76,000 Americans on Bataan Peninsula in the Philippines. Several hundred men were killed. Thousands of Americans and Filipinos were forced to march in the northern part of the Philippine islands for four days through the jungles. They were given no food, little water, and little rest. About 54,000 arrived at the new camp, where many later died of disease and malnutrition in their first few months of imprisonment. MacArthur vowed to return. In 1944, he did just that.

Lesson 10-5: The War on the Home Front

Although the United States had begun preparing for war during the summer of 1940, war production made up only 15 percent of the nation's industrial output in 1941, and U.S. armed forces were seriously understaffed and undersupplied. During the next four years, war production on the home front churned into high gear. In 1940, the U.S. GNP was estimated at $99 billion, but by 1945, it had more than doubled to $211 billion.

During its involvement in World War II, the U.S. government spent between $186 million and $250 million a day on the war effort. By 1943, two-thirds of the U.S. economy was geared to war, and, by 1945, the United States had become the major producer of war goods. Unemployment was virtually nonexistent.

Expanding the Military and the Workforce

In 1942, FDR created the Joint Chiefs of Staff to oversee America's rapidly expanding military. By the end of the war, more than 15 million men had served in the U.S. armed forces. The air force, a minor corps at the outset of the war, grew substantially and gained a measure of autonomy during the war. The Joint Chiefs also established the Office of Strategic Services (OSS) to assess the enemy's assets and liabilities, conduct espionage, and gather information to be used in strategic planning.

More than 400,000 women played active roles in the armed forces as well. Women served in the Women's Auxiliary Army Corps (WAAC), Women Accepted for Voluntary Emergency Service in the navy (WAVES), and the women's auxiliary unit of the Coast Guard, SPARS. Several thousand women also joined the marines, and others signed up for the Women's Air Force Service Pilots (WASPS), where nearly 1,100 female pilots ferried military aircraft across the United States, towed targets for antiaircraft practice, tested new planes, and even ferried planes to Britain. More than 10,000 women served overseas, where 200 of them died and 80 became Japanese POWs.

Nearly half of the Dallas and Seattle aircraft workers during the war were women, and women accounted for 38 percent of government jobs and 36 percent of the entire workforce. The image of **Rosie the Riveter**, a strong-armed woman with a rivet gun, proved persuasive as increasing numbers of women entered the workforce. Although the roles women played in the war helped create new respect for the working woman, women were still paid far less than working men, and traditional notions of gender roles prevailed throughout the war.

Fighting Airmen

In 1941, Congress authorized the formation of an all-black combat unit. The 99th Fighter squadron started their training at the Tuskegee Institute in Alabama. The 99th, along with three other squadrons, were then sent to Europe to assist in escorting bombing raids. The **Tuskegee Airmen** received numerous medals, displayed great valor, and became one of the most successful and highly decorated air combat troops during the war. After the end of World War II, the troops returned home to face racism again, but, because of their bravery and skill, became instrumental in the desegregation of the U.S. troops when Truman issued Executive Order 9981 in 1948, ending years of segregation in the armed forces.

Boosting Production

The War Production Board, created in 1942, oversaw production of thousands of planes, tanks, and artillery pieces. The board allocated resources and shifted production from civilian to military items by offering incentives for firms to produce military goods. Plants were redesigned to produce tanks, planes, weapons, and munitions. By the end of the war, the United States had built about 300,000 aircraft, 85,000 tanks, 375,000 artillery pieces, 2.5 million machine guns, and 90,000 sea ships (more war material than that produced by the four Axis powers combined).

The federal budget multiplied tenfold between 1940 and 1945. U.S. expenditures during World War II totaled nearly twice the amount spent by the government in its previous 150 years of existence. Spending on war production also precipitated a shift in American income distribution: The share of national income allocated to the richest Americans decreased, and the share allocated to the middle class doubled.

War spending, accompanied by the draft, ended the high rates of unemployment. Organized labor grew strong, with union membership increasing by about 60 percent. Although most unions abided by a no-strike policy, they secured new benefits, such as fewer hours and better health plans, for their members, partially as a concession from the National War Labor Board, which limited wage increases to avoid inflation.

The Office of Price Administration waged a battle against inflation and overuse of resources, overseeing a **rationing** program designed to curb new purchases and conserve materials, particularly gas, sugar, coffee, butter, and meat. Americans largely complied with these efforts voluntarily and implemented "meatless Tuesdays," planted "victory gardens," and conducted collection drives to gather materials for recycling.

Another tactic aimed at financing the war was the sale of war bonds, which involved many Hollywood actors (even Bugs Bunny!) doing their part to promote the war effort.

Controlling Information and Advertising the War

The Office of Censorship examined all letters sent overseas and worked with media firms to control information broadcast to the public. The Office of War Information, formed in June 1942, employed artists, writers, and advertisers in a campaign to shape public opinion by explaining the reasons for U.S. entry into the war and by portraying the enemy as barbaric and cruel.

Lesson 10-6: Japanese Internment

On February 19, 1942, FDR issued **Executive Order 9066**, establishing military areas across the United States. More than 120,000 Japanese immigrants and U.S.-born Japanese-Americans were sent to these relocation centers under military police guard. The policy was deemed necessary to prevent acts of sabotage and espionage in support of Japan.

In 1944, the Supreme Court upheld the constitutionality of the order in *Korematsu v. U.S.* Although there was no evidence of Japanese-Americans posing a threat to the country, they were kept in relocation centers until 1944, when they gradually began to be released.

In an ironic twist, the most highly decorated American unit in the European war was the **442nd Regimental Combat Team**, composed of Japanese-American soldiers. They fought bravely in battle. After they liberated the small town of Bruyeres in southern France and rescued the "Lost Battalion" (141st), the Japanese-American soldiers gained that respect. For their performance, 18,000 total awards were bestowed on the 442nd, including 9,500 Purple Hearts, 52 Distinguished Service Crosses, seven Distinguished Unit Citations, and one Congressional Medal of Honor.

Lesson 10-7: Re-Election and Succession

FDR ran for re-election once again in 1944, in the midst of World War II, with Harry S. Truman as his running mate. FDR won an unprecedented fourth term. Shortly after Roosevelt's fourth term began, he died of a cerebral hemorrhage on April 12, 1945, leaving Truman to oversee the war effort. During the 82 days of FDR's fourth term, he never met with Truman nor shared vital information about the U.S.'s new secret weapon.

Lesson 10-8: Advancing the War Effort

As the home front buzzed in support of the war effort, the U.S. armed forces faced a two-front battle, in Europe and the Pacific.

Drive to Victory in Europe

The Allies and the United States agreed to focus on victory in Europe before turning to Japan. For U.S. troops, European involvement began in 1942 with Operation Torch, a North African campaign in which more than 100,000 Allied troops under American **General Dwight D. Eisenhower** forced a German surrender in Tunisia. The Allies eventually gained control of the Mediterranean and paved the way for the invasion of Europe. In the summer of 1943, Allied troops conquered Sicily, and Mussolini was overthrown. After the Battle of Stalingrad in January 1943, Hitler's forces surrendered in battle for the first time, marking the turning point of the war in Europe. Soviet troops then began the long advance toward Germany. By mid-1944, they had succeeded in pushing the Nazis out of the Soviet Union. The Soviets advanced toward Germany, liberating occupied regions from German rule.

In 1944, the United States launched a front against the Germans in France, dubbed Operation Overlord. It centered on the June 6, 1944, **D-Day** invasion of Normandy, in which American, British, and Canadian forces under the command of General Eisenhower, the supreme allied commander in Europe, undertook a massive land, sea, and air assault. An impressive armada of ships and troops were involved in this complex assault. Despite heavy resistance and many casualties in the early hours of the campaign, the Allies pressed on. By the end of the summer, they had liberated Belgium, Luxembourg, and most of France, including the capital city of Paris on August 25th. Nine months later, the war in Europe would come to an end with the German defeat.

In December 1944, Hitler sent the last of his reserves to attack the Allied troops in Belgium and Luxembourg. The reserves penetrated the Allies' line but were forced back in late December and early January. The **Battle of the Bulge** ended with an Allied victory in January 1945, despite heavy Allied losses.

By the end of April, Berlin was encircled by American, British, and Soviet troops. Germany surrendered unconditionally on May 8, 1945, and American citizens celebrated V-E Day in honor of the Allied victory in Europe. In the next few days and weeks, though, the world became horrified at the loss of more than 6 million Jews and several million others who had died in the concentration camps discovered by Allied forces invading Germany.

War in the Pacific

As General MacArthur "leapfrogged" from island to island on a path north from Australia, and the navy island-hopped toward Japan from the Central Pacific, they secured U.S. control of these Japanese islands and put Tokyo, Japan's capital, within range for U.S. bombers. In the summer of 1944, U.S. forces destroyed the imperial fleet, wiping out Japan's naval power.

The final push to victory in Japan began in 1945, when American troops won long, bloody battles on the islands of Iwo Jima and Okinawa from February to June. Japan also suffered heavy loses in the skirmishes but refused to consider surrender. The fierce battle by the Marines for **Iwo Jima** in February and March is famous for the fighting and bravery of the nearly 7,000 soldiers who lost their lives in this campaign and for the image of the Marines raising the flag atop Mount Suribachi during the battle. This battle and image became one of the most enduring battle images of World War II and allowed the United States to gain a foothold in order to get closer to Japan.

Lesson 10-9: The Manhattan Project

In 1942, the American government funded a $2 billion government plan dubbed "the **Manhattan Project**" to develop a new secret weapon. It established a site in Los Alamos, New Mexico, to develop a nuclear bomb. Richland, Washington, supported the project with the creation of plutonium at the Hanford Engineer Works. Oak Ridge, Tennessee, was the site of plants built for diffusing rare and vital uranium-235 from uranium-238. Chicago, Illinois, harbored a number of scientists working on nuclear technology. **Robert Oppenheimer** was the director of this nuclear project, one of the best-kept secrets of the war.

The first test came on July 16, 1945, at White Sands Missile Range at **Trinity Site** between Alamogordo and Socorro, New Mexico. After receiving word of the success of the test, Truman, while meeting with Soviet Premier Joseph Stalin and British Prime Minister Winston Churchill at the Potsdam Conference, issued a secret order to drop an atomic bomb if Japan didn't comply with an ultimatum to surrender unconditionally by August 3rd or face "prompt and utter destruction."

Japan rejected the threat, and on August 6, 1945, an American B-29 bomber, the *Enola Gay*, dropped an atomic bomb on the Japanese city of Hiroshima, killing more than 70,000 and injuring another 70,000. Three days later, a second bomb was dropped on Nagasaki, killing 40,000 and injuring 60,000. On August 15, 1945, **V-J Day** (Victory over Japan) was declared when Japan surrendered, and on September 2, 1945, Japanese leaders officially surrendered on board the *USS Missouri* with General Douglas MacArthur accepting the signed agreement.

Truman made the final decision to use the atomic bombs as a way to end the war quickly with minimal loss of American life. Some believed racism inspired the bombs' use, and some claimed that Truman could have forced Japan's surrender simply by demonstrating the bombs' effect on an abandoned island. Others argued that the bombs were used mainly to intimidate Joseph Stalin and to prevent the Soviet Union,

which declared war on Japan on August 8, 1945, from claiming a share in victory over Japan. Although Truman's motives were questioned, the ultimate responsibility to drop the bomb rested with the president, and he did not back down from his choice.

Lesson 10-10: Negotiating Peace for a New World Order

Even while the war was proceeding, the Allies were meeting to settle details about the post-war world order. Their diplomatic agreements—and disagreements—reached far beyond the war's end.

The Tehran Conference

In 1943, FDR and Churchill arrived in Tehran, Iran, to meet Stalin at the **Tehran Conference**. At this first meeting of the **Big Three**, the Allies planned the 1944 assault on France and agreed to divide Germany into zones of occupation after the war. They also agreed to establish a new international peacekeeping organization, the United Nations.

The Yalta Conference

In February 1945, the Big Three met again in the Soviet city of **Yalta**. This would be the last time all three leaders would meet. Stalin, whose troops had overrun Eastern Europe, leveraged the most bargaining power at the Yalta Conference. At the meeting, they agreed to divide Germany and Berlin into four zones of occupation, and promised free elections in Eastern Europe following the war. Stalin agreed to declare war against Japan soon after Germany surrendered. Plans were approved for a United Nations conference in San Francisco in April 1945.

The Potsdam Conference

After FDR's death and the end of the war in Europe, Harry Truman, new British Prime Minister Clement Atlee, and Stalin met at the **Potsdam Conference** in Germany from July 17 to August 2, 1945. Little was accomplished diplomatically. The United States and Great Britain were becoming wary of the USSR and its goals for Eastern Europe after the war ended.

The three leaders did agree to demilitarize Germany and agreed on the concept of war crimes trials. The Potsdam Agreement divided Germany into four zones, administered by the Soviet Union, France, Britain, and the United States, and established joint administration of Berlin, which lay well within the Soviet zone.

Lesson 10-11: War Crimes Trials at Nuremberg

As the Allies pressed in on German occupied territories in 1944 and 1945 they began to discover one of the greatest tragedies of World War II: the German concentration camps. Sites at Auschwitz, Bergen-Belen, and

Birkenau were among the sites of the **Holocaust**, which was a German attempt to annihilate more than six million European Jews and millions of other "undesirable peoples" in Europe. The end of the war resulted in the liberation of countless people from these death camps. Many high-ranking German officials were arrested and faced trial on criminal charges.

The trials of Nazi war criminals began in Nuremberg, Germany, in 1945. Prosecutors charged 24 Germans with an assortment of crimes, including waging aggressive war, extermination of ethnic and religious groups, and murder and mistreatment of prisoners and inhabitants of occupied territories. The tribunal heard testimony and saw documentation on these "crimes against humanity."

The Nuremberg tribunal concluded that the instigation of aggressive war was a crime, and the defendants' claim that they were just following orders was unsound. Twelve defendants were sentenced to death and seven others to prison sentences of varying length.

Lesson 10-12: Post-War Settlement in Asia

After Japan surrendered on September 2, 1945, American forces under General Douglas MacArthur occupied the country, and democratic reforms were imposed on the Japanese government. By the end of occupation in 1952, Japan became an economically powerful democracy.

Another element of the post-war settlement in Asia was the division of Korea at the 38th parallel, an agreement reached between the Soviet Union and the United States shortly before the end of the war as part of the Japanese surrender. The Soviets occupied North Korea and the United States occupied South Korea, each supporting a government that was antagonistic toward the other. This antagonism would erupt in the Korean War in 1950.

Lesson 10-13: The United Nations

In April 1945, the **United Nations** Conference on International Organization met in San Francisco. Delegates from 50 countries outlined their aims for global peace and collective security. In their charter, they created a General Assembly to make policy and a Security Council to settle disputes. In October 1945, the UN officially came into being, with 51 founding members. Its goals were to save succeeding generations from war, to promote national self-determination, to respect human rights, and to help nations work together to solve problems. Its headquarters would be located in New York City. The General Assembly, comprised of each member nation selecting one representative, and a Secretary General to preside over the group, would assemble to discuss the problems of the world. A Security Council was formed consisting of five permanent members (the United States, Great Britain, the USSR, France, and China) along with 10 other members chosen on a two-year cycle from the General Assembly. The five permanent members have veto power and their goal would be to settle international conflicts with the use of economic and military actions to settle international disputes. The Security Council measures would require the unanimous vote of its five permanent members. The UN soon became entangled in international affairs as World War II drew to a close and the Cold War and nuclear age began.

Review Exam

Multiple Choice

1. The policy of appeasement with Adolf Hitler in Europe prior to the outbreak of World War II did all of the following EXCEPT _____.
   a) stop Hilter's advances in taking over territory in Europe
   b) allow Hitler to take over Austria in 1938 in the Anschluss
   c) allow Hitler to take over the Sudentenland along the border of Germany and Czechoslovakia in 1938
   d) allow Hitler to completely take over Czechoslovakia by March 1939

2. While Great Britain, France, and the United States were largely following the policy of isolationism in the 1930s, _____.
   a) Japan was able to gain control of nearly one-quarter of mainland China
   b) Mussolini came to power in Italy
   c) Hitler rose to power in Germany
   d) A, B, and C

3. U.S. involvement in World War II ended the Great Depression by _____.
   a) increasing output of goods and materials so that before the end of the war the United States was the number-one producer of war materials

    b) creating jobs for millions of Americans, including women and minorities

    c) more than doubling of the GNP figures from 1940 to 1945

    d) A, B, and C

4. Prior to the U.S. declaration of war on Japan on December 8, 1941, FDR's policy actions included _____.

    a) allowing the German luxury liner *St. Louis* filled with Jewish refugees to dock and allow all its passengers entry into the United States

    b) strictly adhering to the Neutrality Acts

    c) meeting with Churchill in August 1941 and issues the Atlantic Charter, outlining war aims

    d) discouraging the adoption of a lend-lease policy with Great Britain

5. The Tuskegee Airmen and the 442nd Army Group proved that _____.

    a) an all-black combat unit of pilots had the necessary skills and desire to fight in combat

    b) blacks would need additional training before allowed into combat

    c) black units could easily be integrated into the white army

    d) they displayed minimal valor in fighting and lost several men and airplanes in battle

6. The goal of wartime rationing was _____.

    a) curbing inflation

    b) curbing the overuse of resources as a patriotic duty

    c) encouraging the conservation of gas, sugar, butter, and meat

    d) A, B, and C

7. _____ was not a leader of an Allied country during the war.

    a) Stalin   c) FDR

    b) Hirohito   d) Churchill

8. The attack at Pearl Harbor on December 7, 1941, _____.

    a) was a surprise attack on a U.S. naval base by the Japanese navy

    b) was successful in drawing America into the conflict of World War II

    c) resulted in the deaths of more than 2,400 people and inflicting great damage to the U.S. naval fleet

    d) A, B, and C

9. The _____ was the turning point of the war in Eastern Europe.

    a) Battle of Berlin   c) Battle of Moscow

    b) Battle of Leningrad   d) Operation Sea Lion

10. The D-Day invasion on June 6, 1944, _____.
    a) allowed for the liberation of France by August 1944
    b) was a frontal assault on the Germans at Normandy and the largest amphibious assault in history
    c) saw the Germans make a costly mistake by delaying the movement of his troops in time to adequately counter the attack
    d) A, B, and C

11. The Battle of Midway was significant in 1942 in that _____.
    a) it was deemed the turning point of the war in the Pacific
    b) the United States was able to defeat the Japanese navy and forced it in to a retreat mode
    c) it allowed the Japanese to gain another victory over the American forces in the Pacific
    d) A and B only

12. During World War II, Executive Order 9066 allowed for the internment of Japanese Americans _____.
    a) by forcing the relocation of nearly 120,000 Japanese Americans to military areas across the United States (mainly in the West and Southwest)
    b) with minimal security
    c) for a two-year period
    d) only to be declared unconstitutional in the 1944 *Korematsu v. U.S.* court case

13. The purpose of the Manhattan Project was to _____.
    a) prepare for a surprise attack on Japan in the spring of 1942
    b) develop the atomic bomb
    c) increase the size of the U.S. naval fleet
    d) develop plans for post-war Europe in 1945

14. In 1945, as the Allied troops began pressing in on Germany from the Western and Eastern fronts, _____.
    a) Mussolini mounted a great counter-offensive
    b) Hitler soon surrendered after the Battle of the Bulge
    c) they began to discover the horrors of the Holocaust and the Nazi concentration camps
    d) Russia made plans for free elections for Poland

15. Truman's ultimate decision to drop the atomic bomb on Japan was to _____.
    a) stop the fighting by bringing a quick end to the war against Japan
    b) intimidate the Russians
    c) demonstrate U.S. resolve by ending the war with the least amount of casualties
    d) A, B, and C

16. Post-war settlements in Asia included the _____.
    a) occupation of Japan under the forces of General MacArthur
    b) the division of Korea
    c) the formation of a democratic government in Japan
    d) A, B, and C

17. Before the end of World War II in August 1945, the biggest issue that emerged causing a degree of dissension within the Allies occurred over the issue of _____.
    a) Truman's threat to use the atomic bomb
    b) the future role of the United Nations
    c) the post-war future of a defeated Germany and the status of the Russian-occupied countries in Eastern Europe
    d) the post-war future of Japan

Matching

a   Doolittle's Raid
b. Iwo Jima
c. Neutrality Acts
d. Battle of Britain
e. Potsdam
f. Rome-Berlin Axis
g. Rosie the Riveter
h. Battle of Guadalcanal
i. Hiroshima
j. Tehran
k. General Dwight Eisenhower
l. blitzkrieg

m. Office of Censorship and the Office of War
n. Code Talkers
o. Trinity Site
p. WAAC and WASPS
q. Battle of the Bulge
r. General Douglas MacArthur
s. Nuremburg
t. V-J Day
u. Robert Oppenheimer
v. Stimson Doctrine
w. V-E Day
x. Yalta

____18. limited the United States in doing business with countries engaged in war; revised in 1939 to allow arms sales on a cash-and-carry basis

____19. the site of the first atomic bomb test in the desert in New Mexico in 1945

____20. site of the first meeting between the three Allies in 1943

____21. site of the first atomic bomb dropped on Japan on August 6, 1945

____22. the director of the Manhattan Project

____23. a poster image of a strong-armed woman proving that women could make a valuable contribution to the war effort at home

____24. battle that is famous for the image of American troops raising the flag bravely on Mt. Suribachi

____25. also known as Operation Sea Lion; dealt with the German attack on Great Britain in 1940

____26. two of the groups in which women served in non-combat military work during the war

____27. lightning-fast warfare developed by the Germans

____28. the last German offensive of World War II (in December 1944)

____29. diplomatic tool that employs the practice of non-recognition of a country because of a difference in policy with the U.S.

____30. Victory over Japan (August 15, 1945)

____31. an attack on Japan in April 1942 that was only four months after the Japanese attack at Pearl Harbor

____32. commander of the Allied troops in Europe; leader of the D-Day invasion in 1944

____33. alliance formed by Germany and Italy in 1936

____34. created to regulate information and communication during the war

____35. after this battle the United States began the series of island hopping with the ultimate goal of closing in on Japan

____36. at this meeting of the Allied leaders after the war ended in Europe the alliance began to unravel because of a lack of trust over Russia's plans for Eastern Europe flowing the end of the war

____37. commander of the Allied troops in the Pacific

____38. the last meeting between three Allied leaders (FDR, Churchill, and Stalin) in February 1945

____39. German location of the Nazi war crimes trials in 1945

____40. Victory over Europe (May 8, 1945)

____41. Navajos who were used for radio transmissions in the Pacific to confuse the Japanese

Short Response

42. To what extent did World War II affect the following groups of people in the United States: women, blacks, and Japanese?

43. Evaluate the roles that *apathy, appeasement, and aggression* played in World War II.

44. What role did the United States play in establishing the terms of peace following World War II?

Answers begin on page 295.

The Early Years of the Cold War

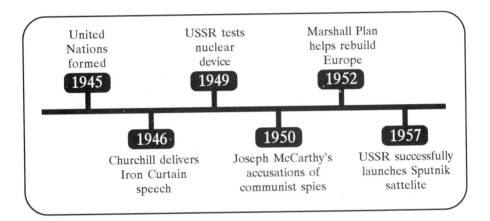

United Nations formed — **1945**

USSR tests nuclear device — **1949**

Marshall Plan helps rebuild Europe — **1952**

1946 — Churchill delivers Iron Curtain speech

1950 — Joseph McCarthy's accusations of communist spies

1957 — USSR successfully launches Sputnik sattelite

Trends and Themes of the Era

▶ The United States and the USSR emerged from World War II as the only superpowers in the world. They quickly became enemies and rivals, battling in politics, technology, and military power.

▶ The arms race, in which the United States and the USSR each developed an arsenal of nuclear weapons that could destroy the other many times over, was a defining reality and metaphor of the Cold War. Though the threat of confrontation loomed, the two sides avoided direct conflict.

▶ Policies for containing communism influenced virtually all U.S. foreign policy decisions.

▶ Fear of communist subversion led to intense domestic anticommunist fervor. Communists and suspected communists were closely watched, and the fear of communism remained part of American culture for decades.

Fears, sympathizers, and threats! After the United States discovered that the USSR had developed and tested a nuclear weapon in the fall of 1949, the race was on to build more nuclear weapons. In the years immediately after World War II, a great rift erupted between the United States and the USSR. Fear was fueled by a growing distrust as the USSR spread into Eastern Europe and set its sights on other places around the globe. Eisenhower warned, "The threat to our safety, and to the hope of a peaceful world, can be simply stated—it is communist imperialism" and "their aim to expand their power, one way or another, throughout the world." Not only was there fear that communism would spread abroad, but the threat of yet another "red scare" on the home front also fueled suspicion. Attempts to contain the spread of communism led to a dramatic increase in military spending, a massive military and weapons buildup, and an intense search for subversives within the country. U.S. strategies to contain the menace of communism were met with continued countermoves by the USSR. Turkey, Berlin, Korea, Vietnam, and ultimately a space race served as flashpoints for confrontation. Truman and Eisenhower dealt with this virtual "chess match" with their counterparts, Stalin and Khrushchev. The world feared that the next global war would be a nuclear one, and people began to make plans for surviving destruction.

Lesson 11-1: The Cold War Begins: The United States vs. the USSR

After World War II, a very different conflict engaged America's attention. The **Cold War** pitted the communist Soviet Union against the capitalist United States and its Western allies, and both sides considered the conflict serious and menacing. Presidents Truman and Eisenhower found themselves in an increasingly difficult and complex battle against communism.

Origins

Even before the end of World War II, the United States and its allies had become wary of the Soviet Union as it continued to advance further into Eastern Europe. Although agreeing to some Soviet concessions, Churchill, Roosevelt, and Truman didn't fully trust Stalin. In a warning to Truman in 1945, Churchill stated, "We do not know what is going on behind the Russian front." The post-war conferences highlighted various concerns and the growing distrust among the World War II Allies. At the last conference, Truman informed Joseph Stalin that U.S. scientists had successfully detonated an atomic bomb, which would become the flashpoint of the nuclear arms race between the two countries.

The Cold War soon became a classic struggle of good versus evil. Many Americans favored a "get tough" policy with the Russians. Following the end of World War II, the United States began to act as international police officers in the name of democratic values. Defense spending reshaped industry and helped stimulate nearly three decades of dramatic economic growth. The Cold War challenged American and Russian economic, political, and military influence around the globe. The U.S.'s goals were promoting democracy in Western Europe, maintaining a strategic military position in relation to the USSR, and preserving U.S. leadership in the world economy. U.S. policymakers promoted a flexible military response with the implied strategy of bankrupting the communists through competitive defense spending.

By the late 1940s, the United States and the USSR had emerged as **superpowers**. The former allies became bitter enemies as they rushed to establish spheres of influence in Europe. In 1946, Stalin claimed that communism and capitalism were incompatible, and wanted to establish a buffer region of pro-Soviet states in Eastern Europe. In the Soviet bloc countries, free elections were canceled, trade and most contacts with the West were cut, travel was limited, Western media was banned, and the USSR claimed the right to intervene in communist countries to counter anti-communist uprisings. In 1945, Stalin disregarded the Yalta Declaration and prevented free elections in Poland. In early March 1946, former British Prime Minister Winston Churchill delivered a speech warning the world that an "**iron curtain** had descended upon the continent of Europe," symbolizing the division of Eastern Europe from the West.

Lesson 11-2: Rebuilding War-Torn Countries

The race was now on to rebuild war-torn Europe and Japan. The war had devastated the economies of many of the major countries in Europe as well and that of Japan. In order to help the U.S. economic growth following the end of the war, it was vital to secure strong trading partners, and, by doing this, stem the threat of the spread of communism.

The Truman Plan in Turkey and Greece

A combination of political, economic, and moral considerations led President Truman to oppose Soviet dominance of Eastern Europe. The economies

and governments of Western Europe were nearing collapse. Early in 1947, allies in Western Europe asked the United States to help fund efforts to prevent the rise of communist governments in Greece and Turkey. Russia was reportedly trying to control the region in order to gain access to the Mediterranean from the Black Sea.

Truman took a strong stance against the Soviet territorial advances, advocating **containment**. Under the policy, the United States would work to prevent further Soviet expansion through military, economic, and diplomatic strategies designed to resist the Russians. In March 1947, Truman asked a joint session of Congress to authorize military assistance to Turkey and Greece. He proclaimed, "It must be the policy of the U.S. to support free people who are resisting subjugation by armed minorities or outside pressures" in order to "assist free peoples to work out their own destinies in their own way." This proclamation, known as the **Truman Doctrine**, committed the United States to a role as global police officer. The United States sent $400 million in economic and military aid to Greece and Turkey because, if they fell, it was feared that the Middle East would be next. The United States felt it had a moral destiny to provide world leadership in the struggle against communism.

The Marshall Plan

The financial counterpart to the Truman Doctrine was the **Marshall Plan**, which pledged financial assistance to Europe to stimulate the post-war recovery; to provide relief for the hungry, homeless, and desperate; and to prevent the further spread and threat of communism. Truman and his secretary of state, George C. Marshall, hoped the plan would eliminate devastation and political instability. By 1952, Congress had appropriated some $17 billion for Marshall Plan aid.

The Marshall Plan became one of the greatest economic success stories of the 20th century. Its support allowed industry to grow to pre-war levels, ushered in a new age of prosperity for Western Europe, and drove a deeper wedge between the United States and the USSR.

The Russians copied the Marshall Plan in 1949 and labeled it **Comecon (Council for Mutual Economic Assistance)**. It provided economic assistance to satellite countries in the Soviet bloc in Eastern Europe.

Helping Rebuild Japan

The United States also stepped in to rebuild Japan's economy after the end of World War II. Japan was demilitarized, and a stable, democratic government was installed. The country's economy revived, eventually to be dominated by the electronics industry, and later, the automobile industry. In 1951, Japan's independence was restored, and it became a U.S. ally. The economic rebuilding program in Japan turned into an economic miracle when, by the 1970s, Japan had become the third-leading industrial nation in the world.

Lesson 11-3: The Arms Race

Nuclear weapons played a central role in the possibility of military engagement between the United States and the USSR. In 1946, Truman proposed a plan to the United Nations that would require the USSR to cease construction on any atomic weaponry, saying that only then would the United States destroy its growing arsenal. The Soviets rejected the plan, and both sides rushed to develop weapons of mass destruction. In 1946, the federal government established the Atomic Energy Commission to oversee the development of nuclear energy and arms. The battle for nuclear dominance became the defining characteristic of the Cold War.

On August 29, 1949, the USSR detonated its first atomic bomb in Kazakhstan. This development, combined with the establishment of a communist regime in China in 1949, inspired a new and fiercer anticommunism stance by the U.S. government. The defense budget more than tripled, and the campaign was on to develop a hydrogen bomb. The National Security Council's report to Truman, **NSC-68**, stated that the USSR was a threat to the free world and, because of the threat to peace and the military disparity between the United States and the USSR, the United States "must engage in a rapid and sustained buildup of the political, economic, and military strength of the free world." It supported the development of a hydrogen bomb, 1,000 times more powerful than those used on Japan, an increase in U.S. armed forces, and tax increases to support massive defense projects. The U.S. role was to function as a state approaching permanent mobilization, whether at war or not.

Before 1950, the U.S. military budget had been around $13.5 billion; six months later, it was $50 billion. This massive military buildup would shape U.S. foreign policy throughout the Cold War. The National Security Act of 1947 also created the **Central Intelligence Agency (CIA)**, responsible for gathering information and conducting covert operations, and the **National Security Council (NSC)**, which assembled top diplomatic and military advisors in one committee.

The drive for the hydrogen bomb succeeded with the November 1952 detonation of an H-bomb in the Marshall Islands in the Pacific. The American advantage was short-lived because, in July 1953, the Russians detonated their own H-bomb. In early 1954, the United States detonated a thermonuclear device at a test site at the **Bikini Atoll** in the Marshall Islands. The blast was the most powerful nuclear test ever conducted by the United States—more than a thousand times bigger than the bombs dropped on Hiroshima and Nagasaki. The radioactive fallout contaminated an area in excess of 7,000 square miles. Natives on the Marshall Islands as well as a crew of Japanese fishermen were affected by the radioactive fallout from this test. In addition, the blast created a huge crater more than a mile wide on the ocean floor. Within a few short years, the United States and the USSR had enough bombs to destroy the world several times over.

Secret U.S. tests on isolated islands in the Pacific and in the desert area northwest of Las Vegas, Nevada, raised questions about the impact of radioactive fallout. In 1952, Great Britain raised the nuclear stakes by becoming the third country with nuclear weapons. Tensions continued to mount as the USSR raised the stakes in the arms race again with the 1957 development of an **intercontinental ballistic missile (ICBM)** that could carry a nuclear warhead.

Lesson 11-4: The Berlin Blockade and a Divided Germany

France, Britain, and the United States gradually united their three zones of occupation within Germany and announced their intention to create a

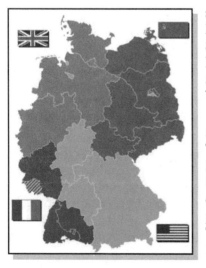

West German Republic in 1948. In opposition to such a republic—which would have included West Berlin—far within the Soviet zone, Stalin established the Berlin Blockade in June 1948, cutting off all rail and highway access to Berlin from the West.

Shortly afterwards, choosing neither to abandon Berlin nor to use military force, Truman ordered an around-the-clock airlift, called **Operation Vittles**. The United States and Great Britain began an airlift of more than two million tons of food, supplies, machines, fuel, and other necessities. The successful airlift continued until May 1949, when the USSR lifted the blockade.

Immediately after the blockade ended, the United States, Britain, and France pulled out of Germany and approved the creation of the **Federal Republic of Germany**, or West Germany. The USSR responded by creating the **German Democratic Republic**, or East Germany, from its occupied region. The city of Berlin was also divided between East and West. In May 1949, the United States and West Germany agreed on the

first major U.S. military treaty since the Revolutionary War, granting $1.3 billion in U.S. aid and creating U.S. army bases in West Germany.

Lesson 11-5: NATO and the Warsaw Pact

The heightened fear of conflict helped persuade Western Europe of the need for a security alliance. In April 1949, 10 Western European nations, Canada, and the United States established the **North Atlantic Treaty Organization (NATO)** and declared that an attack against any member of the alliance would be seen as an attack against all, a policy known as collective security. In July 1949, the United States officially joined NATO, and Congress authorized $1.3 billion for military aid to NATO countries. In 1955, the USSR established a rival alliance, the Warsaw Pact, comprising the members of the Soviet bloc in Eastern Europe.

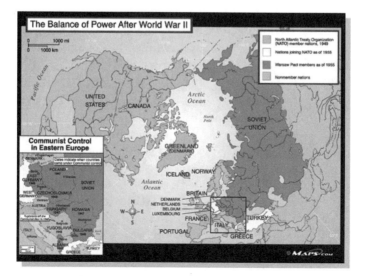

Lesson 11-6: Crisis in Asia

In Asia, as in Europe, Truman tried to contain the spread of communism. The United States denied the USSR any role in the post-war reconstruction of Japan and occupied Japan until 1952, when it officially exited but left troops behind on American military bases. In China, the United States spent almost $3 billion in a failed effort to support Chinese nationalists under Chiang Kai-shek against Mao Zedong's communists. In 1949, the communists won and established the **People's Republic of China**. The nationalists fled to Taiwan, where they formed their own government. Asia, as Germany had, became the site of divisions between competing camps: communist and noncommunist.

Police Action in Korea

On June 25, 1950, communist North Korea invaded South Korea across the **38th parallel**. South Korea immediately appealed to the UN for assistance. At the time, the USSR was boycotting the Security Council, so its vote didn't count in the council. Without asking for a declaration of war, Truman committed U.S. troops as part of a United Nations "police action." **General Douglas MacArthur** was placed in command of the Allied UN forces. Truman authorized an offensive drive across the divide and toward China, but Chinese forces repelled MacArthur in November. Fighting stabilized around the previous border, and in the spring of 1951 Truman sought to scale back the war effort and negotiate peace, despite MacArthur's proposals for bombing attacks north of the Yalu River in China. By July 1951, the communist Koreans had been pushed back past the 38th parallel, and the situation became a stalemate. After a month of publicly denouncing the administration's policy of restraint, MacArthur was relieved of duty in April 1951 by President Truman for advocating that troops go into China, bomb bases in Manchuria, blockade China, and use nuclear weapons if needed.

The Korean War

Peace talks in Panmunjon took two years. (Nearly half of all U.S. casualties occurred during the years of peace talks.) Finally, with the signing of an armistice in 1953, the border was established at the 38th parallel, and a **demilitarized zone (DMZ)** was created on each side of the line. The fighting had stopped, but no formal peace treaty was ever signed.

Civil War in Vietnam

In Vietnam, Truman and later Eisenhower provided U.S. aid to the French, who battled the communist, nationalist Viet Minh for control of the former French colony. Even with limited U.S. support in the Vietnam conflict, France lost control of Indochina in 1954 at Dien Bien Phu. In 1954, the **Geneva Accords**, which included France, Great Britain, the USSR, the United States, China, Laos, Cambodia, and leaders from the north and south in Vietnam, divided Vietnam at the **17th parallel** and set up a free election to unify the country in 1956. **Ho Chi Minh** became the leader of North Vietnam with its capital at **Hanoi**, and **Ngo Dinh Diem**, who was supported by the United States and installed by the CIA) became the leader of South Vietnam with its capital at **Saigon**. Eisenhower, however, refused to sign the Geneva Peace Accords because of his **domino theory**, which contended that if Vietnam fell to Soviet control, as would likely happen if elections reunified the country, the communist forces would soon dominate all of Asia.

Diem's control in the south was tenuous at best, and, in 1960, the National Liberation Front of South Vietnam, backed by North Vietnam, formed in opposition to Diem. Eisenhower sent funds and advisers to aid Diem, committing the United States to involvement in a potentially volatile situation. The United States began to question Diem's rule in South Vietnam, however, as the leader's Catholic beliefs clashed with those of the country's Buddhist majority. Diem appointed family members to government positions, and U.S. aid for economic reform went to the military and corrupt government officials. He moved peasants to communes and, when he intensified his attacks against the Buddhists, several monks retaliated by pouring gasoline on themselves and burning themselves to death.

After the 1960 election, President Kennedy continued U.S. escalation in Vietnam so that, by 1963, the United States had 16,000 military advisers there and had increased military aid. Kennedy then sent Vice President Lyndon Johnson to Vietnam to assess the situation; Johnson claimed that more aid was needed. Kennedy initially reacted by supplying Vietnam with more help because he didn't want to appear soft on communism. The United States then declared that it wouldn't oppose Diem's overthrow. In fact, a CIA plot helped overthrow Diem with his assassination on November 1, 1963, three weeks before Kennedy's assassination.

Lesson 11-7: The Red Scare in America

As Truman and Eisenhower both sought to contain communism in Europe and Asia, their administrations presided over efforts to rid the United States itself of communist elements.

Investigating Loyalty

The American Communist party, which peaked in strength during World War II, had been linked to covert operations designed to aid the Soviet Union; such espionage was known to have involved officials within the federal government. In March 1947, Truman initiated a massive loyalty program with an executive order. The **Loyalty Review Board** became so powerful that it often abridged officials' rights in its search for disloyalty. Employees who criticized American policy were subject to humiliating investigations. By 1956, the program had led to more than 2,500 dismissals and 12,000 resignations from official posts.

As Cold War fears grew, much of the nation became convinced that communists within the country were working on a large scale to subvert the American government. Thirty-nine states passed anti-subversion laws and loyalty programs. Any criticism of the government was likely to meet with investigation and denouncement. In 1947, the **House Un-American Activities Committee (HUAC)**, which included Representative Richard Nixon, led a series of highly publicized hearings in which witnesses were forced into confessions. If they refused to confess, the witnesses faced restrictions on their rights. "Are you now or have you ever been a member of the communist party?" was one of the most famous lines of questioning during the hearings in the late 1940s and early 1950s.

During the 1948 presidential campaign, Truman demonstrated his stance against communism by prosecuting 11 leaders of the Communist party under the 1940 Smith Act, which prohibited any conspiracy to overthrow the government. The Communist Party itself began to fade in strength, with membership falling to about 25,000, but some government officials nevertheless asserted that the communist threat was everywhere.

The HUAC then began to attack a number of prominent screenwriters and directors for supposed "un-American propaganda." Hollywood established an unofficial blacklist that prevented questionable people from getting work. The initial investigation targeted directors, producers, and actors who promoted left-wing ideas. Known as the **Hollywood 10**, the group members refused to discuss past political associations and were blacklisted and sent to jail.

The Hiss and Rosenberg Cases

In 1948, Whittaker Chambers, a senior editor at *Time* magazine and a former Soviet spy, named **Alger Hiss** as an underground member of the Communist Party. Hiss, a graduate of Harvard Law School who had worked within the federal government for years, denied Chamber's claims in court. Nixon, a member of the HUAC, took up the Hiss-Chambers case to investigate subversion. Chambers produced a set of documents known as the *Pumpkin Papers*, which were four rolls of microfilm of various documents from the State Departments. Chambers hid the documents in a hollowed-out pumpkin on his Maryland farm and gave them to Richard Nixon. Nixon used these documents in his investigation. (Television cameras, for the first time, were used at the congressional hearings, signaling another venue for the media to use during the Cold War.) In January 1950, Hiss was convicted of perjury and sentenced to five years imprisonment, emboldening conservatives and raising questions about the past activities of many Democrats in government. The case seemed to prove the communist threat in the United States.

In February 1950, Klaus Fuchs, a scientist involved in the Manhattan Project, was arrested for passing information on nuclear weapons development to the Soviets during World War II. This arrest led to the implication of Harry Gold, David Greenglass, and, most notably, **Ethel** and **Julius Rosenberg**. The Rosenbergs claimed they were victims of anti-Semitism who had been targeted for their leftist beliefs. In March 1951, they were convicted of selling atomic secrets to the Russians and were sentenced to death. Both were executed in June 1953.

McCarthyism

Anti-communism reached its peak in the United States with the rise of **McCarthyism**. In 1950, Senator **Joseph McCarthy** claimed to have a list of 205 people known to be members of the Communist party who were working in the State Department. Although McCarthy later reduced the number of names on his list and modified his allegations to say that the people were merely "bad risks," he continued to make speeches, even after a Senate committee called the accusations a hoax.

Republicans in the Senate soon came to support McCarthy, if only for the political benefits to be gained from attacks on liberals. McCarthy's appeal grew steadily throughout the nation until the Democrats feared that to oppose him would mean certain humiliation and charges of disloyalty. In the spirit of McCarthyism, Congress passed the McCarran Internal Security Act in 1950, which stated that organizations the attorney general deemed communist had to register with the Department of Justice and provide member lists and financial statements. In 1951, the McCarran Committee began targeting diplomats, labor union leaders, professors, and schoolteachers with leftist leanings. The act also barred communists from working in defense plants and allowed the government to deport any alien suspected of subversion. In 1954, at the height of his powers, McCarthy accused the military of being a haven for spies. The army countered by accusing McCarthy of using his power to secure preferential treatment for a member of his staff who had been drafted. In the televised congressional hearings on the matters, McCarthy's behavior eventually turned public opinion against him. The Senate, with support from Eisenhower, voted to censure McCarthy in December 1954.

CBS news journalist **Edward R. Murrow** used his news program, *Person to Person*, to openly challenge Joseph McCarthy in March 1954. The show detailed excerpts from speeches and comments made by McCarthy in an open attack on his credibility. Although Murrow succeeded in starting a public backlash against McCarthy that would ultimately lead to McCarthy's downfall, Murrow's show was eventually cancelled and he had a falling out with CBS news.

Playwright **Arthur Miller** wrote the play *The Crucible* in 1952 to tell the story of the communist witch-hunt in America. He used the story of the Salem Witchcraft Trials in 1692 as a means of relating the McCarthyism scare to the general public. His work on this published play raised communist suspicions and caused the HUAC to have him testify before Congress. In 1957, the HUAC found Miller guilty of contempt of Congress on charges of refusing to reveal the names of literary friends suspected of Communist affiliation. The following year, U.S. Court of Appeals reversed the conviction.

Lesson 11-8: The Space Race

The struggle for nuclear dominance started a battle between the super-powers for technological prowess in all fields. In October 1957, the USSR launched the space satellite *Sputnik*. The United States became alarmed and realized it was falling behind in the arms race. The country rushed to keep up with the USSR in the space race, but its first rocket, the *Vanguard*, exploded on the launch pad. Still, the United States continued its efforts and launched *Explorer I* in January 1958.

America's concern over its technological competitiveness lingered, spurring the 1958 creation of the **National Aeronautics and Space Administration (NASA)**. The United States also placed added emphasis on math and science in the nation's schools. The National Defense Education Act of 1958 provided a fivefold increase in funds available to stimulate and improve science and math education in public and private elementary, secondary, and post-secondary schools.

In April 1961, the USSR launched Yuri Gagarin into space, making him the first person to orbit Earth. The United States countered in May 1961 by launching astronaut Alan Sheppard into space. Within three weeks of Sheppard's feat, President Kennedy pledged in a speech, "I believe that this nation should commit itself to achieving the goal, before this decade is out, of landing a man on the Moon and returning him safely to the Earth."

In 1965, the USSR and the United States both made their first space walks, and by the mid-1960s, the United States had begun to take the lead in the space race with the *Mercury, Gemini,* and *Apollo* rocket programs. The Russians abandoned their plans for the race to the moon and began to initiate plans to live in space with the MIR space station. On July 20, 1969, Neil Armstrong and *Apollo 11* made history after the lunar module, the *Eagle,* landed and Armstrong became the first man to walk on the moon, declaring: "That's one small step for man, one giant leap for mankind."

Lesson 11-9: Brinksmanship

Even though the threat of direct confrontation seemed to be waning by the early 1950s, the Cold War was by no means near an end. Secretary of State **John Foster Dulles** committed the United States to mutual defense pacts with 43 nations. He also created extended controversy with threats of "massive nuclear retaliation" against communist aggression, declaring that the United States must be prepared to "go to the brink" of war in order to attain its objectives, a strategy known as **brinksmanship**.

Convinced that a large nuclear arsenal would deter the Soviets from rash action, Eisenhower advocated military cuts to provide funding for construction of nuclear weapons and planes to drop them. The New Look emphasized massive retaliation rather than ground force involvement in countries threatened by Soviet influence, and it was articulated in the U.S. military doctrine of Mutual Assured Destruction (MAD). Developed in the early 1960s, MAD promised that anyone who launched a nuclear attack would be immediately counterattacked, resulting in total nuclear devastation on both sides.

The focus on massive retaliation, however, didn't detract from interest in extending each superpower's spheres of influence. The focus of the Cold War now turned to various regions where proxy wars were waged by local groups backed by the two powers. The CIA spearheaded U.S. efforts in these proxy wars by providing covert assistance to those opposing Soviet-backed forces. In 1953, the CIA helped to restore the deposed shah of Iran to power, securing an American ally along the Soviet border. Also in 1953, the CIA intervened in elections in the Philippines. In 1954, it backed a military coup in Guatemala. One of the CIA's failures, however, happened in early 1959, when Cuba became a communist state led by **Fidel Castro**.

In 1954, Gamal Abdel Nasser came to power in Egypt and nationalized the Suez Canal, which had been foreign-owned. Israel, Britain, and France then attacked Egypt in October 1956. Eisenhower, enraged at his allies for acting without consulting him, condemned their actions and prepared for a potential war. Finally, Britain, Israel, and France agreed to pull out of Egypt in November 1956. In January 1957, Eisenhower announced that the United States would increase its involvement in the Middle East to oppose Soviet aggression by sending military aid and troops if necessary. The **Eisenhower Doctrine** justified the deployment of 14,000 marines to Lebanon in July 1958 to promote stability.

On May 5, 1960, a U-2 U.S. spy plane piloted by Gary Powers was shot down over Soviet territory, further straining relations between the two countries. The United States had been flying spy reconnaissance missions since 1956, attempting to detect an arms buildup in the Soviet Union. Nikita Khrushchev had been scheduled to meet with Eisenhower in Paris in May 1960, but canceled the meeting after the U-2 incident. At first, the United States tried to deny the U-2 incident, passing it off as a "U-2 weather balloon," but, when the Soviets recovered the pilot and showed him to the world, Eisenhower was forced to admit openly to spying on the Soviets. Even though the spy missions had failed to reveal a Soviet weapons buildup, the president and Congress continued to push for additional defense spending.

Review Exam

Multiple Choice

1. _____ was not a permanent member of the UN Security Council.
   a) China
   b) Germany
   c) France
   d) The USSR

2. The Cold War was a classic struggle of good versus evil and was demonstrated by the _____.
   a) "Iron Curtain" speech delivered by Churchill in 1946
   b) fear in the United States with the Red Scare in the 1950s
   c) buildup of nuclear weapons and military in the United States and the USSR during the1950s
   d) A, B, and C

3. Truman's policy of containment was meant to _____.
   a) stop the spread of communism in Korea

b) prevent further Soviet expansion through military, economic, and diplomatic strategies designed to resist the Russians

c) keep Germany divided after the war

d) diminish Japan's influence in the Pacific region

4. 1949 was a significant year in relations between the Soviet Union and the United States in that _____.

   a) China became a communist country

   b) the Soviet Union tested its first atomic bomb

   c) the United States increased its defense budget to include the development of a hydrogen bomb

   d) A, B, and C

5. NSC-68 was important in that it _____.

   a) committed the United States to war in Korea

   b) recommended a massive increase in military spending

   c) sought gradual increases, in two-year increments, in military spending

   d) scaled back military spending after the success of the Marshall Plan in Europe

6. All of the following are true about the Berlin Airlift, "Operation Vittles," EXCEPT that _____.

   a) all rail and highway access into Berlin was cut off in 1948

   b) Truman ordered a round-the-clock airlift to ship needed supplies into Berlin

   c) military force was reserved for use if necessary

   d) it lasted 11 months and was deemed a success when the Soviets lifted the blockade in 1949

7. In April 1949, the _____ alliance was formed by Western Europeans and was copied in 1955 by the Soviets.

   a) German Allied Defense Group and Warsaw Pact

   b) NATO and the Berlin Alliance

   c) NATO and the Warsaw Pact

   d) Western European Alliance Trust and Berlin Pact

8. Eisenhower's domino theory _____.
    a) was based on the premise that then all of Asia would be threatened by communism if Vietnam fell to Soviet influence
    b) believed that a communist threat in Asia was only doing to take place in Vietnam
    c) minimized the effect of the communist insurgence in North Vietnam
    d) favored a unified country of Vietnam

9. The House Un-American Activities Committee _____.
    a) included Representative Richard Nixon
    b) led a series of publicized hearings about communist activities
    c) began to attack Hollywood screenwriters and directors as producing "un-American propaganda," resulting in many of them being blacklisted in the industry
    d) A, B, and C

10. When the communists in North Korea invaded South Korea by crossing the 38th parallel _____.
    a) they succeeded in taking over South Korea
    b) they received minimal support from the Chinese
    c) they forced South Korea to appeal to the UN for assistance, resulting in the UN pursuit of a "police action" in Korea to combat the communist offensive
    d) MacArthur was placed in charge of the troops and immediately ruled out the use of nuclear weapons against China

11. Ethel and Julius Rosenburg were given the death penalty as a result of _____.
    a) their conviction on selling atomic secrets to the Russians
    b) promoting membership in the Communist Party
    c) increased hysteria in the country with regard to any suspicious communist activity
    d) A and C only

12. In addition to a list that Joseph McCarthy claimed had the names of about 205 communists working for the State Department, McCarthyism also included _____.
   a) a televised news show in which Edward R. Murrow openly challenged the credibility of McCarthy's accusations
   b) the passage of the McCarran Internal Security Act, which began targeting suspected communist activities by diplomats, union leaders, professors, teachers, and military personnel
   c) a series of hearings in which Joseph McCarthy was denounced for his activities and censured by the Senate in 1954
   d) A, B, and C

13. The Cold War became a contest of the American and Russian _____ influence around the world.
   a) economic   c) military
   b) political   d) A, B, and C

14. In 1957, with the successful Soviet launch of the first satellite, *Sputnik*, _____.
   a) the United States became alarmed in keeping up with the Soviets and created NASA in 1958
   b) the United States followed it with the successful launch of the *Vanguard*
   c) the Cold War had now spread to include the "space race"
   d) A and C only

15. Brinksmanship was John Foster Dulles's policy of _____.
   a) Containment
   b) "going to the brink of war" if necessary to halt Soviet aggression
   c) backing away from retaliation against Soviet threats
   d) minimal retaliation against Soviet aggression

16. CIA activities in the 1950s included all of the following EXCEPT _____.
   a) restoring the shah back to power in Iran
   b) intervening in elections in the Philippines
   c) preventing Castro from coming to power in Cuba in 1959
   d) backing a military coup in Guatemala

17. The U-2 spy plane incident involved _____.

   a) a U-2 weather balloon being shot down over Russia

   b) Gary Powers and his spy plane being shot down over Russia

   c) Russia accepting the U.S. apology for the incident

   d) the United States being truthful about its actions

18. The peace talks in Panmunjon in 1953 dealing with the Korean War ended with _____.

   a) only an armistice agreement

   b) a permanent peace agreement between the two nations

   c) both sides agreeing to scale back their military

   d) a formal declaration resolved within the United Nations Security Council

19. Arthur Miller's _____ was written primarily to tell the story of the Red Scare in America by relating it to the witchcraft hysteria in Salem in 1692.

   a) *The Hangings in Boston*   c) *Death of Freedom*

   b) *The Crucible*   d) *My Life Without Freedom*

Matching

a. Smith Act

b. Truman Doctrine

c. Whittaker Chambers

d. CIA

e. 38th parallel

f. General Assembly

g. Republic of Germany

h. Ho Chi Minh

i. Comecon

j. Atomic Energy Commission

k. 17th parallel

l. NSC

m. DMZ

n. George C. Marshall

o. Mao Zedong

p. ICBM

q. Ngo Dinh Diem

r. John Foster Dulles

s. German Democratic Republic

t. Eisenhower Doctrine

u. Loyalty Review Board

v. United Nations

w. MAD

x. Alger Hiss

_____20. Truman's secretary of state; helped devise the plan to rebuild war-torn Western Europe

____21. zones of Germany occupied by the United States, Britain, and France that were combined; also known as West Germany

____22. delegation of countries that would meet in the United Nations to discuss the problems of the world

____23. Central Intelligence Agency; created by the United States as part of the National Security Act of 1947

____24. a program initiated by Truman to check the loyalty of government employees

____25. committed the United States to the role of "world policeman" by giving military and monetary aid to halt the spread of communism

____26. intercontinental ballistic missile; developed by the Soviets in 1957 and feared to have the ability to carry a nuclear warhead

____27. created to oversee the development of nuclear energy and weapons

____28. the Soviet zone of the divided Germany; also known as East Germany

____29. international agency that was formed in 1945 to hear disputes and stop aggression

____30. National Security Council; comprised of top diplomatic and military advisors

____31. leader of South Vietnam

____32. area where the Geneva Accords divided Vietnam into Northern and Southern zones

____33. Council for Mutual Economic Assistance; a Soviet "copycat" of the successful Marshall Plan

____34. the geographical dividing line between North and South Korea

____35. provided the *Pumpkin Papers* to Richard Nixon and the HUAC

____36. leader of North Vietnam

____37. leader of communist China

____38. the demilitarized zone established between North and South Korea along the 38th parallel

____39. mutual assured destruction; upon the launch of a nuclear attack, a counterattack would be launched

____40. prohibited any kind of conspiracy to overthrow the government

____41. singled out as an underground member of the Communist party and was convicted of perjury

___42. Eisenhower's secretary of state; committed the United States to several mutual defense pacts and promoted the use of massive nuclear retaliation against the Soviets in case of an attack

___43. justified the use of military force in the Middle East in 1957 to oppose Soviet aggression (American troops were sent to Lebanon)

Short Response

44. To what extent did the mutual mistrust between the United States and the USSR influence U.S. foreign policy initiatives during the early years of the Cold War?

45. How did Cold War issues affect life on the U.S. home front in respect to *fears, sympathizers, and threats* in the years 1945–1960?

46. How effective was the U.S. policy of containment in the following areas:
   - Turkey and Greece?
   - Korea?
   - Vietnam?
   - Berlin?

Answers begin on page 298.

Domestic Challenges in the 1950s

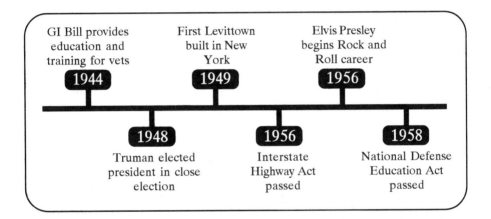

GI Bill provides education and training for vets — **1944**

First Levittown built in New York — **1949**

Elvis Presley begins Rock and Roll career — **1956**

1948 — Truman elected president in close election

1956 — Interstate Highway Act passed

1958 — National Defense Education Act passed

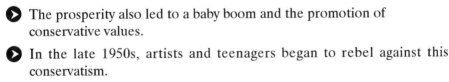

Trends and Themes of the Era

▶ Post-war prosperity in the 1950s helped propel the creation of suburbs and the popularity of the automobile, which in turn led to the decline of cities as wealthy whites left urban areas for the suburbs.

▶ The prosperity also led to a baby boom and the promotion of conservative values.

▶ In the late 1950s, artists and teenagers began to rebel against this conservatism.

▶ The economic programs of Truman and Eisenhower sought to continue, and in some ways expand, New Deal programs.

▶ Strong domestic policies and conformity were also seen as ways to combat the ever-growing threat of communism and subversion.

Happy days are here again! In the late 1940s and the 1950s people believed in the basic strength of the United States. World War II was over, and the United States emerged with the strongest economy in the world. As the nation faced the post-war challenges of becoming a superpower, social, economic, and intellectual conformity assured the nation of a united front against the ominous threat of communism and subversive ideas. It was a time to reinforce traditional values and inspire people with visions of an optimistic future. Ultimately, critics began to challenge the wholesome image of the 1950s. Increasing rates of poverty, the need for a civil rights movement, the obsession with materialism, the growing restlessness of the youth culture, and the USSR's challenge to U.S. preeminence gave rise to the voice of discontent in the 1960s.

Lesson 12-1: Domestic Policies of Truman and Eisenhower

Inflation plagued America's post-war economy, as food prices rose more than 15 percent in 1946. At the same time, American workers demanded higher pay, and strikes were rampant across the country. The railroad system shut down completely in the spring of 1946. When Truman intervened in the strikes, he alienated many working-class interest groups. As a result, Democrats fared badly in the 1946 midterm election, and Republicans gained control of Congress for the first time since 1928.

Truman struggled to push his liberal initiatives through a Republican-controlled Congress. In his attempts to extend FDR's New Deal, Truman secured passage of the **Employment Act of 1946**, which committed the government to stimulating economic growth, but only through significant compromise: Congress stripped the bill of many of its most important elements, such as the stated goal of providing full employment. This opposition set the tone for many of Truman's efforts to create a social safety net for Americans. Congress also blocked Truman's attempts to provide for public housing, the expansion of Social Security, and a higher minimum wage, among other elements derived from the New Deal.

The 1948 Election and the Fair Deal

The Republican Congress passed tax cuts for the rich and kept the minimum wage down in attempts to dismantle the New Deal. Union activities were restricted by the **Taft-Hartley Act** of 1947, which banned certain practices and allowed the president to call for an 80-day cooling-off period to delay strikes thought to pose risks to national safety. Truman vetoed the measure and, although his veto was overridden, his actions roused the support of organized labor, a group crucial to his 1948 election bid. In efforts to maintain the support of this and other groups central to Roosevelt's New

Deal coalition, Truman proposed many liberal reforms aimed at winning the labor, Catholic, Jewish, black, farm, and immigrant vote. He was moderately successful, and, though many assumed he would lose the election to Republican candidate Thomas Dewey, he pulled through with a narrow victory.

Truman also faced a challenge in the 1948 election with a splinter group from his own Democratic Party. Conservative white Southerners joined forces to form the **Dixiecrat Party** and to support Strom Thurmond, governor of South Carolina, and his bid as a third-party candidate running for the presidency. The new party (with its slogan of "segregation forever!") wanted to retain segregation and Jim Crow laws. The split in the Democratic Party not only showed the power of conservative southerners upset with the Party's platform, but it almost cost Truman the election. For the most part, the new short-lived Dixiecrat Party dissolved after the election, but the party members held on to their segregationist ideals that brought about serious problems in the Civil Rights movement in the 1950s and 1960s.

Truman saw his narrow win as a mandate for liberalism. In 1949, he unveiled a new program called the **Fair Deal**, an extension of the gains of New Deal programs. Congress now proved more cooperative and passed bills to increase the minimum wage, expand Social Security, and construct low-income housing. Not all measures in the Fair Deal were passed, however, because some faced fierce opposition from conservative Republicans and southern Democrats. As America entered a period of post-war prosperity and became increasingly interested in international affairs, the Fair Deal and domestic issues lost steam.

Eisenhower and the 1952 Election

Truman decided not to run again for president in 1952, so the Democrats nominated Adlai Stevenson to take on Republican candidate **Dwight D. Eisenhower**. A moderate and a World War II hero, Eisenhower chose as his running mate Richard Nixon, a more conservative Republican and a fervent anticommunist. Eisenhower's choice captured the spirit of the ultraconservative, anticommunist mood of the period and helped push him to a decisive Republican victory in the 1952 election.

Eisenhower called his philosophy of government "dynamic conservatism." He set a moderate, corporate-oriented course for his administration, staffing his cabinet largely with business executives. He was determined to work with the Democratic Party rather than against it, and at times he even opposed proposals made by more conservative members of his own party. "Ike," as Eisenhower was known, advocated a strong government effort to stimulate the economy. He helped sponsor the **Submerged Land Act** (1953), which recovered billions of dollars' worth of oil-rich offshore lands, and gave state government and businesses access to them. Faced with recessions in 1953 and 1957, Eisenhower went against his party's traditional stance by increasing spending rather than trying to maintain a balanced budget. He cooperated with the Democratic Congress in expanding Social Security benefits and raising the minimum wage.

In 1956, Eisenhower supported the **Interstate Highway Act**, the most expensive public works program in American history. It was promoted as a system to allow the rapid movement of military supplies and the evacuation of large urban centers in case of a nuclear strike. The program had a tremendous impact on business and transportation in the country. Eisenhower's success in boosting prosperity and pleasing many different factions while keeping the United States out of war led to his landslide victory in the 1956 election.

In 1958, Eisenhower urged Congress to pass the **National Defense Education Act**. In response to the Soviets' successful launching of *Sputnik*, the United States had to remain on a competitive edge in technical and scientific areas. So, the new legislation provided government funds to further education in math, sciences, and foreign languages. The federal government was even more motivated to remain competitive in the Cold War era.

Lesson 12-2: Social Trends of the 1950s

The decade following World War II was characterized by growing affluence in much of American society, giving rise to high levels of consumption and a boom in population. Consensus, conformity, and economic growth were the major characteristics of the 1950s. Beneath this widespread prosperity, however, lay deepening poverty for some Americans, and the gap between rich and poor widened. During the post-war era, the population grew dramatically and society began to react to a host of new challenges and experiences. On the surface, the ideal of a pleasant life with a new home in the suburbs was the ideal. Below the surface were several challenges that would begin to foster changes in the years and decades ahead.

Education and Training

In 1944, Congress passed the **GI Bill**, officially known as the Servicemen's Readjustment Act of 1944; its goal was to provide educational and training opportunities to returning veterans from World War II. The bill, signed into law by FDR, provided subsidized tuition, fees, and books, and offered assistance for housing while veterans attended colleges or received other forms of training. By the early 1950s, more than eight million veterans received educational benefits for college, vocational, or on the job training for new careers. The costs for this bill was more than $14 billion, but the benefits of further education and training brought about many new opportunities in the 1950s and would help the United States face new challenges at home and abroad in the following years.

Civil Defense

During the 1950s, there was an increased awareness of the threat of a nuclear war. In order to educate the public and to calm fears, the federal government began a massive education program with pamphlets and short films informing the public on how to be prepared in case of a Soviet nuclear attack. The goal was to calm the public and to simply educate them on what to do in case of an attack.

Bert the Turtle appeared in the 1952 Civil Defense short cartoon film, *Duck and Cover*, to promote awareness to schoolchildren of the most up-to-date actions to take in case of an attack. After hearing the warning of an attack, by simply ducking and covering yourself you could be prepared for the nuclear explosion. Furthermore, families could have safety and peace of mind against a nuclear attack by constructing a **fallout shelter** in their backyard and stocking it with food and supplies to be ready in the event of an attack. These films and pamphlets were meant to calm a nervous public. As this was going on, the United States and USSR were both building and testing numerous nuclear weapons, including the H-bombs, in the early 1950s.

Business Growth

Eisenhower's support for government spending greatly stimulated economic growth during the 1950s. Defense spending, which accounted for half of the federal budget, spurred industrial growth and funded scientific and technological advances. The first electric computer was built in 1945, and computer production advanced rapidly throughout the 1950s. The nation's first nuclear power plant opened in 1957, and the chemical and electronics industries both expanded. Industrial plants and American homes alike became automated, with electrical devices performing a wide range of tasks.

Fossil fuel consumption skyrocketed as a result of increased electricity use and the automobile industry's growth. Highway construction led to a boom in the auto, trucking, oil, concrete, and tire industries, and fueled an increase in family vacations and tourism industries. Americans' reliance on the automobile gave rise to suburban sprawl, strip malls, fast-food restaurants, air pollution, traffic jams, and a decline in public transportation.

Boosted by the production benefits of automation, big business flourished, until less than half a percent of American corporations controlled more than half of the nation's corporate wealth. These massive corporations crushed and absorbed their competition, and formed conglomerates to link companies in different industries. Agriculture also mirrored big industry. Technology drastically cut the amount of work needed to successfully grow crops, and many farmers moved to the cities as rich farm companies consolidated family farms, fertilized them with new chemicals, and harvested crops with new machinery.

Unions responded to business consolidation by consolidating as well. In 1955, the American Federation of Labor and the Congress of Industrial Organizations merged to form the AFL-CIO. Prosperity meant high wages and few labor complaints, depriving unions of the high-profile status they had enjoyed in the 1930s and 1940s. The declining number of blue-collar workers, thanks to the rise in automation and the accompanying increase in white-collar jobs, such as office employees, managers, and salespersons, also weakened unions.

The Baby Boom Culture

Prosperous American consumers went on a spending spree in the 1950s. The automobile industry benefited markedly from this surge in spending, as Americans bought nearly 60 million cars during the decade. The resulting increase in mobility contributed to the rise of motels, fast-food restaurants, gas stations, and, most notably, **suburbs**. Areas once considered too far from jobs in urban centers were now accessible and desirable, and middle-class and wealthy Americans began to flee the poverty and congestion of the cities for outlying areas. Suburbs offered a clean, homogeneous, child-friendly, and safe environment.

The American suburban population nearly doubled during the 1950s. **William Levitt** led the suburban revolution in 1949 by developing the first Levittown, a town made up of rows of mass-produced houses, outside New York City on Long Island. As suburban housing developments began to spring up outside major urban areas, "white flight" became a common characteristic of residential areas in large cities, as many middle-class whites moved to suburbia, leaving behind low-income and minority populations. Many of these new suburban communities either explicitly or implicitly excluded minorities, and by 1970 the suburban population of America was predominantly white.

Prosperity inspired Americans to have more children and to start families earlier. The birth rate grew steadily from 1950 to its peak in 1957; at the same time, advances in science and medicine led to lower infant mortality rates and longer life expectancies. The U.S. population accordingly grew from about 150 million to about 180 million during the 1950s. The **baby boom**, as this explosion was called, was both the product of and a cause for conservative views about the family.

The dramatic rise in the number of children created unique challenges for all areas of society in the 1950s and 1960s. Many women who had entered the workforce during World War II left their jobs to return home and raise families. As the birthrate increased, demand grew for diaper services, baby food, toys, and houses. As children entered school, the population surge strained the education system. Many stores and manufacturers also began marketing products for the ever-increasing baby boomer generation.

The rise in population also raised concerns about women's place in American society. **Dr. Benjamin Spock**, author of the successful *Baby and Child Care* (1946), suggested that mothers devote themselves to the full-time care of their children. Popular culture depicted marriage and feminine domesticity as the primary goal for American women, and the education system reinforced this idea. The ideal middle-class woman was portrayed as a housewife, mother, hostess, volunteer, and PTA member who devoted her life to her husband and family.

This revival of domesticity as a social value was accompanied by a religious revival across the country. Religious messages began to edge their way into popular culture as leaders such as evangelist **Billy Graham** became famous faces. Graham and other evangelists not only used radio and newspapers, but they increasingly turned to television as a way to spread their gospel message. Church membership grew dramatically, as did sales of Bibles and religious materials. In 1959, 60 percent of Americans would claim that they believed in God. In fact, it was during the 1950s that Congress added *under God* to the Pledge of Allegiance and *in God we trust* to the nation's paper currency.

The Less Fortunate

Though 1950s' prosperity benefited many Americans, it also obscured widespread poverty. More than one-fifth of the nation lived below the poverty line, some in desolate rural conditions as migrant workers, others in the crowded and dirty slums of American cities. As wealthy whites moved to the suburbs, cities exhausted their funds attempting to provide social services to the growing numbers of poor urbanites, most of whom were minorities. Historically black and immigrant in population, the urban poor now included an increasing number of Hispanic-Americans and Native Americans, who migrated to the cities when they couldn't find work in rural areas. The needs of these disadvantaged groups went largely unanswered, and conditions in cities deteriorated rapidly.

Blacks again migrated to the North, so that, during the 1950s, the black population of Chicago more than doubled. After World War II, more than 5 million blacks relocated to cities including Chicago, New York, Philadelphia, Boston, and Detroit in search of better jobs and housing. Once there, they often fell victim to slumlords, employers who refused to hire blacks, and rising poverty and crime. Many times they were forced to live in all-black housing projects in the inner city. These problems would help give rise to the social unrest of the 1960s.

Lesson 12-3: American Culture Takes Shape

Television rapidly became the medium of choice for Americans. By the 1960s, more than 90 percent of American households owned at least one television. Television brought a message of conformity and consumerism to the American people, and programs fed viewers a steady diet of cookie-cutter idealizations of American life filled with racial and gender stereotypes. Commercials were pervasive, at times dominating the programs themselves. Advertising helped create a mindset of wanting more things.

Television also produced many of the period's heroes and fads, such as the hula-hoop, "Uncle Miltie," otherwise known as Milton Berle ("Mr. Television"), Lucy and Ricky Ricardo of *I Love Lucy*, and the *Mickey Mouse Club*. Television suffered from its share of scandals too, including the infamous game-show incidents of the late 1950s with programs such as *Twenty-One* and *The $64,000 Question*. *The Texaco Star Theater, The Today Show, The Huntley-Brinkley Report, The Ed Sullivan Show*, and *The Red Skelton Show*, in addition to other television shows, transfixed a nation awed by the new medium. As movie studio revenues began to decline, the studios sold off old films and produced Westerns and police shows for television.

Despite the widespread conformity of the period, some elements of the culture rebelled. One source of rebellion that rose to prominence in the 1950s was **rock and roll music**. Rooted in the rhythm and blues of black artists, the music was labeled "rock and roll" for broader appeal and acceptance from white audiences. Chuck Berry, Little Richard, Ray Charles, and other artists drew large audiences.

No one epitomized rock and roll during the 1950s more than **Elvis Presley**, who produced 14 consecutive records between 1956 and 1958 that each sold a million-plus copies. Elvis's long hair, leather jackets, tight blue jeans, sexual innuendos, and hip gyrations shocked many middle-class parents but captured their children's attention. Rock and roll was blamed for the growing delinquency problems among America's youth as a teen subculture began to develop in the country, and rock music would become a major tool of the youth revolt in the 1960s.

In the realm of literature, the spirit of rebellion was embodied in the **Beats**, a group of nonconformists led by writers such as Allan Ginsberg, author of the long poem "Howl" (1956), and Jack Kerouac, author of *On the Road* (1957). These writers rejected uniform middle-class culture and sought to overturn the sexual and social conservatism of the period and experience life on their own terms. The Beats eventually won favor among college-age Americans, who joined in protests against the death penalty, nuclear weaponry, racial segregation, and other facets of American life that went largely unquestioned throughout the 1950s. This burgeoning youth movement would explode in the 1960s.

Review Exam

Multiple Choice

1. In 1956 Eisenhower established the Interstate Highway Act to _____.
   a) repair and maintain the current highway system in the country
   b) build a new highway system to aid in the booming prosperity of the country
   c) promote the new highway system as a way to rapidly move military supplies and allow for the quick evacuation of urban centers in case of a nuclear strike
   d) B and C only

2. The Dixiecrat Party was significant in that it _____.
   a) was another attempt of a third-party political group attempting to push a candidate for the presidency
   b) had the slogan of "segregation forever"
   c) split the Democrat Party and nearly cost Truman the election in 1948
   d) A, B, and C

3. Eisenhower was able to tap into the conservative mood of the country in the 1952 and 1956 campaigns by all of the following EXCEPT _____.
   a) nominating Richard Nixon, an ultra-conservative, as his vice president
   b) advocating a strong government to stimulate the economy
   c) failing to work effectively with the Democratic-controlled Congress
   d) increasing spending in various programs

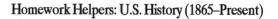
4. The GI Bill, or Servicemen's Readjustment Act, _____.
   a) provided educational and training opportunities to returning World War II veterans
   b) limited the amount of education or training a veteran could receive
   c) was short-lived due to a lack of interest in education after the war
   d) was cancelled because it became too costly

5. The National Defense Education Act of 1958 aimed at having the United States keep a competitive edge with the increase of Soviet threats by _____.
   a) promoting the study of math in schools
   b) providing federal government funds to further education in math, sciences, and foreign languages
   c) promoting the study of science in schools
   d) urging states to finance more of the teaching of math and science in the schools

6. Bert the Turtle and the "duck and cover" campaign _____.
   a) sought to ease the fears of schoolchildren by preparing them to defend themselves in case of a nuclear blast
   b) was a program aimed at hiding from the Soviets
   c) was a program aimed at largely ignoring the threat of nuclear weapons from Russia
   d) was cancelled after one month due to a lack of interest

7. The baby boom generation _____.
   a) was comprised of those born from those born from 1946 to 1964
   b) became the largest segment of the U.S. population
   c) created a dramatic increase in the overall U.S. population due to the large increase in the birthrate
   d) A, B, and C

8. Although the prosperity of the 1950s benefited many Americans, _____.
   a) poverty was still widespread, with more than 20 percent living below the poverty line
   b) as whites moved to the suburbs, a large majority of minorities remained in the inner cities in large urban areas
   c) blacks migrated to the North in search of jobs in the cities of Chicago, New York, Philadelphia, and Boston
   d) A, B, and C

9. Television culture of the 1950s focused on all of the following EXCEPT _____.
   a) producing and promoting many of the heroes and fads of the time period
   b) remaining free of scandal
   c) leading to a decline of movie studio revenue
   d) the popularity of comedies, news shows, Westerns, and police shows

10. Rock and roll shaped the culture of the 1950s _____.
    a) in large part due to Elvis Presley's music and 14 consecutive records
    b) with music that promoted suggestive lyrics and body language, and new styles of clothing
    c) and was blamed for the growing delinquency problems in America's youth
    d) A, B, and C

11. Growth of business in the 1950s _____.
    a) can be in large part attributed to the dramatic increase in defense spending that helped spur industrial growth
    b) was on a 10-year decline, bringing about fears of yet another depression
    c) was spurred by the growth of the highway system as economic growth in industries and businesses gave rise to the suburban sprawl
    d) A and C only

12. 1950s morality is evidenced by all of the following EXCEPT _____.
    a) *under God* being added to the Pledge of Allegiance
    b) *in God we trust* being added to the nation's paper currency
    c) church membership declining dramatically
    d) Bible sales increasing

Matching

a. inflation

b. Billy Graham

c. Submerged Land Act

d. William Levitt

e. suburbs

f. Dixiecrat Party

g. Dr. Benjamin Spock

h. fallout shelters

i. Beats

j. Employment Act of 1946

k. Richard Nixon

l. Fair Deal

m. Taft-Hartley Act of 1947

_____13. legislation that was aimed at extending several New Deal programs, but many Republicans and some Democrats attacked some of the programs as being "too liberal"

_____14. the immediate economic problem facing the Untied States after the end of World War II

_____15. areas on the outskirts of cites that demonstrated the mobility of the affluent society of the 1950s

_____16. Democratic-Party splinter group for which Strom Thurmond ran for president in 1948

_____17. Eisenhower's vice president for eight years

_____18. a popular evangelist of the 1950s who preached the gospel message to large crowds and television audiences

_____19. legislation aimed at recovering billions of dollars' worth of oil-rich offshore lands

_____20. Truman's economic policy program that he saw as an extension of the New Deal by promoting the idea of full employment (the bill was significantly weakened by Congress)

_____21. led the suburban revolution by developing a suburban housing area known as Levittown

_____22. author of *Baby and Child Care*, which became a best seller in the 1950s and suggested how parents might raise their children

_____23. built to help families withstand a nuclear blast

_____24. a group of nonconformists led by writers including Allan Ginsberg and Jack Kerouac, who rejected the uniform middle-class culture and gained popularity, especially among college students

_____25. restricted certain union activities and allowed the president to call for an 80-day cooling-off period to delay strikes that might pose a risk to national safety (vetoed by Truman, and Congress overrode the veto)

Short Response

26. How did the prosperity or *happy days* of the 1950s influence cities, family life, and religion as the United States tried to maintain its role as a superpower in the struggle against communism?

27. How did presidents Truman and Eisenhower begin to address the domestic challenges of the post–World War II society in America?

Answers begin on page 300.

The Civil Rights Movement

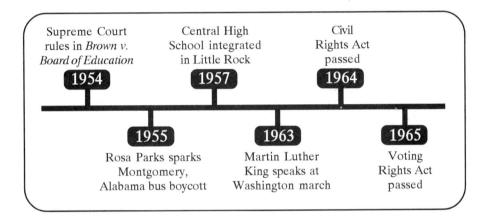

Supreme Court rules in *Brown v. Board of Education*
1954

Central High School integrated in Little Rock
1957

Civil Rights Act passed
1964

1955
Rosa Parks sparks Montgomery, Alabama bus boycott

1963
Martin Luther King speaks at Washington march

1965
Voting Rights Act passed

Trends and Themes of the Era

▶ Bolstered by the landmark 1954 Supreme Court decision *Brown v. Board of Education*, the Civil Rights movement began to come into its own.

▶ Following an ethic of nonviolence, blacks in the South began to win their first battles for equality. The Civil Rights movement gained public support and helped persuade the nation of the power of social action.

▶ Led by Dr. Martin Luther King, Jr., the Civil Rights movement culminated in the 1964 Civil Rights Act and the 1965 Voting Rights Act.

▶ Malcolm X also became a leader of the Civil Rights movement, promoting the use of violence to achieve equality.

▶ With the assassinations of both Malcolm X and Martin Luther King, Jr., the Civil Rights movement began to lose its focus as the Vietnam War overshadowed it and came to dominate the entire nation.

I have a dream....! By the 1950s, America remained very much a divided country, separated by racial lines into black and white. Although segregation had become ingrained into the social consciousness, signs of change were beginning to occur. The momentum for change unfolded in many places: a batter at home plate, a seat on a bus, a jail cell, a lunch counter, the Oval Office, and the highest court in the land. The Civil Rights movement quickly evolved into a campaign that would not only create new social identities for black Americans but would profoundly impact American society. It created an entirely new set of nonviolent and violent challenges for those hoping for change in the status quo. Nonviolent and violent challenges to the movement exposed deeply rooted problems of racism, poverty, militarism, and social status. Events in Vietnam reached a crisis point in 1968, forcing the country's attention away from civil rights and toward the division the war was causing at home and abroad.

Lesson 13-1: The Movement Takes Shape

As the Cold War raged during the late 1940s and the 1950s, American society was undergoing great changes in areas involving civil rights. The Civil Rights movement gathered strength and momentum during the postwar years and would stay strong through the 1960s.

At the beginning of the movement, blacks were still facing widespread discrimination in all areas of life: separate schools, drinking fountains, bathrooms, restaurants, hotels, and waiting rooms. Buses designated "whites only" and "colored only" seating. Initial television broadcasts of civil rights incidents were careful in reporting racial incidents so as not to offend Southern viewers. Black war veterans were harassed, some even killed, for claiming the rights for which they had fought overseas. Presidents walked a cautious political tightrope in attempting to address the issue of civil rights.

Truman and Civil Rights

Trying to preserve Southern white support, President Truman at first avoided issues involving civil rights for blacks, but he couldn't stay removed for long. In 1947, the Presidential Committee on Civil Rights, created a year earlier, produced a report titled "To Secure These Rights," calling for the elimination of segregation. In 1948, Truman endorsed the report's findings and called for an end to racial discrimination in federal hiring practices. He also issued **Executive Order 9981** to end segregation in the military, an initiative that Eisenhower would complete. Although these moves cost Truman the support of many southern whites, the increased support from black voters made up for the political loss.

Eisenhower and the Civil Rights Acts

Eisenhower hadn't been an outspoken proponent of civil rights, and he never publicly supported the Civil Rights movement. Eisenhower believed that such changes had to come from the "heart of the people involved," not from legislative acts. Eisenhower backed the **Civil Rights Act of 1957** and the **Civil Rights Act of 1960**, which would lead to further legislation in the 1960s. The Civil Rights Act of 1957 created a permanent Civil Rights Commission, as well as a Civil Rights division within the Justice Department aimed at combating efforts to deny blacks the vote. The Civil Rights Act of 1960 granted the federal courts the authority to register black voters.

Lesson 13-2: The Supreme Court Weighs In

The fight for civil rights took a major leap forward in May 1954 when the Supreme Court, under the leadership of Chief Justice **Earl Warren**, handed down one of the most famous decisions in American judicial history. Warren had been appointed to the Supreme Court by Eisenhower in 1953, and he issued the unanimous 9-0 decision of *Brown v. Board of Education of Topeka* in 1954. Future Supreme Court justice **Thurgood Marshall,** a leading attorney for the NAACP, argued Linda Brown's case before the Supreme Court. Oliver Brown wanted to send his black daughter, Linda, to the white neighborhood school. This school was much closer than the all-black school that Linda was forced to attend. In the 1954 decision, the Court overturned the 1896 *Plessy v. Ferguson* decision and ruled that segregation of schools was unconstitutional, arguing that separate schools are inherently unequal. The Court stated, "Segregation generates a feeling of inferiority that may affect [the children's] hearts and minds in such a way unlikely to ever be undone." The Court demanded that states desegregate schools immediately with "all deliberate speed."

The *Brown* ruling, along with other previous rulings, demonstrated how the federal court system could be used as a viable weapon against segregation. In the 1939 *Missouri v. Gaines* case, the Supreme Court ruled that the University of Missouri would have to either admit a black law student to the program or build a black law school. Later, in 1950, in **McLauren v. Oklahoma Regents**, the Court agreed with the argument that forcing a black student to eat, sit, and study separated from white students created a badge of inferiority.

Lesson 13-3: Tragedy in Mississippi

In August 1955, the small town of Money, Mississippi, became a major flash point for the Civil Rights movement. The event centered around the brutal murder of **Emmett Till**, a 14-year-old black boy from Chicago who was visiting his uncle, Mose Wright, in Mississippi. Emmett had gone to town with some friends and, when they stopped at a store to buy some candy, Emmett whistled at a white woman in the store. This outraged the whites in the community as a violation of Jim Crow laws. Three days later, on August 28th, two white men, Roy Bryant and J. W. Milam, approached Mose Wright's house after 2 a.m. Emmett was dragged from his bed, and brutally beaten until his body was unrecognizable. He had an ear cut off, had an eye gouged, was shot, and had a 75-pound cotton gin fan tied around his neck with barbed wire. His body was then thrown into the Tallahatchie River. Three days later his body was discovered, identified, and sent back to Chicago. Mamie Till decided to have an open casket funeral because she "wanted the world to know what had happened" to her "little boy." Fifty thousand people attended the funeral.

The killers were arrested and charged with murder. Soon afterwards, the trial began. Despite the fact that Mose Wright identified the killers, the defense claimed that Bryant and Milam did not kill Emmett. At the end of the five-day trial, the all-white male jury acquitted them after about an hour of deliberation.

This incident gained international attention. Before 100 days passed, Montgomery, Alabama, became the scene of a black woman refusing to sit in the back of the bus. The modern Civil Rights movement had begun.

Lesson 13-4: The Movement Gains Momentum

Amid the conflict over *Brown v. Board of Education of Topeka*, a strong Civil Rights movement began gaining momentum in the South. In December 1955 in Montgomery, Alabama, a black, college-educated seamstress, **Rosa Parks**, was arrested for refusing to give her bus seat to a white man. She was jailed for her illegal actions. Led by a minister, **Dr. Martin Luther King, Jr.**, Montgomery blacks organized a boycott of the bus system in response to the actions taken against Rosa Parks, marking the beginning of the nonviolence movement. Shortly after the strike began, bus revenues declined by two-thirds as blacks arranged for rides, formed car pools, or walked. No one had expected the boycott to last for very long, but the protesters scored a major victory when the Supreme Court ruled that bus segregation was illegal, ending the 11-month-long boycott.

The success of the Montgomery bus boycott inspired civil rights leaders to adopt Martin Luther King, Jr.'s philosophy of nonviolent civil disobedience. To direct followers in a campaign against segregation and discrimination, King and other black ministers established the **Southern Christian Leadership Conference (SCLC)** in 1957. Its goal was to mobilize the vast power of black churches on behalf of black civil rights and to work together with the

NAACP to promote racial justice. The SCLC soon found an ally in the **Student Nonviolent Coordinating Committee (SNCC)**, which was formed after a number of sit-ins at businesses that discriminated against blacks.

Lesson 13-5 Crisis in Little Rock

President Eisenhower at first refused to force Southern states to comply with the Court's ruling. Encouraged by this lack of federal backing, Southern state governments engaged in massive resistance by choosing not to desegregate schools and by denying funding to districts that attempted desegregation.

At **Central High School** in Little Rock, Arkansas, nine black students enrolled in the all-white school for the 1957–58 school year. On September 4, 1957, **Elizabeth Eckford** walked alone as she and eight other black students attempted to integrate Central High School. They were stopped at the school entrance by the Arkansas National Guard on orders of **Governor Orval Faubus**. The school board urged the nine to stay home, and the Arkansas governor called out the National Guard to "maintain peace." A judge later ruled that the governor had used the troops to prevent integration, not to preserve law and order.

On September 23rd, the president sent 1,000 members of the 101st Airborne Division to Little Rock and federalized the 10,000-man Arkansas National Guard. On the following day, the army troops escorted the nine black students back into Central High, and while in school each student had his/her own guard. At the end of that school year, **Ernest Green**, one of the original nine black students, became the first black to graduate from Central High School. In retaliation for these acts, Little Rock closed its public high schools during the 1958–59 school year in order to prevent violence and disorder. In 1959, the schools were forced to reopen and integrate.

Lesson 13-6 Civil Rights in the Turbulent 1960s

During the 1960s, the Civil Rights movement built on its achievements of the previous decade by working to counter discrimination and segregation.

In 1960, college students became a major focus of the Civil Rights movement in Greensboro, North Carolina. Four black college students sat down at the counter in a Woolworth's for coffee and doughnuts, and they were refused service. During the next week, the sit-in grew dramatically and received national attention. By the end of the year, blacks had gained access to lunch counters in 126 cities throughout the South. The media images portrayed the black participants as calm, clean-cut college students, in sharp contrast to the angry whites attacking the protesters by pouring condiments on and hurling racial slurs at them. In addition to court rulings and legislation, the media began to play an increasingly significant role in the Civil Rights movement.

Bob Moses began his work with civil rights activists in 1960, when be became the field secretary for the Student Nonviolent Coordinating Committee (SNCC). As the director of the SNCC's Mississippi Project, he worked with the **Congress of Racial Equality (CORE)** to organize the **Freedom Riders** in 1961, in which black and white student volunteers traveled by bus through the Deep South. Although one bus was firebombed on May 14, 1961, the students continued riding. Incidents of increasing violence in the Civil Rights movement made the national nightly news. The public began to take notice of the non-violence of the blacks, and the raging violent attacks by angry whites in the South.

In 1964, Bob Moses continued his work with civil rights in Mississippi when he became the major organizer of the Freedom Summer project in 1964. This project's goal was aimed at increasing black voter registration in Mississippi. In addition, the Freedom Democratic Party was formed in Mississippi along with "freedom schools" and community centers that offered education, medical, and legal assistance to blacks. Although whites harassed, intimidated, and attacked the SNCC volunteers and blacks, the work continued despite the fact that Moses and others were arrested and jailed for their efforts. During their work that summer, more than 60 black churches, businesses, schools, and homes were bombed or burned. Their efforts resulted in 15 civil rights workers being murdered and only 1,600 blacks being registered to vote.

Tragedy occurred in **Greenwood, Mississippi**, when the bodies of James Chaney, who was black, and Andrew Goodman and Michael Schwerner, both white, were discovered missing after they were investigating the burning of a church in June 1964. The investigation and trial found that the disappearance of the civil rights workers was the direct result of a conspiracy between elements of the community police of Neshoba County and the Ku Klux Klan. Three years later in 1967, the trial of the killers resulted in the convictions of seven conspirators. This verdict was significant in that it represented the first ever convictions in Mississippi for the killing of a civil rights worker.

Kennedy and Civil Rights

President Kennedy was cautious about becoming entangled in the complex issue of civil rights. In the spring of 1961, CORE, led by **James Farmer**, held a freedom bus ride through the Deep South to protest illegal segregation in interstate transportation. Buses, waiting rooms, toilets, and terminal restaurants were all used to call attention to illegal segregation. Activists willingly signed on for potentially dangerous trips, even after knowing one of their buses was bombed in Alabama and the riders were beaten with iron bars and clubs. After whites in Alabama assaulted the freedom riders, Attorney General Robert Kennedy sent federal marshals to protect the riders.

In the fall of 1962, Kennedy again sent federal marshals to the South to enforce civil rights, after students and angry white citizens attempted to prevent a black man, **James Meredith**, from attending the University of Mississippi. When Meredith, an Air Force veteran, tried to enroll, the governor defied a federal court order and personally blocked Meredith's path to the admissions office. Attorney General Robert Kennedy dispatched 500 federal troops to the campus, and, after a riot broke out on September 30th, an additional 5,000 federal troops were sent in. A federal guard remained with Meredith until he graduated in 1963.

Also in 1963, Dr. Martin Luther King, Jr., led a series of peaceful demonstrations in Alabama. At a march in Birmingham on May 3, 1963, King and other protesters were jailed for protesting for integrated public facilities and job opportunities for blacks. While serving time in jail, King wrote his "Letter from Birmingham Jail" in which he defended the use of nonviolence in civil disobedience to bring about change. More than one thousand children then marched in place of the jailed protesters. The police commissioner, "**Bull Connor**," was out to crush the protests and used police dogs, clubs, and high-pressure water hoses to disperse the non-violent crowd. The water hit with such force that bark was peeled off trees and children either thrown to the ground or slammed against the sides of buildings. Television cameras captured these horrific events and broadcast them so that others would know what was taking place in the city of Birmingham. Kennedy's administration was forced to intervene and could no longer waver on civil rights. These attacks, along with other high-profile abuses of civil rights, prompted Kennedy to propose a comprehensive civil rights bill to Congress.

Just hours after announcing his support of civil rights legislation, another tragic event occurred with the murder of another civil rights leader, **Medgar Evers**, outside his home in Jackson, Mississippi on June 12, 1963. In 1954, Evers had been appointed field secretary for the NAACP in Mississippi and worked on organizing boycotts and integrating schools, making him a target for radical whites in the state. The trial for Evers's murder in 1963 resulted in

Byron De La Beckwith, a fertilizer salesman and member of the Ku Klux Klan, being tried twice for the murder; both times the all-white male juries were unable to reach a verdict. Beckwith was finally convicted of Evers's murder in 1994.

Recognition of events in the Civil Rights movement continued to grow. A quarter of a million Americans gathered in the mall in Washington, D.C.,

on August 28, 1963, to show their support of Kennedy's proposed legislation and the demand for civil rights action. It was during the **March on Washington** that King gave his famous "I Have a Dream" speech at the Lincoln Memorial, outlining an idealistic view of what America could be. Despite the demonstration and King's speech, however, Republicans in Congress blocked Kennedy's civil rights bill. President Kennedy was assassinated on November 22, 1963, and the next day President Johnson promised he would fight to pass the civil rights bill.

4 Little Girls

In fall of 1963, the **Sixteenth Street Baptist Church** in Birmingham, Alabama, a meeting place for civil rights leaders, became the site of yet another tragedy. Tensions heated up when the SCLC and the CORE became involved in a campaign to register African Americans to vote in Birmingham. On Sunday, September 15, 1963, a bomb exploded under the steps of the church, killing four young girls, Addie Mae Collins, Denise McNair, Carole Robertson, and Cynthia Wesley, who were attending Sunday school. Twenty-three other people were also hurt by the blast. Although it was determined that Robert E. Chambliss, Bobby Frank Cherry, Herman Frank Cash, and Thomas E. Blanton Jr. had planted the bomb, charges had not been filed, and the FBI closed the case in 1968. In 1971, the Attorney General in Alabama reopened the case that resulted in Robert Chambliss's conviction. Herman Frank Cash died in 1994 before a case could be established against him. After reopening the case again in 1998, charged were eventually filed in 2000 that resulted in the convictions of Thomas Blanton Jr. and Bobby Frank Cherry.

Civil Rights Under Johnson

Civil rights advocates were encouraged by Johnson's **Great Society Program**, which aimed to achieve racial equality. After the death of President Kennedy, Johnson called for passage of the tax cuts and civil rights bills as a memorial to the slain president. The **Civil Rights Act of 1964** outlawed segregation in public accommodations, stating, "All persons shall be entitled to the full and equal enjoyment of the goods, services, facilities, and privileges, advantages, and accommodations of any place of public accommodation without discrimination or segregation on the ground of race, color, religion, or national origin." It also gave the government broader powers to enforce desegregation in schools, and established the Equal Employment Opportunity Commission (EEOC) to prevent job discrimination.

After the events of Freedom summer in 1964, the following year King and the Southern Christian Leadership Conference organized a mass protest against black disenfranchisement. The demonstration, which took place in Birmingham, Alabama, drew a violent police reaction. The police attacks were caught on television and cemented national sympathies behind the Civil Rights movement.

In January 1964, the **24th Amendment** was ratified, banning the use of poll taxes as a barrier to voting. Nearly a century since blacks received the right to vote with the 15th Amendment, another obstacle to voting was finally removed. President Johnson then pushed through the **Voting Rights Act (1965)**, which authorized federal examiners to register qualified voters and to suspend literacy tests in voting districts where fewer than half of the minority population of voting age was registered. The bill's passage resulted in an explosion in black voters. The number of registered black voters doubled in many areas. By 1971, 62 percent of blacks were registered to vote in the South, and many black representatives had been elected to office. The two civil rights bills became the highlight of Johnson's Great Society program.

Lesson 13-7: The Black Power Movement and Nonviolence

King and his nonviolent strategies of resistance were supported by the majority of civil rights activists, both black and white. But not everyone believed in nonviolence. The **Black Power** movement expressed the outrage felt by many African Americans. The movement encouraged American blacks to be proud of their "blackness," and promoted violent resistance and separation from white society.

The Black Power movement started with the teachings of **Malcolm X**, who became a prominent spokesman for black rights after joining the Nation of Islam. Rejecting the goal of integration, Malcolm X encouraged his followers to take pride in their African heritage, to consider armed defense rather than relying on nonviolence, and to break free of white domination by "any means necessary." The Nation of Islam became very influential in New York City, Detroit, and Chicago, and claimed more than 10,000 members nationwide, with most of its support coming from urban African Americans. Famed boxer Cassius Clay, known as Muhammad Ali, was a prominent follower of the Nation of Islam philosophy. Malcolm X broke from the Nation of Islam in 1964 and made a pilgrimage to Mecca; upon his return to America, he assumed a new name and new goals focusing on socialism. He was assassinated in February 1965 while giving a speech in Harlem and, with his death, became a martyr for the Black Power movement. Nonetheless, he remained a powerful voice among African Americans, his influence preserved through his teachings and his biography, published the year of his death.

After Malcolm X's death, the mantle of the Black Power movement was carried by **Stokely Carmichael**, the leader of the Student Nonviolent Coordinating Committee (SNCC), who came to reject nonviolence in favor of violent resistance. In 1966, Carmichael's influence helped inspire Huey Newton and Bobby Seale to found the **Black Panthers**. The Panthers carried guns and at times engaged in violent confrontations with police.

The slogan "Black Power," however, didn't apply exclusively to radical groups such as the Black Panthers; it also applied to more moderate groups who worked to reaffirm black culture as distinct from white culture and valuable in its own way. Offshoots of the Black Power movement included Native American Power and Chicano Power, movements that sought to assert the value of ethnic heritage and to counter oppression from mainstream white society.

Within two years after King's "I Have a Dream" speech, black militancy began to grow, sparking race riots throughout the nation during a three-year period. In the summer of 1965, a race riot erupted in the Watts area of Los Angeles. The **Watts Riot** also encouraged similar protests in Detroit, Chicago, New York City, and other major cities across the country. A 1967 report detailed the reasons for the riots, focusing on patterns of inequality and racism embedded in urban life. The report argued that the nation seemed to be moving toward two societies: one black, one white—separate but unequal.

Lesson 13-8: The Assassination of Martin Luther King, Jr.

On April 4, 1968, Dr. Martin Luther King, Jr., the most prominent black leader of the period, was shot and killed in Memphis, Tennessee, by white racist **James Earl Ray**. During his time as the predominant leader of the Civil

Rights movement, King discovered a new and powerful weapon in the form of nonviolent resistance, giving blacks a sense of dignity and destiny. His untimely death set off riots in more than 100 cities, causing enormous property damage and social chaos. The riots led to 46 deaths, more than 3,000 injuries, and 27,000 arrests. With the death of King, the Civil Rights movement had lost the black leader most able to stir the conscience of white America.

King's death occurred at the same time that violence was becoming more predominant in the fight for civil rights and the U.S. involvement in Vietnam was reaching a crisis point. The protests against the war, mounting civil unrest, assassinations of two prominent leaders, and an uncertain 1968 presidential election made the year of 1968 a significant turning point in U.S. history.

Review Exam

Multiple Choice

1. The significance of the *Brown v. Board of Education* ruling in 1954 included _____.
   a) overturning the 1896 *Plessy v. Ferguson* case, which stated "separate but equal" as a policy
   b) a unanimous Supreme Court ruling that schools should integrate with all deliberate speed
   c) the ruling stated that "separate is not equal"
   d) A, B, and C

2. The Emmett Till tragedy that ended with the murder of 14-year old Emmett sparked outrage, as evidenced by all of the following EXCEPT _____.
   a) that his funeral was open-casket so that the world could see what happened
   b) that the two killers, Bryant and Milam, were found guilty
   c) for the gruesome details of his murder
   d) that 50,000 attended his funeral in Chicago

3. The Montgomery bus boycott _____.
   a) was started with Rosa Parks's refusal to give up her bus seat to a white man
   b) lasted for two years with no end in sight
   c) failed to gain the attention of Dr. Martin Luther King, Jr.
   d) witnessed the beginning of violence in the Civil Rights movement

4. Central High School in Little Rock, Arkansas, in 1957 was the site of an integration plan when _____.
   a) nine black students attempted to attend the school
   b) President Eisenhower sent in 1,000 National Guard troops to maintain order and escorted the students around the school
   c) Governor Faubus attempted to block admission of the students
   d) A, B, and C

5. The Freedom Riders organized by James Farmer and CORE in 1961 attempted to _____.
   a) organize bus trips through states in the North to bring attention to the plight of racism in the South
   b) organize a bus trip to plan a march in Montgomery, Alabama
   c) organize a freedom bus ride through the Deep South to protest illegal segregation in interstate transportation
   d) protest the earlier bombing of a bus in Alabama

6. Bob Moses organized the Freedom Summer project in Mississippi in 1964; despite harassment and attacks, the goal of the project was to _____.
   a) with the assistance of the Freedom Democratic Party, establish freedom schools and community centers to offer education, medical, and legal assistance to blacks
   b) increase voter registration in Mississippi
   c) increase support for the project from the white community in the state
   d) A and B only

7. MLK's "Letter from Birmingham Jail" written in 1963 while being jailed for protesting for integrated public facilities was important in _____.
   a) promoting the use of nonviolence in bringing about lasting change in the Civil Rights movement
   b) promoting a combination of nonviolence with limited violent acts to bring about reform
   c) advocating the widespread use of violent resistance to bring about reform
   d) realizing that civil rights reform was not going to be possible

8. The Children's March in 1963 in Birmingham forced JFK's administration to no longer waver on the issue of civil rights, because the country witnessed the _____.
   a) nonviolent protest march of more than 1,000 children, who marched in place of jailed protestors

b) use by police commissioner Bull Connor of police dogs, clubs, and high-pressure water hoses to disperse the crowd

c) televised events due to media coverage of the event

d) A, B, and C

9. The March on Washington in the summer of 1963 was important when MLK delivered his "I Have a Dream" speech because _____.

a) JFK was now ready to send a civil rights bill to Congress

b) a mixed crowd of more than 250,000 gathered at the Mall in Washington to hear the speech

c) people began to increase their demands for civil rights actions by the federal government

d) A, B, and C

10. The 16th Street Baptist Church bombing in the fall of 1963 resulted in all of the following EXCEPT _____.

a) the deaths of four young girls

b) the conviction of the four men responsible for the bombing

c) an FBI investigation

d) the injury of nearly two dozen people in the blast

11. As a major part of LBJ's Great Society program, the Civil Rights Act of 1964 _____.

a) banned discrimination on the grounds of race, color, religion, or national origin

b) outlawed racial discrimination in public facilities and in places of employment

c) created the Equal Employment Opportunity Commission

d) A, B, and C

12. As part of removing barriers for blacks voting, all of the following occurred in the 1960s EXCEPT that the _____.

a) numbers of black registered voters continued to remain low

b) 24th Amendment barred the use of poll taxes

c) Civil Rights Act of 1965 banned the use of literacy tests

d) Civil Rights Act of 1965 also authorized the use of federal examiners to register qualified voters

13. The term *Black Power* _____.

a) began with the teachings of Malcolm X

b) was symbolized by SNCC leader Stokely Carmichael's open defiance

   c) influenced the founding of the Black Panthers, who favored the carrying and use of firearms in violent confrontations with whites

   d) A, B, and C

14. 1968 was a turning point in the history of the country in that _____.

   a) two major political leaders, MLK and Robert Kennedy, were assassinated that year

   b) violence in reaction to Vietnam and the Civil Rights movement continued to erupt across the country

   c) became a turning point in the war in Vietnam

   d) A, B, and C

15. As more violence occurred in the Civil Rights movement, whites who had been charged with criminal charges against blacks were _____.

   a) most likely to be acquitted at first for their crimes

   b) brought to trial at later dates upon the re-opening of cases resulting in the retrial and conviction of the whites who committed the acts o: violence

   c) convicted for their crimes, as evidenced in Greenwood, Mississippi, with the conviction of seven conspirators in 1967

   d) A, B, and C

16. Malcolm X was best associated with the Nation of Islam and _____.

   a) the continued use of nonviolent measures in the Civil Rights movement

   b) the use of violence to achieve civil rights and to break away from white dominance

   c) accepting the role of segregation in society

   d) promoting the use of nonviolent and violent tactics to achieve immediate integration and acceptance in society

17. Martin Luther King, Jr., was the most prominent leader of the Civil Rights movement who _____.

   a) discovered a powerful weapon in the form on nonviolent protest

   b) gave blacks a sense of dignity and destiny with his work in the movement

   c) was assassinated in 1968, resulting in numerous riots and chaos in the months following his death

   d) A, B, and C

Matching

a. Watts Riot
b. Civil Rights Acts of 1957
c. Thurgood Marshall
d. James Earl Ray
e. SNCC
f. CORE
g. segregation
h. Eisenhower
i. SCLC
j. Stokley Charmichael
k. Elizabeth Eckford
l. Medgar Evers
m. Chief Justice Earl Warren
n. Greenwood, Mississippi
o. Ernest Green
p. Governor Orval Faubus
q. Greensboro, North Carolina
r. James Meredith
s. Bob Moses
t. Civil Rights Act of 1960
u. Executive Order 9981

_____18. forced blacks in many places throughout the South to use separate schools, drinking fountains, bathrooms, restaurants, hotels, and waiting rooms

_____19. a group established by Southern ministers in 1957 to mobilize black churches on behalf of civil rights

_____20. Truman ended segregation in the military with this in 1948

_____21. the first president since Reconstruction to order military troops into the South

_____22. field secretary for SNCC and the director of SNCC's Mississippi Project

_____23. Chief Justice of the Supreme Court who overturned the *Plessy v. Ferguson* ruling of "separate but equal" with a new ruling in 1954 that "separate is not equal"

_____24. Martin Luther King, Jr.'s assassinator

_____25. a committee formed after several students were discriminated against in a number of sit-ins

_____26. the site of Klan violence against two white and one black civil rights worker in the summer of 1964

_____27. created a permanent Civil Rights Commission and a civil rights division within the Justice Department

_____28. first black student to graduate from the integrated Central High School in Little Rock, Arkansas

_____29. a congress established to help organize the Freedom Riders in 1961 and was led by James Farmer

_____30. 1965 riot in this area of Los Angeles that was sparked by black militancy

_____31. black Air Force veteran who attempted to attend the University of Mississippi in 1962

_____32. granted federal courts the authority to register black voters

_____33. NAACP lawyer who argued the *Brown* case before the Supreme Court

_____34. a black civil rights leader who was murdered outside his home in Jackson, Mississippi, in 1963

_____35. site of sit-ins by black college students in 1960 at a Woolworth's lunch counter that ultimately resulted in the integration of lunch counters in various places throughout the South

_____36. attempted to prevent the integration of Central High School in Little Rock, Arkansas in 1957

_____37. one of the Little Rock Nine who "walked alone" in 1957 in the integration of Central High School

_____38. leader of SNCC who came to promote violent resistance in the Civil Rights movement

Short Response

39. What role did the federal government play in the black struggle for civil rights during the decades of the 1950s and 1960s?

40. To what extent did the Civil Rights movement achieve its goals? To what extent did the tactics employed by various leaders in the Civil Rights movement achieve success?

41. What was the role of the media in the civil rights movement?

Answers begin on page 301.

Domestic and Foreign Crisis in the Turbulent 1960s

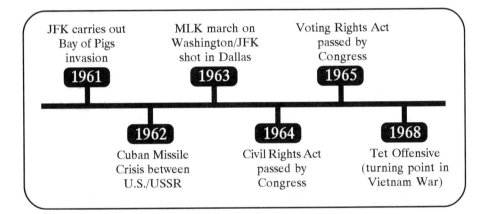

JFK carries out Bay of Pigs invasion
1961

MLK march on Washington/JFK shot in Dallas
1963

Voting Rights Act passed by Congress
1965

1962
Cuban Missile Crisis between U.S./USSR

1964
Civil Rights Act passed by Congress

1968
Tet Offensive (turning point in Vietnam War)

Trends and Themes of the Era

▶ Democrats, who held the presidency in the 1960s, tried to bring about the liberal social reforms that were the hallmarks of their party's philosophy.

▶ The 1960s was a time of dramatic social engagement and action. In addition to the Civil Rights and antiwar movements, a powerful women's rights movement also took root.

▶ The Cold War continued throughout the decade, nearly erupting in nuclear war during the Cuban Missile Crisis in 1962. Cold War anxieties and concerns over Soviet domination in Asia led to the buildup of American forces in Vietnam and the Vietnam War.

▶ In the tradition of social action started during the Civil Rights movement, and in response to U.S. involvement in a foreign war, a vocal minority of Americans organized the anti-war movement.

Burn, baby, burn! Foreign affairs challenges in Vietnam quickly overshadowed the domestic agendas of the New Frontier and the Great Society. President Johnson lamented that the war in Vietnam "killed the only lady he ever loved—the Great Society." The conflict not only resulted in war and political casualties, but also gave rise to a growing counterculture protest movement. The Vietnam War eroded America's confidence at home and called into question U.S. influence around the world. Domestic cutbacks, spiraling inflation, news reports about the war, and a growing unrest inspired a vocal—and sometimes violent— anti-war movement. A credibility gap emerged between what Johnson's administration was saying and what actually was happening in the Vietnam War. America saw its confidence erode as political and civil right leaders fell victim to assassins, protesters and politicians questioned the country's involvement in the war, and misleading official statements about the Vietnam War were disclosed. The conformity of the 1950s and early 1960s quickly came unraveled as the United States became deeply entrenched in the "quagmire" of Vietnam.

Lesson 14-1: JFK and the New Frontier

In 1961, Democrats controlled the White House, and kept that control until 1969. JFK dealt with congressional opposition to his plan for a New Frontier until his assassination in 1963, when Lyndon B. Johnson took office and pushed his predecessor's proposed reforms through Congress under his Great Society program.

The 1960 Election

The 1960 presidential election was one of the closest in American history. The race centered on two very different candidates: Republican Richard Nixon, who had served for eight years as Eisenhower's vice president, and Democratic Massachusetts Senator John F. Kennedy, who, at age 43, would become the youngest person ever to be elected president. During the campaign, Nixon stressed his steadfast commitment to fighting communism, and Kennedy focused on character.

Religious issues also surrounded the campaign because Kennedy was a Roman Catholic, and no Catholic had ever been elected president. Questions arose about his ability to place national interests above the wishes of the pope. He attempted to assuage these fears by committing himself to a complete separation of church and state. Nixon avoided the issue of religion in his campaign.

The decisive battleground of the election proved to be the media, in a series of televised debates. Kennedy arrived for the first debate well tanned and rested, portraying an image of youth and vigor; Nixon looked tired and nervous after recovering from a knee injury. Although radio listeners believed that Nixon was the better debater, the new television audience decided Kennedy was the victor. The election was close: Kennedy won 49.7 percent of the popular vote to Nixon's 49.5 percent. Slightly more than 100,000 popular votes separated the two. Kennedy ended up with a 303–219 margin in the Electoral College.

The New Frontier

Kennedy promised a **New Frontier** for America, encompassing reform at home and victory in the Cold War. In his acceptance speech in the 1960 primary, Kennedy stated, "We stand today on the verge of a new frontier—the frontier of the 1960s, a frontier of unknown opportunities and perils—a frontier of unfulfilled hopes and threats."

To accomplish his goals, Kennedy assembled a group of politically savvy advisers termed "the best and the brightest." **Robert McNamara**, President of Ford Motor Company, served as secretary of defense. McGeorge Bundy, a Harvard University dean, was special assistant for national-security affairs, and the president's brother, **Robert Kennedy**, filled the post of attorney general. **Jacqueline Kennedy** also played an important role as first lady. Kennedy carefully crafted his image as a young, intelligent, and vibrant leader.

Despite Kennedy's reputation, however, he was unable to push much reform through Congress, where he faced opposition from conservative Republicans and Southern Democrats. His plans for increased federal aid to education, urban renewal, and government-provided medical care went unfulfilled. Kennedy's primary achievements at home were raising the minimum wage and, in 1961, establishing the **Peace Corps**, a program to send volunteer teachers, health workers, and engineers to Third World countries.

Kennedy's efforts to support environmental issues came about in 1963. Rachel Carson's publication of *Silent Spring* in 1962, which exposed the environmental hazards of the pesticide DDT, touched off a broad movement to push environmental measures through Congress. In 1963, the campaign spurred passage of the Clean Air Act to regulate factory and automobile emissions. This, along with the 1960 Clean Water Act, marked the beginning of a period when the federal government became increasingly involved in environmental matters.

On November 22, 1963, Kennedy's presidency abruptly ended when he was assassinated by **Lee Harvey Oswald** from the sixth floor of the book depository warehouse as the presidential motorcade drove through Dallas. Kennedy and his wife were on a good-will trip to gain support from Southern

Democrats. JFK was assassinated, Texas Governor John Connally was seriously wounded, and Vice President Lyndon B. Johnson was sworn in as president aboard Air Force One on the return trip to Washington. Jackie Kennedy had the task of planning her husband's funeral to honor his memory. The images of the assassination trip in Dallas, the murder of Lee Harvey Oswald on television two days later, and the solemn state funeral were all captured by the media as a grief-stricken nation tried to come to terms with this crisis.

Lesson 14-2: LBJ and the Great Society

Following President Kennedy's death, Lyndon B. Johnson backed his predecessor's attempted reform as a memorial to the slain president. In 1964, Johnson achieved just that: passage of both a tax cut and the Civil Rights Act, which outlawed segregation in public accommodations, gave the government broader powers to enforce desegregation in schools, and established the Equal Employment Opportunity Commission to prevent job discrimination. A year later, Johnson pushed through the Voting Rights Act, which authorized federal examiners to register qualified voters and to suspend literacy tests in voting districts where fewer than half of the minority population of voting age was registered. The bill's passage resulted in an increase in black voters, with the number of registered black voters doubling in many areas.

Michael Harrington's book, *The Other America*, was a groundbreaking study of American poverty that became the focus of Johnson's domestic policy goals. More than 20 percent of Americans endured bad housing, malnutrition, poor medical care, and other devastations of poverty. Forty percent of all black families lived below the poverty level, and many white Appalachian Mountains people lived in poverty.

Johnson called for a war on poverty in his state of the union address in 1964. His **Great Society** became the most ambitious set of social reform legislation programs since the New Deal. In 1964, Congress passed the work on initial programs. In 1966, the government spent $22 billion on the Vietnam War and $1.2 billion on the Great Society. As Johnson turned his full attention to the war instead of the domestic programs, the Great Society fell. Dr. Martin Luther King, Jr., commented on the decreased amount of money allocated to the programs by saying that the Great Society was "shot down on the battlefields of Vietnam." Johnson's domestic program brought to the forefront the basic issue between liberal Democrats, who promised change with social programs, and conservative Republicans, who opposed tax increases to provide for numerous programs.

Great Society Programs at a Glance

Civil Rights Act of 1964 Outlawed employment discrimination on the basis of race, color, religion, sex, or national origin.

Job Corps and **VISTA** Part of the Economic Opportunity Act that provided vocational training and a domestic Peace Corps to combat rural and urban poverty.

Head Start A pre-Kindergarten program aimed at disadvantaged, poor preschoolers.

Upward Bound Provided college preparation assistance for poor teenagers.

Medicare/Medicaid Established federally funded medical insurance for people over age 65 and federally funded medical insurance for the poor under age 65.

Voting Rights Act of 1965 Suspended literacy and other voter tests, and required federal supervision of registration.

Department of Housing and Urban Development Established public housing units, low-rent housing subsidies, and created the Department of HUD

National Foundation for the Arts and Humanities Provided assistance for painters, actors, dancers, musicians, and other artists; the **Public Broadcasting Corporation** provided financial assistance to noncommercial educational TV and radio broadcasting.

Immigration Act Repealed the national origins quota system.

Higher Education Act Provided grants and loans to students based on need.

Elementary and Secondary Education Act Provided huge federal aid to states based on number of low-income students; established bilingual education, reading programs, and special education programs.

National Traffic and Motor Vehicle Safety Act Promoted the use of safe cars and seat belts.

Highway Safety Act Enacted highway safety laws, such as speed limits.

Minimum Wage Bill Increased minimum wage to $1.40 per hour (effective February 1967) and to $1.60 per hour (effective February 1968); expanded to include workers in retail stores, restaurants, and hotels.

Supreme Court Decisions

During the 1960s, the Supreme Court, under liberal Chief Justice Earl Warren, delivered a number of significant decisions that brought about significant changes as well as sparked a degree of criticism from critics. The *Engel v. Vitale* decision in 1962 prohibited prayer in public schools. In 1963 the *Gideon v. Wainwright* decision obliged the states to provide indigent defendants in felony cases with public defenders. Finally, the 1966 *Miranda v. Arizona* case required police to make suspects aware of their rights to remain silent and to have an attorney present during questioning, the so-called Miranda rights.

Lesson 14-3: Turbulence in the Cold War

During Kennedy's and Johnson's presidencies, tensions with the USSR remained high. These tensions peaked most notably in Berlin, Cuba, and Vietnam.

The Berlin Wall

By 1961, more than four million East Germans had moved to West Berlin. This created a "brain drain" and economic problem for communist East Berlin. In an effort to halt people from moving into West Germany, Khrushchev ordered the building of the Berlin Wall in August 1961. This wall provided a visible symbol of the Iron Curtain, a physical and political barrier between the communist East and free West, and symbolized the division of the entire world into two Cold War spheres. After the construction of the wall in 1963, JFK visited Berlin in June and delivered his famous speech using the phrase "Ich bin ein Berliner" at the Berlin Wall. President Kennedy began what other presidents would demand of Moscow, "Tear down that wall."

The Cold War in Cuba

After **Fidel Castro** and the Cuban communists overthrew the Cuban government in 1959, Cuba became a source of anxiety for the United States, as it represented an extension of the Soviet sphere of influence to within 90 miles

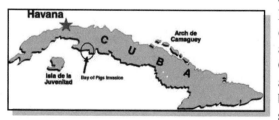

of America. In 1961, President Kennedy authorized a plan, drawn up by the Eisenhower administration, to send 1,500 Cuban exiles, trained and armed by the United States, back to Cuba to spark an insurrection. The **Bay of Pigs**

invasion took place in April. The plan was to rally people in Cuba to revolt, but the exiles met with stiff resistance and failed to get the U.S. backing promised. In a matter of days, the Cuban army had captured or killed the entire force, resulting in an embarrassing defeat for the returning exiles and the United States and casting doubts on Kennedy's approach to foreign affairs.

After the Bay of Pigs, Khrushchev stepped up military aid to Cuba by sending 43,000 troops to join the 271,000 Cuban forces. In July 1962, Khrushchev began to build 42 mis-
sile sites in Cuba. In early October, an American U-2 spy plane discovered the sites that, when completed, would be able to reach American targets as far away as 2,200 miles. One week later, on October 14th, Kennedy announced a blockade of 200 U.S. warships to prevent Cuba from receiving any more missiles.

In what became known as the **Cuban Missile Crisis,** Kennedy vowed use a naval blockade to prevent the shipment of more missiles—and to dismantle the existing missile bases by force, if necessary, if the USSR did not do so. Some 250,000 troops gathered in Florida to prepare to invade Cuba, and U.S. naval forces readied themselves to intercept Russian freighters. Relations between the United States and the USSR became extremely tense, and a nuclear war seemed very possible. B-52s carrying nuclear weapons stayed constantly airborne, ready to strike. The United States and the USSR went on full military alert as the world held its breath. During the next 13 days, the future of the world was at stake. In the end, Khrushchev recalled the Russian freighters and sent Kennedy a message that he would dismantle the Cuban missiles in exchange for a U.S. promise never to invade Cuba and to dismantle missiles in Turkey. Kennedy accepted the compromise. The Cuban Missile Crisis became a defining moment of JFK's presidency.

Soviet Military Build Up in Cuba

Guanajay IRBM sites
San Cristobal MRBM sites
Sagua La Grande MRBM sites
Remedios IRBM sites

SA-2 SAM sites (24) — Ground force installations (4)
SSM cruise sites (5) — IL-28 Airfields (2)
GM patrol craft bases (2) — MRBM Sites (6)
MIG-21 airfields (3) — IRBM Sites (3)

In July 1963, the United States and the USSR signed the

Limited Test-Ban Treaty, prohibiting undersea and atmospheric testing of nuclear weaponry. This effort at easing tensions would later be known as *detente*, from the French for "relaxation of tensions." Kennedy began seeking ways to reduce international tensions. Detente meant that the two countries could negotiate and bargain (as opposed to containment, which called for confronting communists around the world). Later that year, the United States and the USSR established a telephone "hotline" so that the two leaders could contact each other during potential crises. Despite the partial thaw in tensions, the United States and the USSR continued to maintain Cold War tensions and escalated the arms race for yet another 25 years.

Lesson 14-4: The Raging Conflict in Vietnam

Vietnam, divided at the 17th parallel between communist North Vietnam and U.S.–dominated South Vietnam, concerned Kennedy during his presidency. He believed in Eisenhower's domino theory (when one nation fell under Soviet domination, others in the region would soon follow). In efforts to prevent communist advances, Kennedy boosted the number of U.S. forces in South Vietnam to 16,000 by 1963. These forces aimed to protect the South Vietnamese from the procommunist National Liberation Front, called the Vietcong.

After President Kennedy's assassination in November 1963, Lyndon Johnson assumed the presidency and the oversight of American operations in Vietnam. In August 1964, President Johnson announced that two North Vietnamese patrol boats had attacked American warships in the Gulf of Tonkin off the coast of North Vietnam. Johnson declared that Americans had been attacked without cause and ordered air strikes. The incident was never confirmed, but Johnson used it to expand his powers in dealing with the situation. Congress passed the **Gulf of Tonkin Resolution** on August 7, 1964, allowing the president to commit troops and planes to protect South Vietnam. It was the only approval of U.S. intervention in Vietnam ever voted on in Congress and served as a virtual declaration of war. Johnson was determined not to lose Vietnam to communism, and at one point he promised "not to send American boys 9–10 thousand miles away to do what Asian boys ought to do for themselves."

In 1965, Johnson ordered **Operation Rolling Thunder**, which launched continuous bombing raids over North Vietnam. The strategy failed to force North Vietnam to negotiate, and it didn't stop the flow of soldiers and supplies to communist forces in the south. Operation Rolling Thunder began with air raids on the north to try to cripple the economy and force the communists to the bargaining table. War tactics also focused on wearing down the

Vietcong forces (South Vietnamese forces that supported the North Vietnamese) in the south by using search-and-destroy missions (attacking villages, burning huts, killing civilians while trying to kill Vietcong, and using defoliants such as **Agent Orange** to destroy the jungle and aid in spotting enemy movements in the underbrush). As the crisis escalated in the air and on the ground, the number of U.S. troops assigned for one-year duty tours increased from 190,000 at the end of 1965 to more than 540,000 at the height of the war in 1968.

As the conflict intensified, Johnson was faced with the dilemma of whether or not to tell the American public the full extent of the war. Johnson was accused by his critics of using "intentional deceit"—promising to try for a diplomatic settlement while secretly planning never to accept the terms offered by North Vietnam. As the conflict continued, Johnson found it increasingly difficult to hold the line against further escalations or to speak frankly with the American public about the war.

The enemy the American soldiers faced—the North Vietnamese Army and the Vietcong—used nontraditional guerrilla methods of warfare, and they were well supplied, well reinforced, and determined to fight until the United States moved out of Vietnam. The **Vietcong** was a Communist-led army and guerrilla force of Vietnamese in South Vietnam that supported the National Liberation Front and received support from North Vietnamese.

The war became a guerrilla battle with little geographic indication of success or failure, and it cost the Americans $21 billion annually. A 10 percent tax increase was imposed on incomes and businesses, and even the Social Security fund was tapped to fund the war effort. Inflation increased throughout the rest of the war and impacted the economy during the entire decade of the 1970s.

Until 1965, the media had either ignored Vietnam or issued reports of strong patriotic support. Now, claims of human suffering and devastation undermined the administration's reports about the war. In 1966, stories began to surface about the war's realities. By 1967, the media was obsessed with reporting on Vietnam, and the nightly news and newsmagazines had a tremendous impact on turning the public against the war. Scenes such as an execution of a Vietcong suspect on the street in broad daylight, injured soldiers, and screaming children running away from chemical warfare bombings showed the horrors of the war. The American public began to gauge the war's progress by the rising casualty figures and the increasing number of news reports about the conflict.

In January 1968, the North Vietnamese Army and the Vietcong launched a massive offensive on forces in the south, known as the **Tet Offensive**. On the Vietnamese New Year holiday of Tet on January 30th, the Vietcong began a well-coordinated assault on major urban areas and, though American troops

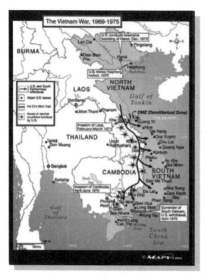

repelled the offensive after about a month of fighting, many thousands American troops were killed, and the North Vietnamese managed to breach many areas thought to be secure. The United States had been caught off guard. Americans began openly protesting the war and questioning the country's role in Vietnam. After the Tet offensive, the American public began to believe that victory in Vietnam would be impossible.

In March 1968 the **My Lai massacre** occurred, with U.S. soldiers killing unarmed Vietnamese citizens, comprised mainly of women and children in the area around the village of My Lai. News of this event were initially covered up, but, as news spread about the incident, it sparked outrage by many and served as another incident to further reduce support for the war effort. One of the soldiers in charge of one of the platoons, **Lt. William Calley**, would later claim in his court martial trial two years later that he was just acting under orders from his commander.

As the growing anti-war movement gained strength and support, Johnson's approval ratings plummeted, coinciding with the beginning of the 1968 presidential campaign. In April 1968, Johnson halted the sustained bombing of North Vietnam and announced that he wouldn't seek reelection. The increasingly unpopular war would be placed in the hands of his successor. The anti-war sentiment among Democrats splintered after **Robert Kennedy** was assassinated by Sirhan Sirhan, following his win in the California primary on June 5th. In August, the Democratic National Convention in Chicago was plagued by serious riots outside the convention hall over the Vietnam War.

Peace talks between North Vietnam and the United States began in May 1968, marking a turning point in the U.S. escalation of the conflict since the 1950s. Leaders began to realize that the form of communism in Vietnam was intensely regional and nationalistic rather than expansionist. The rising cost of the war, increasing taxes, inflation, and the cost of domestic reform led to a series of crises that the Democratic Party had to face. With dissension at the Democratic National Convention in Chicago, the Republican challenger, Nixon, capitalized on the situation by promising a "secret plan to win the war in Vietnam" and announcing a schedule of troop withdrawals that would begin in 1969.

Opposition to the Vietnam War

Opposition to the Vietnam War emerged on many fronts. College campuses around the nation became the focal point of numerous anti-war protests, as the baby boomers of the post–World War II years now became the most vocal protesters against the Vietnam War. Protest speeches, songs, free speech movements, music, hairstyles, and draft-card burning all served as symbols of the anti-war sentiment. In 1965, the first teach-in was held at the University of Michigan to discuss U.S. actions. In 1966, after a wave of military draft calls, mass protests erupted on college campuses.

Many clergy, intellectuals, and politicians joined students in voicing opposition to the war. These critics denounced American involvement in an essentially Vietnamese war, claiming there was no way to win without great cost and loss of life, and noting that the war was being fought predominantly by poor Americans. Senator William Fulbright, who chaired the Senate Foreign Relations Committee, became a vocal critic of President Johnson and declared that the war in Vietnam could not be won and was destructive to domestic reform. In 1967, LBJ fired Defense Secretary Robert McNamara after he expressed his opposition to the war, citing a concern about the moral justifications for war. Television coverage further intensified anti-war sentiments, as Americans saw reports about the war firsthand.

At times, this polarization yielded to violence and clashes with police. Combat soldiers returned from their tours of duty only to rejoin a deeply divided society. Often, returning soldiers boarded a plane headed out of Vietnam, and, within 24 hours, were back in the United States, without being debriefed about the war. They weren't fully prepared to re-enter society, and many felt betrayed. Other veterans were jobless and drug-dependent, and suffered from post-traumatic stress.

Lesson 14-5: More Social Activism in the 1960s

Encouraged by the success of the anti-war and Civil Rights movements during the 1960s, many groups launched their own campaigns to redress perceived wrongs in American government and society.

The Youth Movement

A number of reform movements during the 1960s originated with college students. As college attendance soared during the decade, and campuses became centers for protest movements. The growing opposition to the war was both significant and vocal. Leading the youth movement was **Students for a Democratic Society (SDS)**, founded in 1962 to mobilize support for leftist goals throughout the nation. Students sat in, marched, and rallied to end mandatory ROTC programs at many colleges, halt military research, address racism, and express their disgust with the Vietnam War. The anti-war cause inspired rallies, draft-card burning, and harassment of anyone connected with the military.

Notable student protests included a mass demonstration at Columbia University in the spring of 1968, which resulted in a temporary shutdown of the school. In the fall of 1969, an organized group known as March Against Death held a rally in which about 300,000 people marched in a long, circling path through Washington, D.C., for 40 hours straight, each holding a candle and the name of a soldier killed or a village destroyed in Vietnam.

The youth movement was challenged on May 4, 1970, when **Kent State University** students in Ohio who were protesting Richard Nixon's expansion of the Vietnam War into Cambodia were met by armed National Guardsmen and inundated with tear gas. A panicked troop of guardsmen then fired into the crowd, killing four and wounding nine; two of the dead hadn't even been a part of the demonstration.

Hippies and Woodstock

The counterculture movement of the 1960s found its dissenting voice through the **"hippies"** who could be easily recognized by their long hair, blue jeans, and wild t-shirts. Unhappy with many of the domestic and foreign events of the decade, they resorted to sit-ins, peace signs, "flower power," drug use, and music to get their message across. The height of the hippie movement was the **Woodstock Music and Art Festival** held in August 1969, at a dairy farm near Bethel, New York from August 15–August 18, 1969. Several famous artists, including Joan Baez, Janis Joplin, The Grateful Dead, Creedence Clearwater Revival, The Who, Jefferson Airplane, and Jimi Hendrix, performed to the crowd of more than 500,000. It remains one of the most famous rock festivals that has ever been held.

Women's Liberation

The feminist movement gained strength during the 1960s. The most prominent symbol of this resurgence was the 1963 publication of Betty Friedan's *The Feminine Mystique*, which urged women to break free from the domestic role and seek "something more." Kennedy's Presidential Commission on the Status of Women issued a report in 1963 detailing the lingering inequalities between men and women in the work force. The Civil Rights Act of 1964 prohibited sexual as well as racial discrimination in hiring practices. The **National Organization for Women (NOW)** formed in 1966 to lobby

Congress, file lawsuits, and publicize the feminist cause. By 1970, more than 40 percent of all women worked outside the home.

Many women involved in the liberation movement had started out in the anti-war or Civil Rights movement, and they used the same tactics for the feminist cause. They encouraged women to meet in small groups to discuss their problems, and they met in larger groups to burn bras and beauty items as a form of protest. They founded health centers geared to women and advocated abortion education. Demonstrations were held to demand the right to equal employment and legal abortions.

Women's issues continued to dominate the political spotlight when Congress passed **Title IX** in the Educational Acts in 1972, barring discrimination on the basis of sex in any educational program receiving federal money. The law dramatically impacted women's sports in high school and college athletic programs. Participation in girls' athletic programs nearly tripled at some schools.

Pro-choice activists won a major victory in 1973, when the Supreme Court legalized abortion in the landmark decision *Roe v. Wade*. The seven–two ruling stated that abortion was "a private matter" and that "privacy was a constitutionally protected right." The ruling spurred the formation of pro-choice and pro-life groups that now rank among the most powerful political lobby groups.

A major setback in the women's movement involved the debate over the **Equal Rights Amendment (ERA)**. Congress passed the measure in 1972, but it failed to be approved by the necessary 38 states needed for ratification. In addition, some women's groups began to disagree among themselves about strategies to achieve equality in society. The anti-ERA push received national attention through the activities of Phyllis Schlafly, a devout Roman Catholic who claimed that adherents of the ERA were "rejecting womanhood—the God-given roles of wife and motherhood."

Review Exam

Multiple Choice

1. All of the following were issues in the 1960 presidential campaign EXCEPT _____.
    a) the omission of any religious talk or references to religion
    b) the narrow margin of votes in the popular vote
    c) youth and character
    d) the televised presidential debates

2. LBJ's Great Society program _____.
   a) was an ambitious social program aimed at ending poverty in America
   b) included massive increases of spending for Medicare, Medicaid, education, and other programs
   c) was "shot down on the battlefields of Vietnam"
   d) A, B, and C

3. JFK's New Frontier Program encompassed the optimism of the country standing on the edge of a new frontier that _____.
   a) was one of unknown opportunities and perils, and a frontier of hopes and threats
   b) was more perilous than hopeful
   c) chose to focus only on the hopes and opportunities of a new era
   d) relied on minimal advice from his cabinet and other advisers

4. All of the following were true about the Berlin Wall EXCEPT that _____.
   a) it was a physical barrier between East and West Berlin
   b) it allowed movement of people from East Berlin to West Berlin
   c) JFK visited the Wall and delivered a speech in which he sided with the people of West Berlin
   d) it came to symbolize the guarded Cold War spheres of the communist East and free West

5. The Bay of Pigs invasion in 1961 _____.
   a) was a CIA attempt to overthrow Castro from power in Cuba
   b) was a successful CIA operation
   c) increased JFK's standing in foreign affairs
   d) succeeded in getting the people of Cuba to rally against Castro

6. The Cuban Missile Crisis _____.
   a) was a 13-day standoff between U.S. and USSR troops and leadership over the shipment of missiles to Cuba
   b) began when the United States detected missile sites in Cuba that would be capable of launching missiles that could virtually attack any area in the United States
   c) resulted in a blockade of Cuba by more than 200 warships intent on preventing Cuba from receiving any more missiles from the Soviets
   d) A, B, and C

7. The Gulf of Tonkin Resolution _____.
    a) was a formal declaration of war against the Vietnamese
    b) allowed LBJ to commit troops and planes to protect South Vietnam
    c) was a temporary order allowing limited use of troops in Vietnam
    d) allowed for more military advisors to be sent to South Vietnam

8. Operation Rolling Thunder was a plan devised to _____.
    a) get the Vietcong to come out of hiding
    b) cut off the flow of supplies coming into the South from North Vietnam
    c) launch continuous bombing raids over North Vietnam to attempt to cripple their economy
    d) B and C only

9. The Tet Offensive in January of 1968 _____.
    a) was a surprise attack on various sites throughout South Vietnam
    b) caught the United Sates off guard and began to undermine support for the war effort
    c) was repelled by American troops after about a month of fighting
    d) A, B, and C

10. After 1968, military leaders and presidents began to realize that _____.
    a) the form of communism was nationalistic—meaning that the goal of communism in North Vietnam was only to take over South Vietnam
    b) they needed to keep the public perception of a worldwide threat of communism to add credibility to the war effort in Vietnam
    c) peace talks were needed to end the escalating conflict
    d) A, B, and C

11. Protests to the Vietnam War included all of the following EXCEPT _____.
    a) continued support for the war effort from all of those on LBJ's staff
    b) college students using anti-war speeches, songs, and free speech movements
    c) the burning of draft cards
    d) members of the clergy and many politicians

12. The women's movement included all of the following EXCEPT the _____.
    a) passage and ratification of the ERA in 1972
    b) Title IX program
    c) formation of NOW to lobby members of Congress
    d) landmark ruling in *Roe v. Wade* in 1972

13. The My Lai massacre was an incident that included all of the following EXCEPT _____.
   a) a court martial trial for Lt. Calley, who claimed to be only operating under orders from his commander
   b) the senseless killing of innocent Vietnamese women and children
   c) honest reporting about the event
   d) a further erosion of public support for the war effort in Vietnam

14. Nixon campaigned in 1968 with his platform of _____.
   a) having a "secret plan" to end the war in Vietnam
   b) making plans to bomb Cambodia
   c) ending the use of Agent Orange
   d) insisting on immediate negotiations with the leadership of North Vietnam

15. Kent State University in 1970 was the site of a _____.
   a) peaceful student protest about continued involvement in the Vietnam War
   b) war protest that ended with the deaths of four students being shot by National Guard troops
   c) campaign speech by Nixon announcing a change in policy in Vietnam
   d) debate between supporters and protesters of the war movement

Matching

a. *Engel v. Vitale*
b. Fidel Castro
c. New Frontier
d. Clean Air Act of 1963
e. Robert McNamara
f. Jacqueline Kennedy
g. SDS
h. Nixon
i. *Gideon v. Wainwright*
j. Peace Corps
k. Lee Harvey Oswald

l. *Miranda v. Arizona*
m. Great Society
n. President Johnson
o. Robert Kennedy
p. hotline
q. Woodstock
r. détente
s. Senator William Fulbright
t. Vietcong
u. Clean Water Act 1960
v. Agent Orange

____16. JFK's domestic policy agenda
____17. JFK's assassin

____18. 1962 court decision that prohibited prayer in public schools

____19. lost the presidential debates to JFK in 1960 as well as losing the presidential election to JFK in a very narrow margin of votes

____20. an effort at relaxing tensions between the United States and the USSR that involved negotiations between the two countries

____21. JFK's secretary of defense

____22. court ruling that states were obliged to provide a defense lawyer for indigent defendants

____23. LBJ's domestic policy agenda that promoted great changes in social reform but began to be sidelined by spending for the Vietnam War

____24. began to regulate factory and automobile emissions

____25. became the communist leader in Cuba in 1959

____26. established the reading of rights for suspects upon their arrest

____27. first lady who played a vital role in JFK's election and presidency

____28. a defoliant used to destroy the jungles in Vietnam

____29. volunteer organization established by JFK to send volunteer teachers, health workers, and engineers to Third World countries

____30. one of the most outspoken organizations against the war in Vietnam

____31. marked the beginning of a period when the federal government became increasingly involved in environmental issues

____32. a communist-led army and guerrilla force of Vietnamese in South Vietnam that supported the National Liberation Front and received support from North Vietnam

____33. one of the most outspoken critics of Johnson's policies in Vietnam and chairman of the Senate Foreign Relations Committee

____34. a telephone communication set up between the White House and the Kremlin so that U.S. and USSR leaders could quickly communicate during a crisis

____35. shot by Sirhan Sirhan after winning the California primary in 1968 in his bid for the presidency

____36. a music and art festival held at the height of the hippie movement at dairy farm in New York in the summer of 1969

____37. was accused of using "intentional deceit" in his dealings with Vietnam—promising a diplomatic solution to end the crisis— while secretly planning to not accept any of the terms of the North Vietnamese

Short Response

38. To what extent did the United States achieve its objectives in Vietnam?

39. Why is the year 1968 often viewed as a turning point in the nation's history?

40. To what extent did the antiwar movement influence national policy in Vietnam?

Answers begin on page 302.

From Watergate to Reaganomics

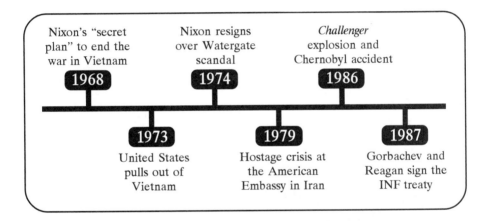

Nixon's "secret plan" to end the war in Vietnam — **1968**

Nixon resigns over Watergate scandal — **1974**

Challenger explosion and Chernobyl accident — **1986**

1973 — United States pulls out of Vietnam

1979 — Hostage crisis at the American Embassy in Iran

1987 — Gorbachev and Reagan sign the INF treaty

Trends and Themes of the Era

▸ Domestically, the United States underwent cycles of economic boom and bust as inflation, government spending, and the deficit became major concerns.

▸ America suffered from the political fallout of Vietnam and Watergate. These events would shape politics for the remainder of the century as the country shifted between Republican and Democratic presidents, and faced a decline in voter participation and lack of trust in the government.

▸ The Cold War intensified. It dominated foreign policy throughout the era and influenced domestic policy, as well. The Cold War began to end with the fall of Eastern Europe in 1989 and the fall of the Soviet Union in 1991. As the sole superpower, the United States debated about but ultimately maintained its role as an international policeman.

A cancer is growing on the presidency! Vietnam. Watergate. OPEC. Energy crisis. Inflation. Stagflation. Environment. Hostages. Boycotts. America seemed to be a nation in a state of flux by the mid-1970s. The withdrawal of troops from the lost war in Vietnam was soon followed by a political scandal that toppled the commander-in-chief and another crisis in which the commander-in-chief was himself held "hostage" as a crisis unfolded in Iran. America was being forced to face limits on the world stage and at home. American society was fractured by political dissension between liberals and conservatives, and a general mistrust of political leaders and government. Voter turnout continued to decline. America was adrift as it questioned its role in the world and looked not only for guidance but also for a new vision for the country. The Republican era of the 1980s would reshape American foreign policy along with the political and economic climate of the country. These challenges would influence America well into the 21st century.

Lesson 15-1: The Nixon Presidency: Secret Plans and Détente

Richard Nixon was elected president at a major turning point of the county in 1968. Nixon announced a "secret plan" to end the war in Vietnam. His conservatism appealed to a nation weary from a decade of social activism and political reform. Nixon opposed racial integration, denounced the liberal Supreme Court, and promised a return to order, stability, and decency in America. In office, he scaled back progressive reforms, eventually pulled U.S. troops out of Vietnam, and focused on détente between the U.S. and its Cold War enemies. Despite all these activities, Nixon is best remembered for the Watergate scandal that ended his presidency.

Nixon portrayed himself as the representative of the **"silent majority,"** a label he used to designate American citizens who had grown tired of progressive reforms, student protests, and racial integration of schools. However, Democrats in Congress blocked many of Nixon's conservative efforts and succeeded in pushing through progressive reforms, including bills to extend social welfare programs and protect the environment.

Although many of Nixon's conservative initiatives failed in Congress, including his attempt to hold off the integration of Mississippi schools and his opposition to the extension of the Voting Rights Act of 1965, his efforts did succeed in winning the support of the white South. This support proved key to Nixon's crushing defeat of liberal Democrat George McGovern in the election of 1972.

Vietnamization

The Vietnam War was the most pressing issue Nixon faced in 1969. The war, now widely opposed by the American public, was sapping the nation of military strength and economic resources. Nixon and his top adviser on foreign affairs, National Security Adviser, and, later Secretary of State, **Henry Kissinger**, devised three main strategies to "Vietnamize," or "de-Americanize," the Vietnam War and bring about "peace with honor." First, the United States gradually pulled out American ground troops, reducing forces from about 500,000 in 1968 to about 30,000 in 1972. Kissinger announced the **Nixon Doctrine**, which acknowledged limits of U.S. power. It meant that U.S. allies would have to rely more on their own resources for their own defense, indicating that the United States did not have unlimited resources to unconditionally and continuously aid the cause of freedom. The second tactic was to send Kissinger to North Vietnam to negotiate a treaty. Third, at the same time Nixon was withdrawing troops from Vietnam, he secretly authorized a massive bombing campaign in March 1969 that targeted North Vietnamese supply routes throughout Cambodia and Laos. Knowledge of the secret raids was kept quiet for nearly a year.

The **Kent State** protests on May 4, 1970, were staged in response to the bombing in Cambodia. The protestors targeted the ROTC building, and National Guard troops were called in and were harassed by the students. The Guard then opened fire, killing four students and wounding 11 others. This led to other protests on college campuses across the country, including one against racism at Jackson State College in Mississippi that resulted in the deaths of two black student protestors. Tensions were still at a fever pitch in 1970 over the issues of Vietnam and racism.

In November 1972, Nixon ran for re-election, promising an end to the war and to "bring the boys home." More than 36,000 tons of bombs were dropped at the Christmas bombing of Hanoi and North Vietnam. By the end of December, North Vietnam was willing to meet for negotiations, and the USSR, China, and other nations began calling for an end to the war. On January 27, 1973, a cease-fire was finally announced.

In 1971, **Daniel Ellsberg**, who had worked as an analyst under Secretary Robert McNamara at the Department of Defense, went public with the **Pentagon Papers**, a lengthy report of America's three decades of involvement in Indochina that led to the Vietnam War. The report revealed government deception, miscalculation, and bureaucratic arrogance. Furthermore, it revealed that President Lyndon Johnson had been committing an increasing amount of troops to the war while at the same time telling the nation that he had no long-range plans for the war. Most damning was the impression that the U.S. government did not believe it was possible to win the war and that the government had not been honest in reporting about the war to the general public. This disclosure demoralized many Americans.

The **Paris Accords**, signed in January 1973, finally settled the terms of U.S. withdrawal, ending the war between the United States and North Vietnam, but it left the conflict between North and South Vietnam unresolved. The last American troops left South Vietnam in March 1973. By the time U.S. involvement ended, 58,000 Americans had died, 300,000 had been wounded, and conditions in Vietnam remained unstable and war-torn. The war in Vietnam continued until 1975, when North Vietnam won control of the entire country. The war resulted in a loss of U.S. prestige and a loss of self-confidence at home.

In response to the end of the conflict in Vietnam, Congress passed a joint resolution, known as the **War Powers Act** in November 1973. It severely limited the actions a president can take in a conflict. It gave the president 48 hours to notify Congress after an action begins, limited the action to 60 days of action, and stated that the troops have an additional 30 days to withdraw. After 90 days, a formal declaration of war needs to take place for action to continue.

The gradual reduction of U.S. troops in Vietnam was part of Nixon's plan to achieve **détente**, an easing of tensions between the United States and its Cold War enemies. In April 1971, the communist People's Republic of China hosted the U.S. table-tennis team, and in February 1972, Nixon himself visited China for a highly publicized tour and meetings with Mao Zedong. Though official diplomatic relations between the two nations were not established until 1979, this visit resulted in greatly improved communication between the two nations. In May 1972, Nixon went to Moscow, where he signed the first **Strategic Arms Limitation Treaty (SALT I)**. SALT I limited each of the superpowers to 200 antiballistic missiles and set quotas for intercontinental and submarine missiles. Though largely symbolic, the agreement sparked hope for cooperation between the two superpowers.

Lesson 15-2: OPEC

On October 6, 1973 (Yom Kippur, the holiest day in the Jewish calendar), Egypt and Syria opened a coordinated surprise military attack against Israel. The attack was in retaliation of the Israeli six-day war with Egypt in 1967. Nine Arab states openly supported the Egyptian-Syrian war effort. The Soviet Union supplied the Arab states with weapons while the Untied States came to the aid of Israel. The fighting ended on October 22nd with a United Nations resolution calling for all parties to cease firing. But the war was not over.

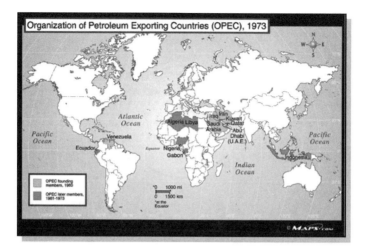

On October 17, 1973, **OPEC, the Organization of Petroleum Exporting Countries** (Saudi Arabia, Kuwait, Iran, Iraq, and Venezuela), which provided 80 percent of the world's oil exports, placed an oil embargo on nations who were supporting Israel. OPEC sought to use oil as a weapon to punish the West. The resulting rise in oil prices was also accompanied by a decrease in oil production. The embargo lasted from October 17, 1973, until March 18, 1974. By December 1973, oil prices had more than quadrupled, with oil prices soaring to more than $12 per barrel and the price of gasoline more than doubled in price.

The impact of this crisis on the public and the economy was dramatic. Fuel and utility rates soared raising prices in all other areas. It created a tightening of money as consumers curtailed spending. During the embargo, OPEC oil production declined by 25 percent, causing temporary shortages of gasoline and heating oil. Some filling stations ran out of gasoline, and cars had to wait in long lines for gasoline during the height of the crisis. By the end of the 1970s, the price of oil had soared to $34 per barrel.

The United States relied heavily on foreign oil: The United States consumed 70 percent of the oil in the world, and 36 percent of U.S. oil was imported. As a response to the embargo, the United States adopted the following measures: lowering the speed limit to 55 MPH, extending daylight savings time, turning thermostats down to 68°, cutting back on air travel, buying smaller cars, encouraging energy conservation, and closing gas stations on Sundays.

The increase in oil prices continued to "fuel" inflation throughout the 1970s. Arab countries grew wealthy as oil prices skyrocketed—while at the same time industrialized countries that relied on Arab oil experienced the worst economic slump since the Great Depression. Oil had now become a bargaining chip in world affairs and would continue to play a dominant role in world affairs for the remainder of the 20th century.

Lesson 15-3: Watergate: Break-In and Cover-Up

Nixon's presidency ended with the Watergate scandal. During the 1972 presidential campaign, Nixon created the **Committee to Re-elect the President (CREEP).** In June 1972, five men carrying cameras and wiretapping equipment were caught breaking into Democratic National Committee headquarters in the Watergate office complex in Washington, D.C. The burglars were later found to be employed by CREEP. A massive cover-up effort began, while Nixon vowed that no one in his administration was involved in the break-in. The break-in was a very minor issue in the re-election campaign, and Nixon easily won re-election in November.

It was later revealed that, six days after the break-in, Nixon ordered his chief of staff, **H. R. Haldeman**, to instruct the CIA to tell the FBI not to probe too deeply into connections between the White House and the burglars. Attempts to destroy paperwork and bribe key individuals were gradually exposed, most prominently in a series of articles in *The Washington Post*. Reporters **Carl Bernstein** and **Bob Woodward** unmasked the Nixon administration's corruption and attempted cover-up, having received much of their information from an unnamed informant known as **Deep Throat**. (In 2005, former FBI Associate Director Mark Felt confirmed that he was Deep Throat.)

In January 1973, the burglars were convicted and sent to jail. After being "bribed" by White House Counsel **John Dean** with $400,000 of hush money, the convicted men began to talk. Soon afterward, a Senate committee was formed to investigate the "cancer that was growing on the presidency" with Senator Sam Ervin as chairman. In February 1973, the Senate established an investigative committee to look into the growing scandal. During the summer of 1973 a series of hearings were held by the Watergate Committee. John Dean implicated Nixon in the cover-up and another witness stated that Nixon had a secret taping system in the Oval Office. The president himself was named as a co-conspirator in the cover-up. Nixon cited **executive privilege** when subpoenaed to turn the tapes over.

By July 1974, the public Watergate hearings had disclosed evidence of illegal White House activities and the House of Representatives recommended that Nixon be impeached. The House Judiciary Committee then adopted three articles of impeachment, charging Nixon with obstruction of justice, abuse of presidential powers, and trying to impede the impeachment process by defying committee subpoenas. Following that action, on August 4, 1974, the Supreme Court issued a unanimous ruling stating in *U.S. v. Nixon* (1974) that Nixon must turn over the tapes. Nixon turned over the tapes on August 5th—within eight hours of the ruling. The tapes made it clear that Nixon had been involved actively in the cover-up from the onset.

Because of the inevitability of impeachment by the House and probable conviction by the Senate, Nixon resigned from the presidency effective August 9, 1974, becoming the first U.S. president to resign his office.

Nixon never admitted guilt in Watergate, only that it represented an "error of judgment." **Gerald Ford**, who had been appointed vice president following Spiro Agnew's resignation in October 1973, assumed the presidency. Coming on the heels of the Vietnam War, the Watergate scandal inflamed the American public's mistrust of, and antagonism toward, the national government.

Lesson 15-4: Domestic Issues

Nixon left office with a mixed legacy. In addition to Vietnam, Watergate, OPEC, and foreign policy issues, Nixon was active in other areas as well.

In 1970, he urged Congress to create the **Environmental Protection Agency (EPA)**, a government agency aimed to protect environmental interests by controlling the rates of air and water pollution.

The economy posed a great challenge for Nixon as the expense of the Vietnam War drained the economy and brought about spiraling inflation that would persist throughout most of the 1970s. Cost of living began to rise for the average American, and the early 1970s saw a recession, a rise in unemployment, and an unfavorable trade balance. In an effort to deal with this "crisis," Nixon instituted a 90-day freeze in wages and prices in August 1970.

Nixon nominated four justices to the Supreme Court: Warren Burger to replace Earl Warren as Chief Justice, Henry Blackmun, Lewis Powell, and William Rehnquist. In 1973, the Supreme Court issued one of its most controversial rulings in the *Roe v. Wade* case that legalized abortion. This set up a struggle between right-to-life groups and pro-choice groups over the issue of abortion and attempts to regulate or overturn the 1973 ruling.

The women's movement scored a victory with the passage of the **Equal Rights Amendment (ERA)** that aimed to "provide equality of rights under the law" by not denying it on account of sex. As the states began to vote on ratification of the amendment, opposition forces organized in part by **Phyllis Schlafly** claimed that the new amendment would degrade the status of women and erode the family. The **National Organization of Women (NOW)** fought back in support of the proposed amendment. When the time for ratification passed in 1982, it was three states short of the number needed for ratification.

Lesson 15-5: Ford: "WIN"

Gerald Ford served as little more than a caretaker in the White House until the 1976 election. Ford's announcement on September 8, 1974, granting an "unconditional pardon" to Nixon for any crimes he might have committed as president was widely criticized by both parties. Although no formal charges were pending against Nixon after he left office, Ford said he feared "ugly passions" would be aroused if former president Nixon was put on trial. Though he received bad press after pardoning Nixon, Ford's presidency was unblemished by scandal. However, Ford was challenged by economic problems at a time when many were disillusioned by politics in general.

Domestic Affairs

Ford vetoed measures aimed at social welfare, environmental protection, and civil rights. A Democratic Congress overrode most of these vetoes. Ford's woes increased with the Arab oil embargo, which devastated the U.S. economy. Rising oil prices sparked enormous inflation, which hit 12 percent in 1974. In October of that year, Ford initiated the **"Whip Inflation Now" (WIN)** program. He planned to encourage a slow but steady growth of the economy by keeping interest rates stable, raising taxes to reduce the deficit, and restraining federal spending. His voluntary WIN program used big red, white, and blue buttons to foster support for the program. Instead of reversing inflation and stabilizing the economy, his efforts threw the economy into a recession, with unemployment and interest rates soaring, and business production declining. That year, the country entered its deepest downturn since the Great Depression, but the government refused to increase spending or cut taxes.

The Republicans feared a conservative candidate, namely Ronald Reagan, on the ticket in the 1976 campaign, so they nominated Gerald Ford and Bob Dole to run against Democrats Jimmy Carter and Walter Mondale, his vice-presidential candidate. During the 1976 election Ford was quoted as saying, "There is no Soviet domination" and "things are more like they are now than they ever have been." These comments continued to erode Ford's standing with the public. Carter beat Ford with less than 50 percent of the popular vote and a 297–241 margin in the Electoral College.

Foreign Affairs

In 1975, Ford and Soviet Premier Leonid Brezhnev, along with the leaders of 31 other states, signed the Helsinki Accords, which solidified European boundaries and promised to respect human rights and the freedom to travel. Ford kept Kissinger as Secretary of State and continued policies began during Nixon's term. Ford met with Soviet leaders in Vladivostok to begin work on another round of weapons reduction agreements on SALT II, but little progress on arms control was made. In fact, when it came up for ratification under the Carter administration, the SALT II treaty was never ratified by the U.S. Senate. In the Middle East, Iran was receiving continued U.S. support while anti–U.S. sentiment began to grow among the fundamentalist Muslim faction of the population.

Lesson 15-6: Carter: Human Rights and Hostage Crisis

Jimmy Carter was elected president in 1976. He sought to restore the White House to a new simplicity and directness. He ran as a "born-again" Christian and Southern Democrat. A former governor of Georgia, Carter presented himself as a political outsider. His presidency was marked by a commitment to morality, but scarred by economic and foreign policy challenges. The biggest legacy of the Carter administration was its lack of direction. At the end of his term, he stated, "We have a crisis of the American spirit."

Domestic Affairs

Carter supported a tax cut and the creation of a public works program, which helped reduce unemployment to 5 percent by late 1978. However, Carter failed to push many of his other economic programs through Congress. By the end of Carter's term, unemployment, inflation, and interest rates rose dramatically.

The economy was further hurt in 1979 by the decade's second energy shortage, provoked by OPEC's hike in oil prices. In efforts to promote conservation and responsible energy use, Carter created the **Department of Energy** in 1977, proposed taxes on fossil-fuel use, and supported research on alternative energy sources. The 800-mile Alaskan Pipeline was completed in 1977 at a cost of more than $7.7 billion. Environmental concerns ran high as the project continued. It was feared that an oil spill might occur at the Valdez oil terminal in Prince William Sound. Those concerns came true when the *Exxon Valdez* ran aground, causing a massive oil spill in the region in 1989. Carter also encouraged the passage of an energy bill in 1978 and encouraged the federal government to provide the Chrysler Corporation with a $1 billion tax credit as a "bailout" to prevent its bankruptcy.

Foreign Affairs: A Mixed Record

Carter is best known for his foreign affairs. He supported human rights around the world, working to unveil and halt abuses. Carter also worked to improve relations with nations previously hostile to the United States. In 1977, he negotiated a treaty with Panama to transfer the Panama Canal back to the Panamanians in 1999, and he officially recognized the People's Republic of China in 1979.

Carter's biggest success and biggest challenge in foreign affairs involved the Middle East. In September 1978, Carter invited Israel's leader, Menachem Begin, and Egypt's leader, Anwar el-Sadat, to Camp David, where they worked out a treaty. The **Camp David Accords** were signed by the two leaders at the White House in March 1979, but they fell apart when Sadat was assassinated by Islamic fundamentalists in 1981.

In June 1979, Carter and Leonid Brezhnev signed **SALT II (Strategic Arms Limitation Treaty)**, but the Senate failed to ratify the treaty. The treaty was meant to further limit the arms race between the United States and USSR. However, by the time Brezhnev and Carter met to sign the agreement in July 1979 in Vienna, the United States had ordered the construction of a new category of ballistic missiles and the Soviets went ahead with new missiles of their own. Ratification of the treaty by the Senate never occurred because of the Russian invasion of Afghanistan in December. Grain sales were curtailed to the Russians and the United States, and several of its close allies, boycotted the 1980 Summer Olympics in Moscow in response to the Afghanistan invasion. Because of increased U.S.–USSR tensions, Carter asked for an increase in military spending. Détente was dead during the Carter administration.

Adding to this tension, in January 1979 the Shah of Iran, a U.S. ally, fled his country to escape a revolution. The religious leader **Ayatollah Khomenei** assumed control of the country in February 1979. The shah was admitted to the U.S. for medical treatment for cancer, but religious fundamentalists wanted him returned to Iran for a trial. When the United States allowed the shah to enter the United States, the U.S. embassy in Tehran was put under siege and 54 Americans were taken hostage for 444 days. During this **hostage crisis,** the Iranians referred to the United States as the "great Satan." The crisis dramatized the decline of U.S. power abroad, and the Shiite fundamentalists continued to spread their beliefs throughout the Middle East. The United States froze Iranian assets, suspended arms sales to Iran, and threatened to deport Iranians in the United States back to Iran. Ted Koppel's *Nightline* program kept the nation informed about the crisis. An attempt to rescue the hostages in 1980 failed, and once again, the United States was at the mercy of the fundamentalists. President Carter seemed helpless in bringing an end to this situation. It plagued him until his last day in office. Despite all of his efforts, the hostage crisis continued until the release of the hostages on January 20, 1981, within minutes of Reagan's swearing-in as president. Carter's inability to resolve the Iran hostage crisis was a major blemish on his presidency.

Lesson 15-7: Reaganomics and "Win One for the Gipper"

Republican Ronald Reagan won the 1980 election by promising to end the "tax and spend" policies of his liberal predecessors and to revive the patriotism needed to win the Cold War. Reagan's slogan for the 1980 campaign was "Are you better off now than you were four years ago?" His economic goals dominated his presidency. During his two terms, Reagan and his conservative allies reshaped the nation's political and social landscape. He was given the nickname of the "great communicator." He also developed a style of governing in which he left the actual work to his aides, while he concentrated on speaking and fundraising. Reagan survived an assassination attempt on March 30, 1981. In his bid for re-election in 1984, he garnered 59 percent of the popular vote and 49 states in the Electoral College.

Domestic Affairs and Reaganomics

Ronald Reagan's economic program, dubbed **Reaganomics**, was founded on the belief that a capitalist system free from taxation and government involvement would be most productive and that the prosperity of a rich upper class would **"trickle down"** to the poor. This term came to stand for tax cuts and domestic budget reductions along with the supply-side economic theory. The theory stated that the tax cuts would give businesses and individuals more to invest, and investments would grow the economy. Because of investments, tax revenues would grow and government expenditures would be trimmed because of the lack of need for them. This, in turn, would cause the federal deficit to go down. Reagan pushed a three-year, 25-percent tax cut through Congress in 1981, as well as a $40 billion cut in federal spending on school lunches, student loans, and public transportation, among other services.

To curb inflation, the Federal Reserve Board hiked interest rates in 1981, plunging the country into a recession. Unemployment soared to 10 percent and, because of Reagan's cuts in social spending, the impoverished found themselves without social programs. Along with unemployment, trade and federal deficits skyrocketed. (The federal deficit rose because the government offset its cuts in social spending with huge increases in military spending.) Recession, however, gave way to a rebound in early 1983, when inflation stabilized and consumer confidence returned.

From 1983 to 1987, the economy boomed, spurred by speculation in the stock market. The bubble burst, however, on October 19, 1987, when 20 percent of the stock market's value was lost, the largest single-day decline in history. The crash exposed the economic problems concealed by the four boom years: a high trade deficit and the widening gap between rich and poor and growing problems in the savings and loan industry. These problems were still unresolved when the economy began to recover in 1988.

The Supreme Court

Reagan's appointed three conservatives to the Supreme Court: **Sandra Day O'Connor**, the Court's first female (1982), Antonin Scalia (1987) and Anthony Kennedy (1988). He elevated Justice William Rehnquist, a conservative Nixon appointee, to Chief Justice in 1986.

Deficit Spending

Because of lower tax revenues, deficit spending increased dramatically during the Reagan years. Before the 1980s, the largest single-year deficit was $66 billion. In 1986, the deficit was $221 billion. The 1980 debt was $907 billion, and, in 1986, it was more than $2 trillion. In 1989, the debt rose to $2.8 trillion and the 1992 figure was $4 trillion! In addition to the deficit, the United States also owed other countries $340 billion in 1985 and became the world's biggest debtor nation by the mid-1980s.

Wealth in America

The **Yuppies** lived by the slogan "you can have it all." These new "young urban professionals" became synonymous with upward mobility, greed, and selfishness of the 1980s. At the same time, people at the lower part of the economic ladder saw declines, because the Reagan tax cuts did little to help middle-income taxpayers. Social Security taxes continued to increase, and many families became dependent on two incomes. In 1989 the richest 1 percent of Americans accounted for 37 percent of the nation's wealth. The percentage of Americans in poverty grew drastically during the decade.

AIDS

When the AIDS outbreak hit in the early 1980s, it was perceived only as a threat to gay men. Later, it would be identified as HIV, human immunodeficiency virus. Within a short time, the epidemic spread and began to appear among intravenous drug users, hemophiliacs who received blood transfusions, and heterosexuals. The Reagan administration was slow to respond, and little money was appropriated to AIDS research. Surgeon General C. Everett Koop challenged the public in 1986 with his bold proposals of AIDS education and awareness. As deaths rose and public concern grew, Congress approved just more than $1 billion for the battle against AIDS in 1987. Despite these efforts, the number of AIDS cases in the United States exceeded 100,000 by the end of the decade. The U.S. death rate from AIDS began to decline during the 1990s due to education and new medications, but the AIDS epidemic is still ravaging parts of the world, leaving many people in poor and underdeveloped Third World nations at great risk in the 21st century.

The *Challenger* Explosion

January 28, 1986, was to be the date of the successful launch of the *Challenger*, with teacher Christa McAuliffe on board. Tragedy struck just 73 seconds into the flight when a seal on the solid rocket booster failed, causing a leak in the fuel tank and an explosion that resulted in the loss of the entire crew. That evening, instead of delivering his state of the union address, Reagan led the nation in mourning in a speech he concluded with: "The crew of the space shuttle *Challenger* honored us by the manner in which they lived their lives. We will never forget them, nor the last time we saw them, this morning, as they prepared for their journey and waved good-bye and slipped the surly bonds of earth to touch the face of God." NASA halted flights for two years while investigations and improvements were made.

Lesson 15-8: Foreign Affairs and the "Evil Empire"

The Reagan administration's distrust of the Soviets and their allies led it into a scandal known as the **Iran-Contra affair**. In 1982, the CIA organized a force of 10,000 men in Nicaragua, who called themselves "Contras," to fight against the Sandinista regime, which had military ties to the Soviet Union and Cuba. Reagan hoped to establish a democratic, U.S.-friendly government in

Nicaragua, but Congress voted to ban aid to the Contras. The administration maintained secret support, organized from within the White House by Oliver North, a member of the National Security Council. A series of investigations in 1987 uncovered the plan: The United States had been selling arms to the anti-American government in Iran and using profits from these sales to secretly finance the Contras. Although there was no evidence that Reagan knew of the plan, the Iran-Contra scandal rekindled the American public's distrust of the U.S. government.

Soon after coming to the White House, Reagan referred to the USSR as the "evil empire," and he sought to "find peace through strength." His administration's Cold War strategy was military buildup. Reagan was responsible for a $1.7 trillion increase in military spending over a five-year period in order to make America the leading superpower again. This spending included development of the B-1 Bomber (stealth bomber), the MX Missile, and the **Strategic Defense Initiative** ("Star Wars") program that amounted to a satellite and laser shield to detect and intercept incoming missiles before they could ever strike. The Pentagon's budget nearly doubled during Reagan's first term in office, paralleling an increase in nuclear weapons and alarming the nation about a seeming increase in the likelihood of nuclear war. "Star Wars" never came close to completion because technology lagged behind the program's defensive aims, and the massive arms buildup forced the USSR to spend itself into bankruptcy by the late 1980s.

In 1985, when **Mikhail Gorbachev** became the new leader in the USSR, he ushered in the economic and political reform programs of glasnost (openness) and peristroika (restructuring). On April 26, 1986, a reactor at the **Chernobyl** nuclear power plant in the Soviet Union experienced a steam explosion resulting in a fire, a series of explosions, and a "nuclear meltdown." The radioactive fallout drifted Westward over, Eastern Europe, Western Europe, Scandinavia, and the Eastern part of North America. Although the USSR reported nothing for nearly 24 hours, world demand forced the Soviet Union to admit to the accident. Although a major part of the data about the incident remained secret, it forced an "openness" of the communist government.

Despite Reagan's anti-communist stance and the largest military buildup in history, between 1985 and 1988 Reagan and Gorbachev held four separate summit meetings. The 1986 summit saw Gorbachev propose a 50-percent reduction in all strategic nuclear weapons and a reduction of Soviet and American missiles in Europe. The **INF Treaty**, signed by Gorbachev and Reagan on December 8, 1987, provided for the elimination of more than 2,600 missiles and on-site inspections; it also provided a breakthrough in the Cold War mentality. In December 1987, Gorbachev visited the United States, and, in 1988, Reagan visited Moscow. These talks led to the eventual end of the Cold War during the early years of George Bush's administration.

In a speech at the Brandenburg Gate in West Berlin, Germany, on June 12, 1987, leaders had gathered to commemorate the 750th anniversary of Berlin. Reagan spoke to the German audience and General Secretary Gorbachev, by stating, "If you seek peace, if you seek prosperity for the Soviet Union and Eastern Europe, if you seek liberalization...Mr. Gorbachev, tear down this wall!" This plea was, the same one began by JFK, of tearing down the wall separating East and West Berlin. This wall had long served as a visible symbol between free countries in Western Europe and Soviet-dominated counties in Eastern Europe. Regan's plea began a series of events that would eventually lead to

the tearing down of the wall on November 9, 1989, and the collapse of the USSR on December 31, 1991.

Review Exam

Multiple Choice

1. The Pentagon Papers released by Daniel Ellsberg and printed in the *New York Times* in 1971 revealed that _____.
   a) the government had relied on a series of deceptions, miscalculations, and arrogance in dealing with the U.S. involvement in Vietnam
   b) even as LBJ kept increasing troops in Vietnam, he had no long-range plan to end the war
   c) the government had not been totally honest in reporting events of the war to the general public
   d) A, B, and C

2. The War Powers Act of 1973 had the intent of _____.
   a) increasing presidential power during a military crisis by giving him up to six months to conduct military actions without a formal declaration of war
   b) limiting presidential power during a military crisis by giving him 48 hours to inform Congress of his actions, 60 days of action, and 30 days to withdraw (after 90 days, a formal declaration of war would need to take place)

    c) allowing the president the authority to declare war

    d) bringing a formalized end to the Vietnam crisis

3. OPEC placed an embargo on oil that increased inflation worries in the United States because it _____.

    a) included all oil-producing countries in the organization with the intent of using oil as a bargaining chip in foreign affairs

    b) created an oil crisis in which oil prices more than quadrupled

    c) more than doubled the price of gasoline

    d) A, B, and C

4. The Watergate break-in into the Democratic National Headquarters in 1972 included all of the following EXCEPT that _____.

    a) it appeared at first to be a minor story about an insignificant break-in

    b) it was a major issue in Nixon's 1972 re-election campaign

    c) Nixon claimed that no one in his administration was involved in the break-in

    d) CREEP began a cover-up of the incident

5. The investigation by Woodward and Bernstein of *The Washington Post* into the Watergate Scandal _____.

    a) relied heavily on secret information supplied by an informant known only as "Deep Throat"

    b) exposed a complex scheme of deceit and cover-up from the highest levels of the Nixon administration

    c) would lead the House of Representatives in the summer of 1974 to draft articles of impeachment based on obstruction of justice, abuse of presidential power, and attempts to impede the investigation process

    d) A, B, and C

6. "A cancer is growing on the presidency" began to be a reality in the Watergate Scandal when _____.

    a) John Dean, White House counsel, implicated Nixon in the cover-up

    b) Senate investigations into the Watergate scandal discovered the secret taping system used by Nixon

    c) Nixon cited executive privilege when subpoenaed to turn the tapes over to the Senate committee and attempted to defy the committee by not turning the tapes over

    d) A, B, and C

7. Carter created the Department of Energy in 1977 as an effort to _____.
   a) promote conservation and responsible energy use, as well as promote the Alaska Pipeline to increase the domestic supply of oil
   b) propose taxes on fossil fuel usage
   c) support research into alternative fuels
   d) A, B, and C

8. All of the following were foreign affairs issues during the Carter administration EXCEPT _____.
   a) the Soviet invasion of Afghanistan in 1979
   b) negotiating a treaty with Panama to return control of the Panama Canal to Panama in 1999
   c) negotiating a successful SALT II arms limitation treaty with the Soviets that was ratified by the Senate in 1979
   d) sponsoring a boycott of the 1980 Moscow Summer Olympics in protest to the military actions in Afghanistan

9. The hostage crisis in Tehran, Iran, in 1979 included all of the following EXCEPT that _____.
   a) it created an international crisis when 54 Americans were taken hostage at the American embassy in Tehran
   b) it was supported by the Ayatollah Khomenei
   c) it ended successfully with Carter's negotiations before Reagan was sworn in to office as president
   d) after a rescue attempt in early 1980 failed, the United States was at the mercy of the fundamentalist extremists

10. _____ was not nominated to the Supreme Court by Reagan.
    a) Sandra Day O'Connor
    b) William Rehnquist
    c) Anthony Kennedy
    d) Antonin Scalia

11. The AIDS crisis in the 1980s _____.
    a) was at first largely ignored by the Reagan administration as just affecting gay men
    b) initially saw limited federal funding to investigate the spread of the disease
    c) saw Reagan's Surgeon General, Everett Koop, promoting AIDS awareness and education in 1986
    d) A, B, and C

12. All of the following items dealt with the *Challenger* explosion in 1986 EXCEPT that it _____.
    a) resulted in the loss of the entire crew of seven aboard the shuttle
    b) was the flight that the first teacher, Christa McAuliffe, was on board
    c) ended the shuttle program
    d) resulted from a faulty seal on a solid rocket booster

13. The Iran-Contra Affair in 1987 involved _____.
    a) secretly selling arms to Iran and using the profits to secretly finance the Contras in Nicaragua
    b) a government-sponsored plan to sell weapons to both Iran and Nicaragua
    c) an executive order issued by Reagan authorizing the arms sale
    d) a CIA initiative to rid the region of the Contras

14. _____ was part of Reagan's nearly $2 trillion increase in military spending in the 1980s to combat the impending Soviet threat.
    a) The B-1 bomber (Stealth Bomber)
    b) The MX missile program
    c) The "Star Wars" program (Strategic Defense Initiative)
    d) A, B, and C

15. The Chernobyl incident in Russia that involved a nuclear plant near meltdown in 1986 resulted in all of the following EXCEPT _____.
    a) glasnost
    b) perestroika
    c) a continuance in the Cold War philosophy that had been adhered to for nearly 40 years
    d) Gorbachev leading a series of reforms that also included summit meetings with the United states to discuss a reduction in all strategic nuclear weapons

16. The 1980 presidential campaign was significant in that _____.
    a) one question changed the campaign ("Are you better off now that you were four years ago?")
    b) Reagan's election as a conservative Republican meant the end to an era of tax and spend liberalism
    c) Carter nearly won the election when it was announced th.t the hostages in Iran were to be released
    d) A and B only

17. All of the following are true about Reagan in office EXCEPT that he ____.
   a) survived an assassination attempt two months into office
   b) was not an active president and did not do much to end the Cold War
   c) was an extremely popular president
   d) was nicknamed the "great communicator"

Matching

a. silent majority	i. Kent State University	p. the "evil empire"
b. Brandenburg Gate		q. *Roe v. Wade*
c. CREEP	j. John Dean	r. Reaganomics
d. detente	k. Nixon Doctrine	s. SALT II
e. yuppies	l. *U.S. v. Nixon*	t. INF Treaty
f. Henry Kissinger	m. SALT I	u. WIN
g. EPA	n. human rights	v. deficit spending
h. H. R. Haldeman	o. Gerald Ford	w. Camp David Accords

____18. committee created by Nixon; money from this group going to pay off the five men ordered to break in to the Watergate building

____19. a label used by Nixon to describe Americans who were discontent with reforms and racial integration of schools

____20. Ford's domestic program intended to "whip inflation now"

____21. Nixon's secretary of state who promoted a "peace with honor" end to the Vietnam War

____22. directed the CIA not to probe too deeply into the Watergate break-in

____23. an easing of tensions between the United States and its Cold War enemies

____24. unanimous Supreme Court decision that ordered Nixon to turn over all of the tapes that implicated Nixon in the scandal of the break-in and cover-up)

____25. location of Reagan's famous Berlin Wall in 1987 that ended with "Mr. Gorbachev, tear down this wall!"

____26. Kissinger announced this statement, saying that there were limits to U.S. power abroad

____27. assumed the presidency in August 1974 after Nixon's resignation

_____28. treaty signed by Nixon and Brezhnev in 1972; the first agreement limiting the numbers of anti-ballistic missiles that the two superpowers were permitted to keep

_____29. White House counsel who bribed the Watergate spies with $400,000 of hush money

_____30. agency established in 1970 to protect environmental interests

_____31. site where four college student protesters were shot by National Guard troops on May 4, 1970, which led to other college riots including the one at Jackson State College in Mississippi 10 days later)

_____32. legalized abortions in 1972

_____33. young urban professionals of the 1980s

_____34. U.S.-USSR arms agreement aimed at limiting nuclear weapons

_____35. this involved the government spending more money than it had; it increased to $2 trillion-plus by the end of Reagan's term in office and rose to nearly $4 trillion by the end of Bush's term in office in 1992

_____36. in 1978 Carter was able to get Israel's leader, Begin and Egypt's leader, el-Sadat, to sign a treaty ending hostilities between the two nations

_____37. Jimmy Carter began to support this around the world as a means of halting abuses to people in various countries

_____38. Reagan's reference to the Soviet Union made soon after taking office in 1981

_____39. founded on the belief of tax cuts to the wealthy to promote economic growth ("trickle down economics")

_____40. provided for the elimination of missiles and allowed for on-site inspections; hailed as a major breakthrough in U.S.-USSR relations

Short Response

41. What was important about presidential power in the Watergate Scandal?

42. How did the Iran hostage crisis cripple the Carter presidency?

43. How did the Reagan presidency shape the country in the 1980s?

Answers begin on page 304.

A New World Order

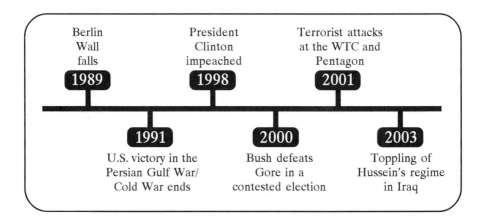

Berlin Wall falls
1989

President Clinton impeached
1998

Terrorist attacks at the WTC and Pentagon
2001

1991
U.S. victory in the Persian Gulf War/ Cold War ends

2000
Bush defeats Gore in a contested election

2003
Toppling of Hussein's regime in Iraq

Trends and Themes of the Era

❯ The United States gets involved in the Persian Gulf War in 1991 and invades Iraq again in 2003.

❯ The economy begins to surge during the later part of the 1990s. Democrats take the credit for economic growth.

❯ President Bill Clinton is impeached in 1998 but remains in office for the remainder of his second term.

❯ The 9/11 attacks on the World Trade Center and Pentagon in 2001 have a profound effect on America.

❯ The War on Terrorism shapes politics at home and abroad.

Dawn of a new era! The world at the end of the 20th century and the beginning of the 21st century was changing quickly. With the collapse of the Soviet Union in 1991, the United States remained a superpower on the world stage and was faced with numerous challenges both abroad and at home that would severely call into question her role in world and domestic affairs. Presidents focused on economic challenges, such as jobs, trade, oil, the stock market, and immigration, and challenges on the world stage at times eclipsed domestic challenges. America will continue to stand strong and face the new challenges while looking back on the past for guidance and support.

Lesson 16-1: George H. W. Bush: A Kinder, Gentler...

After serving as Reagan's vice president, and after service as head of the Republican Committee, UN ambassador, envoy to China, director of the CIA, and World War II veteran, George Herbert Walker Bush ran for president in 1988. Dan Quayle was his running mate, and he ran a negative campaign against Democrat Michael Dukakis. Bush promised to bring "a kinder, gentler administration" to Washington, and "Read my lips: no new taxes" became the new catch phrase. Bush's legacy was his handling of foreign affairs. He became so involved in foreign affairs, that domestic affairs received less attention during his presidency.

The Economy

A recession began in 1990 and, in 1991, unemployment and layoffs increased, and many began to fear about job security. The federal deficit, overburdened state and local governments, and a decrease in consumer confidence all affected recession recovery. Cutbacks in military spending meant the closing of military bases and affected the economies in those areas. The downturn in the economy cost Bush in his 1992 re-election bid.

As the Cold War ended, both Russia and the United States faced economic challenges due to massive amounts of military spending. During the 1980s, the deficit soared, and the surplus from the Social Security fund was used to spend on government programs, thereby masking the true size of the deficit.

The Supreme Court

Bush nominated David Souter (1990) and Clarence Thomas (1991) to the Supreme Court. Although Souter has tended to vote more on the liberal side of the court, Clarence Thomas, who replaced Thurgood Marshall, has voted conservative consistently. Thomas faced a challenge during his confirmation hearings from Anita Hill of sexual misconduct before being confirmed.

News Programs and Legislation

In 1990 Bush encouraged the spirit of volunteerism by talking about "a thousand points of light," referring to people reaching out in service to others. The **Points of Light Foundation** began its work as an organization supporting volunteer-based organizations and advocates community service.

The **North America Free Trade Agreement (NAFTA)** with Canada and Mexico aimed at easing trade restrictions between the three nations was negotiated by Bush and signed into law by Clinton in 1993. The agreement lifted tariffs on most goods produced by the three nations. It called for the gradual elimination, of many remaining barriers to investment and to the movement of goods and services among the three nations. Agriculture, automobile and textile manufacturing, telecommunications, financial services, energy, and trucking were among the major industries affected by the agreement.

In 1990, Bush signed the Clean Air Act, which imposed new government regulations on smog, automobile exhaust, acid rain, and toxic air pollution. He also approved legislation to expand the Head Start Program and enhanced his image as the "education president." June 1990 was a turning point for Bush when he agreed to a tax increase to deal with the deficit, losses from the savings and loan crisis in the late 1980s, and rising healthcare costs for Medicare and Medicaid. His promise no new taxes was broken—something voters remembered two years later.

Bush signed the **Americans With Disabilities Act (ADA)** in 1991, prohibiting discrimination in hiring, transportation, and public accommodations, and the following year called for public buildings to be made handicap accessible.

Foreign Affairs

Bush's presidency would be defined by his role on the world stage with foreign affairs. Part of his legacy deals with the fall of the Berlin Wall on November 9, 1989. This event would also lead to the spread of democracy throughout Eastern Europe and see a united Germany in 1990.

Events unfolded in the USSR that, in the words of Gorbachev in a 1988 UN address, resulted in a "new world order." Talks of reform and disarmament continued. As democratic reforms swept across communist Eastern Europe, Boris Yeltsin attempted a coup in August 1991 to remove Gorbachev from power in Russia. It failed, but, by the end of December 1991, Gorbachev resigned, signaling the end of the 74-year reign of the Communist Party in the USSR. Boris Yeltsin became the leader of the new democratic Russia. Conversion from communism to democracy and from a controlled market economy to a free economy for the USSR and countries in Eastern Europe would prove challenging in the 1990s. Former Russian Republics and Eastern Europe turned to the Untied States for assistance.

In 1989, Bush received broad support for his "war on drugs" when he ordered the invasion of Panama on December 20th to dispose drug lord and dictator **Manuel Noriega**. He was later tried and convicted in U.S. federal court on drug trafficking and racketeering charges.

The Persian Gulf War

The other defining moment of Bush's presidency came with his leadership in the war against Iraq in the Persian Gulf War. On August 2, 1990, Iraq invaded the oil-rich country of Kuwait, the "19th province of Iraq." The United States led a broad coalition of UN countries as more than 200,000 troops were sent to the Gulf region in **Operation Desert Shield** to discourage further aggression by Iraq's leader, **Saddam Hussein**. Tensions mounted in the region as the troop strength doubled by January 1991.

UN sanctions failed to deal effectively with Hussein, so on January 16, 1991, with a unanimous vote of the UN Security Council (in which Russia was a member and a major supporter of weapons for Iraq), UN forces began a six-week bombing raid against Iraq. Media images showed the superiority of the new U.S. weapons: Patriot Missiles and the Stealth Bomber. **Operation Desert Storm** began on February 24th when ground troops, led by **General Norman Schwarzkopf**, took only 100 hours to force Saddam out of Kuwait. The offensive freed Kuwait and forced Hussein's forces to retreat. As his troops retreated towards Baghdad, countless oil wells were set on fire. Once the independence of Kuwait was secured, Bush withdrew the troops, acting on advice from **General Colin Powell**, chairman of the Joint Chiefs of Staff. Saddam Hussein remained in power in Iraq; as a result of the actions in the war, in the next few years he crushed Iraqi dissident Kurds in northern Iraq and Shi'ite Muslims in the south; was suspected of harboring biological, chemical, and nuclear weapons of mass destruction; and ignored repeated UN resolutions. The war was extremely popular in America (Bush's approval rating was greater than 80 percent), the United States scored a major victory in a war,

helping to blot the image of loss from Vietnam. At the same time, the war fueled anti-American sentiment among some radical, conservative Muslims including that of Saudi-born **Osama bin Laden**.

The 1992 Campaign

Americans were disillusioned about the economic recession following the end of the war in Iraq and were growing discontent with the deficit, morality issues, and two-party politics in general. They were clamoring for change. The public wanted a leader with a vision for the nation's future.

During the 1992 campaign, Ross Perot, a Texas billionaire who financed his own campaign, jumped into the race as an independent candidate of the Reform Party. In the end, although Ross Perot failed to gain any Electoral College votes, he gained 19 percent of the popular vote. Bill Clinton won with 43 percent of the popular vote; Bush received 37 percent.

Lesson 16-2: The Clinton Era: A New Kind of Democrat

Clinton carefully crafted his image as a new kind of Democrat that would be sensitive to the needs of the middle class while at the same time working to balance the federal budget. He campaigned on the platform of higher taxes for wealthy Americans, universal healthcare coverage, and continuing to develop and strengthen America's infrastructure. Although ads attacked his character and lack of war experience, Clinton kept the campaign focused on the economy. "It's the economy, stupid" became one of the sound bites of the campaign.

During the 1992 campaign, one issue surfaced that sought to discredit Clinton: rumors of a 12-year affair with Gennifer Flowers. At the time, Clinton denied the affair, and Hillary Clinton came to her husband's defense. This was not the last time this scenario would be played out.

Once in office, Clinton appointed many women and minorities to key positions: **Janet Reno** as the first female attorney general, **Ruth Bader Ginsberg** as the second female on the Supreme Court, **Madeleine Albright** as the first female secretary of state, and his wife and First Lady, **Hillary Clinton** was named to chair the government committee to draft a healthcare plan. In addition, Clinton took credit for a remarkable turnaround of the economy by helping erase the budget deficit of more than $250 billion and creating a budget surplus of more than $500 billion by the time he left office after two terms.

Domestic Agenda

One of Clinton's first actions in office was to issue an executive order banning discrimination in the armed forces by not allowing gays to be discharged from the military because of their sexual preference. A compromise was reached in which "don't ask, don't tell" became the policy, in which commanders could not specifically ask recruits about their sexual preference.

In addition, Clinton signed legislation approving the **Family Medical Leave Act (FMLA)** in 1993, requiring large corporations to grant unpaid leave for employees who were pregnant or suffering from a serious medical condition. Clinton also signed the **Brady Bill**, in late 1993, limiting the accessibility of handguns and mandating a seven-day waiting period and background check for gun purchases.

In 1993, Clinton's committee on healthcare convened with its goal of reforming **healthcare coverage** for Americans by providing a plan for universal coverage. Hillary Clinton was placed in charge of this committee, which presented its plans to Congress in late 1993, and, by the following September, the proposal was dead in Congress. Clinton suffered a major defeat by Republican opposition to the plan. The public became dismayed with the apparent gridlock in Congress, setting the stage for the Republicans to gain control of both houses of Congress in the 1994 mid-term elections.

The Republican Revolution

In 1994, **Newt Gingrich**, the new Speaker of the House, led the conservative backlash against Clinton's liberal polices by endorsing the Contract with America. Its programs endorsed tax reduction, reduced federal regulations, reduced the size of the federal government, and worked to balanced the budget by 2002. When the Republicans gained control of Congress in the 1994 election, it was the first time in 40 years that they had been in charge of both houses. This set the stage for a divided government: a Democratic president and a Republican-controlled Congress. Gingrich became one of the most outspoken critics of Clinton's policies over the next two years.

Oklahoma City

Terrorism took a new turn on April 19, 1995, when an explosion rocked the federal building in Oklahoma City, resulting in 168 deaths (including 19 children in a daycare center in the building), countless injuries, and destruction of the building. The bomb was the work of extremist **Timothy McVeigh** and Terry Nichols, who were angry with the federal government for its actions at Waco in a government siege in 1993 against the Branch Davidians. Clinton used this opportunity to further his presidential leadership by not only reaching out to families and survivors of the blast, but the nation as a whole in the days following the blast to comfort and encourage people. McVeigh was sentenced to death for his actions, and was executed in June 2001.

Welfare Reform

Clinton began the year of 1996 on a high note when in his State of the Union Address he promised to "end welfare as we know it." His political agenda focused on welfare reform, resulted in the **Personal Responsibility and Work Opportunity Act of 1996**, signed into law in August of that year. This bill provided sweeping changes in the welfare program by establishing a time limit of five years for benefit payments. It also provided block grants to states to distribute and manage under federal guidelines. The bill encouraged getting people off the welfare rolls by having them find jobs and get training.

The WTC Bombing

On February 26, 1993, the **World Trade Center** was the scene of a terrorist attack when a group of Islamic terrorists detonated a bomb in the underground garage of Tower One. The resulting explosion killed six people and injured more than 1,000 but failed to topple the structure. The group, al-Qaeda, was behind this plot. The main conspirator, Sheik Omar Abdel-Rahman, received a life sentence for his part in the bombing, and the other 10 conspirators received lengthy prison terms. The nation was alarmed at this terrorist attack on its own soil. Terrorism had come to America.

The 1996 Campaign

Clinton led in nearly every poll during the 1996 campaign in which he and Vice President Al Gore ran against Bob Dole and his running mate Jack Kemp. During the campaign, Clinton faced several issues. **Paula Jones** sued him in 1994 for sexual harassment. He tried to claim presidential immunity from the case. Clinton's appeal to delay the case while he was acting president went to the Supreme Court in 1996. The case was on hold until after the 1996 fall election, and in May 1997 the Supreme Court ruled that Paula Jones could continue to pursue her case against the president. Depositions in this case led to another scandal in 1998: a failed real-estate venture known as the Whitewater scandal. He and his wife lost money in this venture, but two close partners had been convicted of fraud. The Clintons claimed that **Ken Starr**, the independent counsel from the Justice Department in the Whitewater case, was using this case as a "right-wing conspiracy" to defraud them.

Despite the external issues surrounding the election, Clinton maintained more than a 50-percent majority popularity in opinion polls during the campaign. In the November election, Clinton became the first Democrat since FDR to win reelection. Although Clinton's popularity was still intact, the Republicans remained in charge of Congress. Clinton's goal in the campaign became that of "building a bridge to the 21st century" by continuing to focus on the strength of the economy during his second term in office.

Foreign Affairs

Clinton inherited two major foreign affairs problems that he would be forced to deal with. President Bush had ordered a small contingent of U.S. troops to Somalia in 1992 in order to assist in relief operations in Somalia in a program dubbed Operation Restore Hope. Clinton continued to follow this policy, which also became a UN operation of coalition troops. In October 1993, 18 American troops were killed in a raid in **Mogadishu**. Americans became outraged when television reports showed the naked corpse of a U.S. helicopter pilot being dragged through the streets of the capital in Somalia. The Somalia warlord in charge of the attack on U.S. soldiers was receiving support from an organization that would become known as **al-Qaeda**, led by Osama bin Laden. Due to a lack of clear focus for intervention in the first place, the United States withdrew its troops in 1994.

The United States, again with UN coalition forces, was also drawn into the ethnic conflict in Bosnia with the breakup of the former nation of Yugoslavia. UN peacekeeping troops were sent in to secure peace. In 1995, the Dayton Agreement divided the country into a Bosnian Croat Federation and Serbia. President Slobadan Milosevic was intent upon crushing any dissent. In 1999, NATO forces authorized the use of air strikes to halt Milosevic's aggression. The world soon discovered that President Milosevic was involved in "ethnic cleansing" in Kosovo when the dead bodies of more than 10,000 Albanian civilians were discovered. While facing charges from a war crimes tribunal, Milosevic was overthrown in a coup.

In August 1998, terrorist bombing attacks at U.S. embassies in Kenya and Tanzania that were the work of bin Laden's al-Qaeda organization resulted in numerous deaths and injuries. Clinton ordered Operation Infinite Reach to begin. It froze all of bin Laden's assets and began a series of air strikes against suspected al-Qaeda bases and a major pharmaceutical plant in Afghanistan. Despite this limited attack, it did not harm bin Laden and his operatives.

An attack in 2000 on the *USS Cole* in Yemen was also the work of bin Laden's al-Qaeda organization. The attack at the port in Aden resulted in the deaths of 17 Americans and extensive damage to the ship.

Clinton also supported Britain and other allies in maintaining UN sanctions and boycotts against Hussein in Iraq as well as patrolling flights over the no-fly zone. The fear was that Saddam Hussein was still a major threat in the region due to his suspected harboring weapons of mass destruction.

Impeachment

In January 1988, allegations arose that Clinton was involved in a sex scandal with White House intern Monica Lewinsky from 1995 to 1997. In a televised speech, Clinton denied the affair and blatantly stated that he never had "sexual relations with that woman, Monica Lewinsky." Hillary Clinton, the vice president, and other members of Clinton's staff immediately defended him. Independent prosecutor Ken Starr had his powers broadened to investigate the allegations. By mid-August, President Clinton admitted that he had "misled" the public and that he indeed had a sexual relationship with Lewinksy.

The next order of events led to a long list of charges of **impeachment** against the president. Clinton's supporters claimed that the affair was a private matter and did not impact the manner in which Clinton ran the country. In the midterm elections in 1998, Republicans felt they could make significant gains for further control in Congress because of pending impeachment proceedings. In the outcome of the election, the balance remained the same in the Senate, and Democrats gained seats in the House. On December 19, 1998, the House voted, for the second time in history, to impeach a sitting president. They settled on two articles of impeachment: perjury and attempting to obstruct justice.

The Senate trial began in January 1999 and lasted nearly five weeks. In the end, the Senate did not have the two-thirds vote majority to remove him from office. The Senate decided Clinton's actions did not meet the Constitutional definition of "high crimes and misdemeanors" needed to remove a president from office. Clinton expressed sorrow and faced censure in the Senate, but remained in office. He spent the last two years of his presidency attempting to restore his image and reputation.

The Clintons' Legacy

After the impeachment proceedings, Clinton set out to save social security, improve education, work on the environment, deal with the role of the military in foreign affairs, and craft his lasting legacy by planning his presidential library. He also set out to assist the Democratic Party in holding on to the presidency in the upcoming election.

Hillary had plans of her own: a Senate race in New York. This meant a move to New York, and she conducted her campaign while continuing her role as First Lady. Hillary Clinton won the New York Senate race in 2000, gaining 56 percent of the vote, becoming the first First Lady to run for and to be elected to public office.

Lesson 16-3: George W. Bush: Governor Turned President

The **2000 campaign** involved Democrat Vice President **Al Gore** and Republican Texas Governor **George W. Bush,** son of former president George H. W. Bush. Gore struggled to define his character within the Party under the shadow of Clinton-era scandals. Bush campaigned as a "compassionate conservative" and made broad appeals to conservative Republicans.

The outcome of the election was close and showed a deeply divided nation. Only 500,000 popular votes separated the two major candidates, with Gore leading in the popular vote. Bush won a majority of the states with electoral votes with a final tally of 271 to 266. Despite the Republican victory with a majority of states and Electoral College votes, the Democrats won in major metropolitan areas and in the larger states.

After assuming office, Bush set out to make conservative appointments to his cabinet: Donald Rumsfield as secretary of defense, Colin Powell as secretary of state, Condoleezza Rice as national security advisor, and John Ashcroft as attorney general.

No Child Left Behind

Bush set out to work on education reform. In December 2001 Bush signed the **No Child Left Behind** bill into law, which sought to reshape education in the nation by calling for annual performance reports from states as well as mandating annual testing to demonstrate progress, especially in the areas of math and reading. Its ultimate goal aimed to improve the quality of education. (It continues to face opposition about funding, testing, and other provisions.)

September 11, 2001

September 11, 2001, forever changed how America and the world view terrorism. On that morning, 19 Islamic militants, supported by al-Qaeda and Osama bin Laden, boarded four airliners and hijacked them, turning them into live bombs aimed at destruction. Two planes crashed into the **World Trade Center** towers in New York City shortly after 9 a.m., causing their collapse and the deaths of nearly 3,000 people.

Just after 9:30 that morning, an aircraft crashed into the **Pentagon**, killing 189 personnel and civilians and damaging a wing of the building.

The horror continued as **Flight 93** turned around in mid-flight over Ohio and took aim at Washington, D.C. Its intended target was the Capitol

Building or White House. Before it could reach its target, several men became instant heroes when they helped take down the flight, causing it to crash in a Pennsylvania field, killing all 44 passengers and crew shortly after 10 a.m.

As the events unfolded, President Bush was in Florida visiting a second-grade class. Once informed of the attacks, President Bush took action, and demonstrated leadership and determination in the coming days and weeks, visiting Ground Zero, speaking to the American public and Congress, and reaching out to console fellow Americans. As he spoke to the nation on the evening of 9/11, he reminded the nation of the need to "go forward to defend freedom." This began the **War on Terrorism**. Bush vowed in a speech to a joint session of Congress on September 20th that this nation would strike back against terrorism and that nations would be put on notice when he stated, "Either you are with us, or you are with the terrorists. From this day forward, any nation that continues to harbor or support terrorism will be regarded by the United States as a hostile regime." This terrorist attack reshaped the image of the president put the United States on a new course in the early 21st century.

Afghanistan became the first target in this new war. Bush planned an invasion of **Afghanistan** in October 2001 in order to go after the Taliban government that was supporting al-Qaeda, to destroy al-Qaeda, and to capture bin Laden. Despite intelligence reports and bombing raids, bin Laden proved elusive to U.S. troops.

The War on Terrorism also took on various aspects on the homefront. Bush created a new cabinet level office, the **Department of Homeland Security**, with former Pennsylvania governor Tom Ridge filling the post. In addition, safety measures were enacted at the country's airports and borders in an attempt to secure U.S. borders against enemy combatants. Furthermore, a new bill, the **Patriot Act**, was signed into law in October 2001 with a goal of expanding the authority of American law enforcement to counter terrorism and terrorist activities in the country and overseas.

In March 2003, the invasion of Iraq began with the aid of Britain. The intent was to use force to get Saddam Hussein to disarm for his failure to comply with UN inspectors searching for weapons of mass destruction. The armed invasion led to American troops marching into Baghdad within three weeks, and the toppling of a statue of Saddam Hussein in Baghdad on April 9, 2003. The war was declared to be "over" with the aid of coalition forces and in May, President Bush declared an end to the armed conflict phase of the invasion and an end to Hussein's regime. The task

ahead was to secure a new, democratic government and rebuild the country of Iraq. Despite the work going on in the country, armed rebel forces continued to resist the troops as roadside bombings and other tactics tried to dissuade the work being done in Iraq. Conflicts of interest between the three major groups (Kurds, Shi'ite, and Suni) within Iraq also threatened to stall the mission in Iraq. In December 2003, American troops successfully captured Saddam Hussein in a hole in the ground within miles of his hometown, Tikrit.

Review Exam

Multiple Choice

1. George H. W. Bush served in all of these positions EXCEPT as _____.
   - a) the director of the CIA
   - b) Republican Committee chairman
   - c) secretary of state
   - d) envoy to China

2. Negotiations between Bush and Gorbachev that began in the Reagan presidency led to _____.
   - a) the end of communism in the Soviet Union
   - b) the end of the Cold War between the two superpowers
   - c) escalation of the nuclear crisis between the United States and USSR
   - d) A and B only

3. Operation Desert Shield _____.
   - a) was a result of Iraq's invasion of Kuwait in August 1990
   - b) saw the use of UN coalition forces in the Gulf region to discourage any further aggression by Hussein
   - c) saw the beginning of bombing raids against Iraq on January 16, 1991, with full approval of the UN Security Council
   - d) A, B, and C

4. Operation Desert Storm in February 1991 witnessed all of the following EXCEPT _____.
   - a) the rapid ground assault in Iraq that lasted only 100 hours and the successful freeing of Kuwait
   - b) Saddam Hussein being removed from power in Iraq after securing the independence of Kuwait
   - c) the destruction of oil wells throughout the country by Iraqi forces
   - d) Hussein beginning to crush dissident Kurds and Shi'ites after the end of the war

5. Osama bin Laden _____.
   a) began to secretly finance al-Qaeda
   b) is a conservative Muslim who harbored anti-American sentiment
   c) began to plot several attacks on American targets after the Persian Gulf War
   d) A, B, and C

6. The 1992 presidential campaign focused on all of the following EXCEPT _____.
   a) Ross Perot gaining a significant number of electoral votes
   b) the campaign being a three-way race between the Republican, Democrat, and Reform parties
   c) the campaign focusing on the economy with the catch phrase "it's the economy stupid!"
   d) allegations of sexual improprieties by candidate Bill Clinton and Gennifer Flowers

7. One of Clinton's first actions as president was to _____.
   a) begin to work immediately on healthcare reform
   b) reach a compromise with military leaders in establishing the "don't ask, don't tell" policy
   c) sign the Family Medical Leave Act
   d) promote the passage of the Brady Bill on handgun control

8. Clinton kept his campaign promise in addressing the issue of healthcare reform in 1993 by _____.
   a) naming his wife, Hillary Clinton, as chairman of the committee on healthcare reform
   b) endorsing a plan of government-managed healthcare
   c) signing the new bill into law in early 1994
   d) A and B only

9. The Republican Revolution began in 1994 when _____.
   a) the Republicans took control of the House of Representatives
   b) the Republicans took control of the Senate
   c) Speaker of the House Newt Gingrich led a conservative backlash to Clinton's liberal policies
   d) A, B, and C

10. Welfare Reform in 1996 aimed at all of the following EXCEPT _____.
    a) "reforming welfare as we know it"

b) establishing a 10-year limit for federal payments

c) providing block grants to states to distribute and manage welfare funds under federal guidelines

d) encouraging people to get off of welfare rolls and moving them into jobs and or training

11. In 1994, President Bill Clinton was charged with a sexual harassment lawsuit from Paula Jones. As the lawsuit proceeded in 1997, all of the following are true about events about that lawsuit EXCEPT that _____.

a) it had a major impact on Clinton's re-election campaign in 1996

b) Clinton tried to have the lawsuit dismissed, citing "executive privilege"

c) during the deposition phase of the lawsuit allegations of yet another affair surfaced when the name Monica Lewinsky came up

d) Clinton's popularity with the public remained higher than 50 percent

12. Actions that were the work of the Islamic terrorist organization al-Qaeda included _____.

a) the bombing raids on U.S. embassies in Kenya and Tanzania in 1998

b) Mogadishu, Somalia, in 1993, resulting in 18 American troops being killed

c) the attack on the *USS Cole* in Yemen in 2000

d) A, B, and C

13. One of George W. Bush's plans for reform in 2001 was the _____.

a) No Child Left Behind bill

b) anti-terrorist funding in early 2001

c) passing the Patriot Act in February of 2001

d) creation of a new cabinet level office for homeland security

14. The attacks on September 11, 2001, _____.

a) resulted in two planes crashing into the World Trade Center

b) Flight 93 being forced down in a crash landing in Pennsylvania

c) a plane crash into a wing of the Pentagon

d) A, B, and C

15. All of the following came about as a result of the War on Terrorism EXCEPT _____.

a) the creation of the cabinet level office of Department of Homeland Security

b) the invasion of Afghanistan in the hunt for Osama bin Laden

c) the assassination of Saddam Hussein in Iraq

d) going after the Taliban government that was supporting al-Qaeda

16. During the Iraq invasion in 2003 all of the following groups within Iraq were in conflict with one another EXCEPT for the _____.

a) Kurds   c) residents of Tikrit

b) Shi'ites   d) Suni

17. In 2001, George W. Bush was responsible for declaring _____.

a) "war on terrorism"

b) anyone harboring or supporting terrorism an enemy of the United States

c) that the war was one of "defending freedom"

d) A, B, and C

Matching

a. Hillary Clinton   h. David Souter   o. al-Qaeda

b. Clarence   i. weapons of nass   p. Colin Powell
   Thomas   destruction   q. Janet Reno
c. Ken Starr   j. World Trade Center   r. Clean Air Act
d. ADA   k. NAFTA   (1990)
e. Tom Ridge   l. Timothy McVeigh   s. Condoleezza Rice
f. recession   m. Norman Schwarzkopf   t. Madeline Albright
g. Al Gore   n. Points of Light Foundation u. Bill Clinton

_____18. George H.W. Bush appointed this person to the Supreme Court in 1990

_____19. a downturn in the economy following the Persian Gulf War that hampered George H. W. Bush's re-election campaign in 1992

_____20. carried out the bombing of the federal building in Oklahoma City on April 19, 1995

_____21. Clinton's attorney general

_____22. an act signed into law in 1991 to promote greater accessibility for the handicapped in public buildings and to prohibit discrimination in hiring, transportation, and public accommodations for those with disabilities

_____23. the charge levied against Saddam Hussein as it was widely reported that he had chemical, biological, and possible nuclear weapons in his control and in defiance of UN sanctions

____24. site of a bombing attack when terrorists detonated a bomb in the underground garage of this building in 1993

____25. George W. Bush's national security advisor in his first term in office in 2001

____26. Bush's nominee to the Supreme Court; replaced Thurgood Marshall in 1991

____27. a terrorist organization led by Osama bin Laden that began planning attacks against American interests

____28. the general in charge of the ground troops in Operation Desert Storm

____29. a service organization promoted by George H.W. Bush

____30. Clinton's secretary of state

____31. agreement signed into law by Clinton in 1993 to promote free trade between Canada, the United States and Mexico

____32. the first Democrat since FDR to be reelected president

____33. imposed new government regulations of smog, automobile exhaust, acid rain, and toxic air pollution

____34. first person to fill the cabinet-level post of Department of Homeland Security

____35. chairman of the joint chiefs of staff during Operation Desert Storm in 1991 and secretary of state in 2001

____36. ran for president in 2000 and lost the election in the Electoral College with a 500,000-vote majority in the popular vote

____37. led the Justice Department investigation into the Whitewater Scandal and Paula Jones case

____38. elected senator from New York in 2000

Short Response

39. How did foreign affairs shape the presidency of George H. W. Bush?

40. What is significant about the impeachment of Bill Clinton?

Answers begin on page 305.

Answer Key

Chapter 1 Answers

Multiple Choice

1. **D**	4. **A**	7. **D**	10. **A**	13. **A**	16. **D**
2. **D**	5. **A**	8. **C**	11. **D**	14. **A**	17. **C**
3. **B**	6. **D**	9. **B**	12. **C**	15. **D**	

Matching

18. **E**	21. **F**	24. **Q**	27. **L**	30. **J**	33. **K**
19. **A**	22. **C**	25. **P**	28. **M**	31. **R**	34. **B**
20. **G**	23. **H**	26. **O**	29. **N**	32. **I**	35. **D**

Short Answer

36. Role of the president:
    ▶ Both Lincoln and Johnson felt that the president should be in charge of the Reconstruction efforts.
    ▶ Lincoln favored a lenient plan in order to bring the rebellious states back into the Union as quickly as possible in order to preserve the Union.
    ▶ Johnson was extremely sympathetic to the plight of Southerners, being a Southern Democrat himself.

    Role of Congress:
    ▶ Congress quickly passed the Wade-Davis Bill, which stipulated the active role of Congress in Reconstruction efforts.
    ▶ Congress, under the control of the Radical Republicans, felt that it, not the president, should dictate the terms of reconstruction.
    ▶ Congress overrode a presidential veto in order to pass the Civil Rights Act of 1866.
    ▶ Congress established the Freedmen's Bureau.
    ▶ Congress also worked to pass the 13th, 14th, and 15th amendments.
    ▶ Congress passed the Reconstruction Act of 1867, which established military rule in the South during Reconstruction.

As Reconstruction efforts were underway, the president attempted to remove his secretary of war, Edwin Stanton, from office. This action greatly angered the Radical Republicans in Congress and they began impeachment proceedings for his violation of the Tenure of Office Act. Johnson was impeached by the House, but the Senate failed to remove him from office by one vote. These actions demonstrated the contentious relationship between the president, a Democrat, and the Congressional leadership, dominated by Radical Republicans. Because of the political nature of the Reconstruction efforts and the impeachment proceedings, both groups became distracted in their attempts at Reconstruction.

37. The courts began to narrowly define the provision of equal rights and due process in the 14th Amendment by claiming that those provisions only applied to "national citizenship." This interpretation encouraged state governments to begin enacting their own state/local segregation restrictions on blacks.

   ▶ *Slaughterhouse Cases* (1873) claimed it was the state's right to enact laws allowing the state of Louisiana to create a 25-year monopoly for one company to slaughter livestock.

   ▶ *U.S. v. Cruikshank* (1876) overturned a case in which three men were convicted of violating the civil rights of their victims.

   ▶ *U.S. v. Reese* (1876) gave states the right to legally deny people the right to vote by using nonracial reasons.

   ▶ *Plessy v. Ferguson* (1896) allowed for the concept of "separate but equal" to be applied to public accommodations allowing for segregation.

38. **Restore:** Lincoln sought to preserve the Union (his goal during the Civil War and for Reconstruction) on the grounds he did not believe that secession was possible. He wanted to be lenient on the South and to bring them back into the Union quickly. He proposed a 10 percent plan and pardons. His plans ended with the assassination plot in 1865 that sought to kill not only him, but also the vice president and secretary of state.

   Rebuild: Once the Radical Republicans took over Reconstruction, they wanted to rebuild Southern society and to ensure that the Republican Party would be in place in the South. Congress felt that it should control the process of Reconstruction, which conflicted with the president's view that he should dictate the terms of Reconstruction. Johnson, a Southern Democrat, wanted to be lenient on the South and to restore political power to former Confederate soldiers. He did not believe in civil rights for blacks. This conflicted with the goals of Congress, which put plans into place with the 13th, 14th, and 15th amendments as well as the Civil Rights Act and Reconstruction Act that granted broad civil rights to blacks, established programs to assist them, and amended the constitution to ensure those rights.

   Retreat: Although civil rights were being granted to blacks at the federal level, actions were taking place at the state level in the South to restrict or deny those rights. Black Codes and Jim Crow laws began restricting voting rights and equal use of public accommodations as well as other restrictions on weapons, juries, and other rights. Reconstruction efforts seemed to lose steam after the impeachment proceedings of President Johnson in which the Republicans attempted to remove the Democratic president from office. During President Grant's terms in office his administration was rocked by scandals and an economic crisis. The contested election of 1876 ended up with Hayes being awarded the victory in the presidential election with the agreement that troops would leave the occupied South. Troops left the South, a new Republican president was in place, the Democrat Party was back in power in the South, and black civil rights were being severely limited in a segregated South.

Chapter 2 Answers

Multiple Choice

1. A	4. B	7. D	10. A	13. B	16. D
2. D	5. D	8. C	11. D	14. A	17. B
3. A	6. C	9. D	12. C	15. C	

Matching

18. M	22. E	26. C	30. K	34. J
19. D	23. O	27. L	31. R	35. P
20. G	24. F	28. S	32. B	36. N
21. H	25. A	29. I	33. Q	

Short Answer

37. Land for settlement:
   ▶ Get-rich-quick goals with the discovery of mineral deposits.
   ▶ Moving "out West" meant opportunity.
   ▶ Native Americans were simply in the way of progress.
   ▶ Life of the cowboys on long cattle drives.
   ▶ Many former Confederate soldiers and blacks went West and became cowboys.
   ▶ Beauty of land that was set aside for national parks.
   ▶ Dime novels about characters in the West.
   ▶ Rugged individualism.

38. Rails:
   ▶ Many railroad companies were established.
   ▶ Trade and travel greatly increased.
   ▶ Thousands of miles of track were laid.
   ▶ Immigrant labor was used to construct the transcontinental railroad.
   ▶ Railroad improvements helped standardize and increase travel.
   ▶ Many railroad companies and their owners became rich as others were driven out of business.

   Roundups:
   ▶ Long cattle drives took millions of cattle to market.
   ▶ Barbed wire and climate conditions brought an end to the open range era.
   ▶ Railroads aided greatly in providing transportation to get cattle to markets.
   ▶ The myth of the cowboy leading an "idyllic" life encouraged many.

▸ Trade and travel greatly increased.

▸ Thousands of miles of track were laid.

▸ Immigrant labor was used to construct the transcontinental railroad.

▸ Railroad improvements helped standardize and increase travel.

Reservations:

▸ Native Americans were seen as a threat to progress.

▸ Violence continued to occur.

▸ As some Native Americans were being killed off, others were being forced to relocate to reservations.

▸ Reservation land was most often desolate.

▸ The Dawes Act sought to relocate Native Americans to reservation lands.

▸ Once-nomadic tribes were forced to change their lifestyle by farming and herding. This became increasingly difficult in the barren regions of the reservation territories.

▸ Some Native Americans resisted this change; others surrendered and gave in to the demands of the white man's culture.

▸ Details of the federal government's treatment of Native Americans were published and challenged.

▸ The use of force continued as Native Americans were forced to assimilate into the white society.

Chapter 3 Answers

Multiple Choice

1. **D**	4. **D**	7. **A**	10. **C**	13. **D**	16. **B**
2. **D**	5. **C**	8. **D**	11. **B**	14. **C**	17. **D**
3. **B**	6. **A**	9. **D**	12. **A**	15. **D**	

Matching

18. **C**	22. **M**	26. **B**	30. **N**	34. **P**
19. **E**	23. **J**	27. **H**	31. **R**	35. **O**
20. **I**	24. **A**	28. **F**	32. **S**	36. **Q**
21. **G**	25. **D**	29. **K**	33. **L**	

Short Answer

37. The relationship between business leaders and unions:

▸ Big businesses grew at the expense of labor.

▸ Heads of corporations became extremely wealthy.

▸ Workers endured long hours, low pay, and unsafe conditions.

▸ Workers attempted to join labor unions (NLU, Knights of Labor, AFL, IWW).

▸ Unions resorted to strikes to get businesses to meet their demands.

- Many strikes ended in violence, with workers and policemen often wounded or killed.
- The president resorted to using the army to break up two different railroad strikes.
- Scab labor was hired to replace striking workers, often at lower pay.
- Unions would fight for better wages and better working conditions, including an eight-hour workday.

38. How "big business" shaped the economy:
    - Formation of giant corporations.
    - By the 1890s the United States was the leading industrial nation in the world.
    - One of every three items manufactured worldwide was made in the United States.
    - Dramatic economic growth.
    - Railroads grew dramatically (largest users of coal, largest carriers of goods and people, largest single employer of labor).
    - Technological innovations.
    - Big cities such as New York and Chicago grew as hubs for jobs.
    - Vertical integration (businesses acquiring all the resources they needed to produce and market goods)
    - Horizontal integration (businesses acquired competitors and began minimizing competition)
    - Monopolies were formed.
    - Businesses followed the concept of laissez-faire. They favored minimal government interference in the economic realm (and felt it was best to let businesses regulate themselves).
    - Businesses such as Carnegie Steel and Standard Oil dominated the economy.

39. Growth:
    - America became the leading industrial country in the world by the 1890s.
    - America began exporting a wide range of goods.
    - The population of big cities grew as people moved in search of jobs.
    - Monopolies were formed (for example, Standard Oil).
    - Business growth was largely unregulated (or businesses fought regulations that were trying to be imposed).

    Wealth:
    - Rockefeller and Carnegie became multi-millionaires, the two richest men in America.
    - Some of the wealthy used their money for philanthropy. Rockefeller and Carnegie, for example, both gave away millions for education, research, and so on.
    - The income gap between business leaders and workers widened.
    - Business leaders were referred to as captains of industry and sometimes robber barons.
    - Business leaders often used their wealth to increase the size and scope of their business.

‣ Business leaders would always look for ways to cut costs (labor, materials, production, and marketing) in order to increase their profits.

Challenges:

‣ Unions would try to organize laborers to fight for demands (pay, working conditions, and so on).

‣ Union activity often turned violent and businesses used this against the unions as they struggled for acceptance in the workplace.

‣ Monopolies (Standard Oil and Carnegie Steel, U.S. Steel) forced out competition in a variety of methods.

‣ Business mergers often wiped out other businesses.

‣ The government passed some legislative acts to regulate business practices (Interstate Commerce Act, Sherman Anti-Trust Act), but they were often not strongly enforced or businesses would find ways to get around regulations.

‣ The growth of business activity would set the stage for needed reforms in the early 20th century.

‣ Unions would keep working for the demands of laborers but would not find general acceptance until the 1930s.

Chapter 4 Answers

Multiple Choice

1. D	5. B	9. C	13. A
2. B	6. C	10. D	14. B
3. D	7. D	11. B	15. D
4. D	8. A	12. D	16. C

Matching

17. P	21. D	25. A	29. N	33. M
18. E	22. C	26. R	30. Q	34. I
19. G	23. F	27. L	31. K	35. O
20. J	24. B	28. H	32. S	

Short Answer

36. The political landscape from 1865 to 1900

‣ Weak Republican presidents were mostly elected.

‣ Congress took the lead in setting the political agenda.

‣ Corrupt politics were the rule, especially in New York City with the operations of Tammany Hall and Boss Tweed.

‣ Machine politics in the big cities tended to control local and state politics.

‣ Women still not given the right to vote.

‣ Lots of public participation in national elections (80 percent or better).

‣ The Congress majority was often the opposite party from that of the president.

- "Waving the bloody shirt" was a tactic to get increasing amounts of veterans benefits for aging Civil War veterans who were continuing to decrease in number.
- Third-party politics proved its potential power in the form of from the Populist Party.
- Congress passed protectionist measures through the McKinley Tariff of 1890 that raised the rates of tariffs to protect American business interests.
- The president and Congress were challenged by how they dealt with the Panic of 1893 when Coxey's Army marched on Washington, D.C.
- Presidents used their power to use the military to break up two railroad strikes.
- The government was beginning to pass legislation to control the economy and businesses, but often these measures were not strictly enforced.

37. The impact of consumerism in the late 19th century:
   - New inventions, such as the telephone, lightbulb, cameras, and sewing machines, became available.
   - Brand names of items became important.
   - Advertising played a huge role in marketing items to consumers.
   - New companies were being formed (AT&T, General Electric).
   - Chain stores became popular (A&P, Kroeger).
   - Mail-order catalog business was big (Sears, Montgomery Ward, JC Penney).
   - New products from Quaker Oats, Heinz, Coca-Cola, Armor, Swift, Nabisco, and so on.
   - Patents were being issued for new inventions.
   - Concept of "consumer is always right" developed.
   - New business created jobs, especially in the big cities.

38. Social:
   - Largest influx of immigrants to the United States, averaging around 800,000 per year
   - New immigrants changed the "social fabric" of the nation as Greeks, Slavs, Poles, Russians, Jews and others immigrated to America.
   - New immigrants had different religious beliefs, different levels of education, and different levels of job skills than those considered "old" immigrants.
   - Immigrants came to the country with the dream of a better life.
   - The first image for immigrants entering the county through Ellis Island was that of the Statue of Liberty, the symbol of freedom and democracy.
   - The immigrants endured great hardships to immigrate to America.
   - Many immigrants living in big cities tended to live with cultural groups in those cities.
   - Many poor immigrants ended up living in tenements in the big cities.
   - Many new immigrants made many significant contributions to the United States.
   - Many immigrants tried to preserve family values from the "old country."
   - As immigrants' children were born and raised in the United States they became more "Americanized."

Political:

▶ Although the United States had an open immigration policy, the first major roadblock to immigration was the 1882 Chinese Exclusion Act, which barred Chinese immigrants from entering the country.

▶ The 1907 Gentlemen's Agreement with Japan limited the number of Japanese immigrants to the United States.

▶ The great influx of immigrants, especially from Southern and Eastern Europe, led to the Immigration Act of 1924, aimed at severely limiting numbers of immigrants based on national origin.

▶ Immigrants often fled Europe due to unsettling political situations and persecution there.

Economic:

▶ Originally, Chinese and Irish immigrants were employed in the construction of the transcontinental railroad, which was completed in 1869.

▶ The new immigrants who came to America often had the lowest paid jobs in the workplaces.

▶ Immigrant laborers often faced discrimination in the workplace.

▶ The jobs that the immigrants filled helped fuel America's economic growth in the last part of the 19th century.

Chapter 5 Answers

Multiple Choice

1. C	4. A	7. A	10. A	13. A	16. A
2. C	5. B	8. B	11. B	14. D	17. C
3. D	6. B	9. D	12. B	15. C	

Matching

18. E	21. K	24. B	27. R	30. P	33. U	36. D
19. C	22. G	25. F	28. Q	31. S	34. L	37. N
20. A	23. J	26. I	29. H	32. M	35. O	38. T

Short Answer

39. Factors that shaped late-19th-century U.S. foreign policy:

▶ Turner thesis in 1893 (closing of the frontier).

▶ Acquisition of Midway Island in 1867.

▶ Anti-imperialists did not favor imperialistic policies.

▶ Imperialists sought U.S. dominance overseas.

▶ Jingoes were even willing to go to war if necessary.

▶ Acquisition of Hawaii as a territory in 1898.

▶ Building of a naval base at Pearl Harbor in 1898.

▶ Involvement with war against Spain in Cuba in 1898.

▶ Sinking of the **USS Maine** in the Havana harbor 1898.

- ▶ Imperialism by European nations (United States was behind).
- ▶ United States needed new markets for goods and raw materials.
- ▶ Negotiated the Treaty of Paris 1898 and received Puerto Rico, Guam, and the Philippines as territories.
- ▶ Negotiated the Open Door Policy in China (1901).
- ▶ Sought trade with China.
- ▶ Negotiated with Panama for the construction of a canal that was completed and opened in 1914.
- ▶ Became a "policeman" of the nations in the Western Hemisphere with the Roosevelt Corollary.

40. Major U.S. actions as an imperialistic nation:
    - ▶ Helped remove Queen Liliuokalani from power in Hawaii.
    - ▶ Most Hawaiians did not favor the U.S. actions in Hawaii.
    - ▶ Most Hawaiians did not favor becoming a territory in 1898.
    - ▶ Went to war with Spain over events in Cuba.
    - ▶ Became involved in a civil war in the Philippines after the Spanish American War.
    - ▶ Acquired new territory after the Spanish American war.
    - ▶ The Supreme Court ruled that a U.S. possession was not necessarily granted the process leading to eventual statehood.
    - ▶ Some people challenged the U.S. imperialism on the basis of racism.
    - ▶ In the *Insular Cases*, the Supreme Court ruled in 1901 "that the Constitution did not automatically apply to people in acquired territories" and upheld the right of Congress to establish an inferior status for Puerto Rico as an unincorporated territory without promise of statehood.
    - ▶ A large navy would be required to protect American interests abroad.

41. American foreign policy with regard to *expansion, growth, and power"*:
    - ▶ Prior to the 1890s, had basically limited its U.S. expansion to Alaska and Midway island.
    - ▶ Russia, Japan, and European nations were involved with imperialist pursuits prior to the 1890s.
    - ▶ China had been divided into spheres of influence without a zone for the United States.
    - ▶ Was growing economically and needed new outlets for goods as well as increased natural resources.
    - ▶ Some people saw the U.S. imperialistic goals as an extension of Manifest Destiny.
    - ▶ Some people believed in the White Man's burden—that it was up to the United States to help "regenerate" other less fortunate countries.
    - ▶ With the closing of the frontier and the Oklahoma land rush, land became limited. What could be done for further expansion?
    - ▶ Anti-imperialists criticized the U.S. subjugation of others, saying it violated principles of self-government.

▶ Others questioned whether or not dark-skinned people were worthy of U.S. citizenship.

▶ In 1899, the anti-imperialists had nearly succeeded in preventing the Senate from ratifying the expansionist Treaty of Paris. The forces of imperialism won out, and the Anti-Imperialist League lost whatever strength it might have had.

▶ Began to influence countries in the Caribbean and Central America.

▶ The U.S. victories in wars and negotiations strengthened its dealings with foreign nations.

▶ Some U.S. actions in Latin America were viewed with suspicion by the Latin American nations.

Chapter 6 Answers
Multiple Choice

1. C	4. C	7. D	10. D	13. D	16. B
2. D	5. D	8. C	11. B	14. A	17. D
3. C	6. A	9. D	12. C	15. C	

Matching

18. H	22. O	26. Q	30. B	34. V	38. F
19. M	23. E	27. U	31. L	35. T	39. W
20. R	24. J	28. C	32. X	36. P	40. S
21. K	25. A	29. I	33. N	37. D	41. G

Short Answer

42. Strengths and weaknesses of the Progressive Movement:

Strengths

▶ Involvement of a cross-section of society (men/women, Democrat/Republican/ Socialist, wealthy/middle class/laborers).

▶ Local, state, and federal government agencies were seen as allies in bringing about reform efforts.

▶ The reform efforts targeted many of the abuses brought about during the Gilded Age.

▶ New laws were enacted to protect workers, make buildings safer, protect food, change business practices, and so on.

▶ Constitutional amendments targeted reform by banning alcohol (18th Amendment) and granting suffrage to women (19th Amendment).

▶ Presidents, both Republican and Democrat, were taking an active role in establishing policy agendas targeting reform.

▶ The media, with the work of the muckrakers, became an important tool of communicating the need for reform.

▶ Strikes and marches were used as powerful tools of labor unions to get their message of reform out to the general public.

▶ New laws were enacted to combat abuses.

▶ Monopolies were being attacked and forced to break up.

Weaknesses

▶ Anti-union actions still tried to prevent workers from joining unions.

▶ Black civil rights failed to be adequately addressed during this time.

▶ Most of the Progressive Movement measures lost steam with the involvement of the United States in World War I in 1917.

▶ Race riots and lynchings continued to increase (Oklahoma City, Rosewood, and so on).

▶ Failure of anti-lynching legislation to be passed.

43. Role of the presidents during the Progressive Era:

▶ Presidential agendas focused on progressive reform measures.

▶ Presidents were seen as taking an active role in setting these agendas.

▶ Roosevelt was seen as a "trust-buster."

▶ Reforms involved both domestic and foreign issues.

▶ New laws were enacted to bring about reform.

▶ Both Republicans and Democrats focused on issues of reform.

▶ Roosevelt began the image of an "active president" in establishing an agenda.

▶ Presidents were active in attacking monopolies, signing new laws, pushing for legislative measures, and so on.

▶ Presidents were seen as an ally of reform efforts during this time.

▶ Presidents generally wanted the United States to take a leading role in foreign affairs.

44. Reform:

▶ A variety of new laws were enacted.

▶ A cross-section of people (men/women, Democrat/Republican/Socialist, white/black, wealthy/middle class/laborers) were involved with the reform movement.

▶ The new laws made viable changes in the workplace, with people's rights, the Constitution, and so on.

▶ The reform measures sought to bring about lasting change.

Remake:

▶ The new laws sought to bring about a measure of equality.

▶ The new laws affirmed the involvement of government, especially at the state and federal levels.

▶ The new foreign affairs proposals sought to reshape American involvement with foreign countries.

▶ The new regulations attempted to regulate unfair business practices.

Revolutionize:

▶ A variety of new laws were enacted.

▶ A cross-section of people (men/women, Democrat/Republican/Socialist, white/black, wealthy/middle class/laborers) were involved in the reform movement and would set the stage for future changes.

- The new laws made viable changes in the workplace, with people's rights, the Constitution, and so forth, by specifically granting rights to people and protecting those rights.

- New regulations sought to protect people and the environment.

- New political agendas sought to reshape America's involvement in foreign affairs by having the country take an active role in shaping policy.

- The Progressive Era was marked by optimism—that change could actually happen and that people's lives could be made better by taking action in various areas.

Chapter 7 Answers

Multiple Choice

1. C	4. A	7. D	10. D	13. D	16. D
2. B	5. B	8. C	11. A	14. A	17. D
3. D	6. D	9. D	12. A	15. A	

Matching

18. N	21. O	24. K	27. G	30. S	33. J	36. B
19. D	22. E	25. Q	28. L	31. U	34. C	37. H
20. T	23. R	26. I	29. F	32. A	35. M	38. P

Short Answer

39. U.S. neutrality-turned-involvement in World War I:
    - Proclaimed neutrality in 1914.
    - Continued to trade with both Allied and Central Powers.
    - Carnegie donated $10 million to organize a Peace Fund to keep the United States out of war.
    - Remained neutral even after the attack on the *Lusitania* in 1915.
    - Wilson campaigned in 1916 on the platform of "he kept us out of war."
    - Began to be swayed by allied propaganda.
    - The Zimmerman telegram in 1917 greatly outraged the United States.
    - In March 1917, Germany resumed unrestricted submarine warfare.
    - On April 2, 1917, Wilson asked congress for a declaration of war.
    - Wilson's 14 Points was a possible way to end the conflict in Europe.
    - Wilson personally went to Europe to negotiate the Treaty of Versailles.
    - Following the rejection of the Treaty of Versailles in the Senate, the United States retreated into isolationism in the 1920s.

40. Americans' reaction to dissent and suspicion:
    - During World War I propaganda played a huge role in swaying U.S. public sentiment against the Germans and anything related to Germans during the war.
    - New laws were enacted (Espionage Act, Sedition Act) to attack anyone or any group speaking out against the war, the government, its policies, or its leaders.

- ▸ Propaganda in the forms of posters, music, and so forth began to be used to promote a pro-war image.
- ▸ Because of the fear of communism in Russia, many feared communism at home in America.
- ▸ They reacted quickly against any person or group that was seen as a threat to the United States.
- ▸ Sacco and Vanzetti, Italian anarchist immigrants, were arrested for suspected crimes ad given the death penalty.
- ▸ Attorney General Palmer began a series of raids aimed at rooting out any subversive activity. More than 4,000 arrests were made, and more than 500 people were deported from the country following the 1920 raids.

41. U.S. role on the world stage after World War I:
    - ▸ Wilson's idealism led him to ask Congress for a declaration of war in April 1917 to "make the world safe for democracy."
    - ▸ The United States had some limited involvement on the world stage during the era of imperialism but was not considered a leading world power.
    - ▸ The war at the beginning was perceived as another European conflict "over there."
    - ▸ Wilson proposed his 14 Points: his plans on how to resolve the conflict in Europe and prevent war from happening again.
    - ▸ Wilson saw the League of Nations as the best way to prevent future conflicts.
    - ▸ Wilson, a Democrat and a progressive reformer, was at odds with a Republican Congress, especially the Republicans in the Senate.
    - ▸ Wilson went on a trip across the country in 1919 to promote the ratification of the treaty and the U.S. involvement in the League of Nations (on this trip, he suffered a stroke).
    - ▸ The Senate defeated Wilson's plans when it did not ratify the in the Treaty of Versailles.
    - ▸ Following the defeat of the treaty the United States retreated into isolationism and in the 1920 election looked for a candidate to return the country to a sense of "normalcy."

Chapter 8 Answers

Multiple Choice

1. D	4. D	7. B	10. B	13. D	16. C
2. D	5. D	8. C	11. B	14. C	17. D
3. A	6. D	9. A	12. D	15. B	

Matching

18. G	21. H	24. R	27. F	30. K	33. D	36. U
19. M	22. J	25. A	28. Q	31. L	34. B	37. T
20. I	23. S	26. P	29. O	32. N	35. C	38. E

Short Answer

39. Isolationism and 1920s foreign policy:
   ▶ People wanted to forget about the horrors of war.
   ▶ The 1920 campaign promised a return to "normalcy."
   ▶ Although a policy of isolationism was pursued, the United States took limited involvement with various measures seen as an attempt to maintain peace and prevent future conflict of war from occurring.
   ▶ The United States favored a reduction in German war reparations.
   ▶ The United States signed a naval-reduction pact.
   ▶ The United States signed an agreement with 13 other nations outlawing the use of war as a means of resolving international conflicts.

40. Effect of Republican policies on the 1920s economy/comparisons between the economic policies of the 1920s and the Gilded Age:
   (Note: You may want to refer back to chapter 3 and 4 to review the Gilded Age business practices.)
   ▶ Presidents were Republican during the 1920s.
   ▶ Presidents during the Gilded Age were generally Republican.
   ▶ Presidents during the 1920s pursued policies that were pro-business in nature.
   ▶ Presidents during the 1920s favored policies that had minimal government interference in the economy.
   ▶ Presidents during the Gilded Age generally pursued policies of "laissez-faire" (government non-interference).
   ▶ Although Gilded Age presidents signed legislative acts aimed at controlling business actions, the measures were often not strictly enforced.
   ▶ Businesses grew dramatically during the Gilded Age as well as in the 1920s.
   ▶ Businesses in the Gilded Age and the 1920s had few regulations imposed on them; they were left to largely regulate themselves.

41. Influences of Harlem and Hollywood on 1920s culture:
   ▶ Jazz music that came out of the Harlem Renaissance movement was widely popular in nightclubs and radio programs.
   ▶ Jazz appealed to a cross-section of American society.
   ▶ Movies and the actors had great appeal to audiences across the nation.
   ▶ People became very interested in the personal lives of the actors.
   ▶ The number of radio stations and movie studios increased during this decade.
   ▶ People from all parts of the country began to share in the same movies and music, helping to create a "national culture."

42. American lifestyle and *Fords, flappers, and fanatics*
   ▶ The automobile proved increasingly popular (production increased, sales increased, competition increased, prices dropped).
   ▶ Flappers became the symbol of the Twenties with their radical hairstyle (bobbed or short hair), shorter dress lengths that revealed more "skin," and involvement in dance crazes. They sought to do things they thought modern women should be doing.

> Fanatics were part of the Twenties lifestyle: KKK membership dramatically increased to nearly 5 million, people fought against the teaching of evolution in schools, people bought stock on margin by speculative buying in the stock market, people went to speakeasies to consume alcohol, gang violence increased, and people began to elevate people to "hero" status and follow their lives.

Chapter 9 Answers

Multiple Choice

1. A	4. D	7. B	10. D	13. C	16. D
2. D	5. C	8. C	11. D	14. B	17. C
3. D	6. D	9. A	12. D	15. A	

Matching

18. E	22. C	26. V	30. P	34. L	38. R
19. N	23. G	27. S	31. H	35. M	39. J
20. B	24. A	28. I	32. Q	36. O	
21. D	25. K	29. F	33. T	37. U	

Short Answer

40. Role of the federal government and the Great Depression:
> The federal government began slowly to get more involved with assisting businesses under Hoover.

> During Hoover's administration, the federal government still resisted direct assistance to people.

> During Hoover's administration, it was still the goal of the federal government to have people rely mainly on the local and state governments for assistance. It was not the role of the federal government to offer assistance directly to people.

> Late in his term, Hoover began to support the concept of assistance from the federal government in order to ease the effects of the Depression, but it is often viewed as "too little, too late."

> FDR greatly changed the role of the federal government by getting it directly involved in the lives of people.

> FDR helped create programs that put people back to work.

> FDR used deficit spending in order to get the economy going again.

> FDR realized that drastic measures were needed in order to deal with the crisis.

> FDR was able to restore hope back into lives of millions of Americans.

> Many of the FDR's programs, CCC, PWA, WPA, FDIC, Social Security, and TVA, had long-lasting effects.

> Many of the programs sponsored by FDR improved the quality of life.

> Although massive amounts of money were invested into New Deal programs they failed to fully end the effects of the Great Depression.

> World War II brought a final end to the 12 years of the Great Depression.

41. Hoover's and FDR's solutions with regard to *hardship, hunger, and hope*:
   ▸ Within a few weeks of the Depression unemployment rose and would continue to rise until its peak in 1932.
   ▸ By 1932 the unemployment rate was 25 percent.
   ▸ Businesses and banks were failing.
   ▸ Despite the assistance of New Deal programs unemployment rose again in 1937, sparking new fears.
   ▸ Despite the numerous New Deal programs, unemployment averaged about 17 percent for the entire decade of the 1930s.
   ▸ Soup kitchens and bread lines were common sights in the early years of the Depression.
   ▸ Hoover's response to people initially at the outset of the Depression was simply that "hope is just around the corner."
   ▸ Hoovervilles began springing up in many communities.
   ▸ FDR used his inaugural address and fireside chats to instill hope in people.
   ▸ Eleanor Roosevelt traveled for FDR and spoke to people in various places of the country.
   ▸ FDR used New Deal programs to create jobs for Americans.
   ▸ FDR also created the Social Security program to offer assistance to the elderly and needy.
   ▸ FDR called for a bank holiday, during which he developed the Emergency Banking Relief Act that would allow banks to reopen with federal support.
   ▸ Programs such as the TVA reached out to provide assistance to some of the people hit hardest by the Depression.
   ▸ Many of the New Deal programs provided jobs to put people to work.

42. New Deal relief programs and *recovery, reform, and relief*:
   Recovery:
   ▸ Although billions of dollars were spent on programs, the effects of the Depression still lingered at the end of the decade.
   ▸ Unemployment reached a record 25 percent by 1932 and began to decline with New Deal programs.
   ▸ Although unemployment went down, it spiked again in 1937.
   ▸ The Supreme Court challenged many of FDR's programs.
   ▸ Others challenged FDR's programs as not doing enough to help people (Long, Coughlin, Townsend).
   Reform:
   ▸ Government began playing a big role in people's daily lives.
   ▸ The Social Security Act provided government assistance to the elderly in the form of a monthly pension.
   ▸ Various New Deal programs provided jobs that helped rebuild and revitalize the infrastructure of the country.
   ▸ Hoover's attempts were deemed too little, too late.
   ▸ World War I finally ended the Depression.

▸ Blacks switched their allegiance as a bloc of voters by beginning to vote Democrat in 1936.

▸ FDR attempted to alter the makeup of the Supreme Court by adding more members who would be more sympathetic to his reform efforts.

▸ The banking system received assistance from the FDIC.

▸ Safeguards were placed on the stock market.

Relief:

▸ Millions were provided jobs.

▸ As more people began working and earning wages they could again afford to buy food and other items to help the economy get going again.

▸ FDR encouraged people via the radio in fireside chats.

▸ Eleanor Roosevelt expanded her role as first lady as a "diplomat" for the president in promoting the programs to various people.

▸ FDR and Eleanor Roosevelt listened to people and read their letters; people were encouraged by this personal touch.

▸ The programs did provide various forms of relief for jobs, money, and so forth.

43. People's responses to the effects of the Great Depression:

▸ They looked to the federal government for help.

▸ They turned to local and state government agencies for assistance.

▸ They turned to soup kitchens and bread lines.

▸ They sold apples from street corners.

▸ They turned to entertainment as a means of escape. Movies, games, and radio programs became increasingly popular.

▸ People in some of the most severely effected regions simply had to move to find jobs, new homes, and so forth.

▸ Some poor people had to live in Hoovervilles.

▸ Money was tight. People did not trust the banks and they had little to spend. (When they did have money to spend, they were very frugal in their spending.)

▸ Dorothea Lange's photographs showed the impact of the Depression in the lives of ordinary people.

▸ John Steinbeck portrayed a "slice of life" look at the effects of the Depression in his novel The *Grapes of Wrath*.

▸ People voted in large numbers and demonstrated their support for FDR by electing him to four terms in office.

Chapter 10 Answers

Multiple Choice

1. A	4. C	7. B	10. D	13. B	16. D
2. D	5. A	8. D	11. D	14. C	17. C
3. D	6. D	9. B	12. A	15. D	

Matching

18. C	22. U	26. P	30. T	34. M	38. X
19. O	23. G	27. L	31. A	35. H	39. S
20. J	24. B	28. Q	32. K	36. E	40. W
21. I	25. D	29. V	33. F	37. R	41. N

Short Answer

42. Effects of World War II:

On women:

▶ More than 400,000 participated in women's auxiliary military groups (WACS, WAVES, WASPS, SPARS).

▶ Women served in numerous non-combat roles.

▶ Women filled jobs that were traditionally filled by men.

▶ More than one-third of government jobs and aircraft jobs were filled by women.

▶ Women gained a measure of respect in the workplace, but they still dealt with discrimination.

▶ Women earned less than men.

On blacks:

▶ Tuskegee Airmen demonstrated their bravery and skill in air combat.

▶ Blacks worked in numerous jobs that were created by the wartime effort but still faced discrimination in the workplace.

▶ Black units were still segregated in the military in World War II.

On Japanese:

▶ Japanese attacked Americans at Pearl Harbor.

▶ More than 120,000 Japanese Americans were relocated to internment camps under Executive Order 9066 in 1942.

▶ Fred Korematsu, a Japanese American, challenged the internment policy and lost his court case at the Supreme Court.

▶ Japanese captured more than 76,000 Americans on the Bataan Peninsula in the Philippines.

▶ The United States dropped two atomic bombs on Hiroshima and Nagasaki in August 1945.

▶ The United States occupied Japan after the war and rebuilt the government and economy of the country.

43. Roles of *apathy, appeasement, and aggression* in World War II:

Apathy:

▶ The United States ignored the aggression in Europe in the 1930s.

▶ The United States passed Neutrality Acts to remain out of the conflict in Europe.

▶ The United States, Britain, and France followed a policy of isolationism in the 1930s.

▶ Britain and France negotiated with Hitler and under the policy of appeasement. They gave in to Hitler's demands for territory in 1938.

▶ The United States basically ignored the ominous threats of the Japanese before December 7, 1941, and the attack at Pearl Harbor.

▸ Although neutral, the United States began the lend-lease agreement with Britain in 1941.

Appeasement:

▸ Britain and France wanted to avoid another war.

▸ Britain and France felt that if they gave in to the demands of Hitler that they could prevent any further aggression by Hitler.

▸ The actions of this policy only encouraged Hitler to pursue more territory and aggressive actions in 1939 leading up to the invasion of Poland in September 1939. (This policy failed miserably.)

▸ The League of Nations was weak and ineffective in dealing with Germany, Italy, and Japan.

Aggression:

▸ Hitler controlled Austria, Czechoslovakia, Netherlands, Belgium, Denmark, and northern France by 1940.

▸ Hitler began a two-front attack by attacking the countries of Britain and Russia.

▸ This two-front war again forced Germany to divide its troops and war materials.

▸ The Japanese attacked the United States in a surprise attack on December 7, 1941.

▸ The Japanese were fierce fighters in the Pacific.

▸ The United States retaliated against the Japanese on December 8, 1941 by declaring war on Japan.

▸ The United States began the secret Manhattan Project to develop an atomic bomb.

▸ The United States dropped bombs on Hiroshima and Nagasaki in 1945.

▸ The United States emerged victorious from World War II.

▸ Russia began secretly making plans for the occupied regions of Eastern Europe that were under its control by 1945.

44. U.S. role in establishing post-war terms of peace:

▸ The United States participated in conferences with the Allies during the war at Tehran, Yalta, and Potsdam.

▸ FDR took an active role in leading the United States in the war.

▸ The United States helped create the United Nations, with its headquarters to be established in New York City.

▸ The United States used the atomic bombs in order to get an unconditional surrender from Japan and to intimidate the Russians.

▸ The United States took the lead in making postwar plans with dividing Germany.

▸ The United States took the lead in reorganizing the country of Japan.

▸ The strong stance that the United States was taking with postwar actions ended U.S. isolationism.

▸ The United States took the lead in the Nuremberg trials that brought Nazi war criminals to trial for the horrors of the Holocaust and "crimes against humanity."

▸ The U.S. use of the atomic bomb began the era of the Cold War with increasing tensions building between the Untied States and Russia.

▸ With the use of the atomic bomb in 1945 the United States became a superpower.

Chapter 11 Answers

Multiple Choice

1. **B**	5. **B**	9. **D**	13. **D**	17. **B**
2. **D**	6. **C**	10. **C**	14. **D**	18. **A**
3. **B**	7. **C**	11. **D**	15. **B**	19. **B**
4. **D**	8. **A**	12. **D**	16. **C**	

Matching

20. **N**	24. **U**	28. **S**	32. **K**	36. **H**	40. **A**
21. **G**	25. **B**	29. **V**	33. **I**	37. **O**	41. **X**
22. **F**	26. **P**	30. **L**	34. **E**	38. **M**	42. **R**
23. **D**	27. **J**	31. **Q**	35. **C**	39. **W**	43. **T**

Short Answer

44. Influence of U.S.-USSR mistrust on U.S. foreign policy early in the Cold War:
   ‣ Soviets began influencing events in Eastern European countries.
   ‣ Eastern European countries became known as "satellite countries" of the USSR.
   ‣ Winston Churchill warned of an "iron curtain" that had descended upon Europe.
   ‣ The United States was the only country with nuclear weapons and technology in 1945.
   ‣ The Soviets succeeded in testing their nuclear weapon in 1949.
   ‣ The United States feared that the Soviets were out to spread communism over the entire world and that it had to combat that goal.
   ‣ Very little formal communication was done between the two countries early in the conflict. It was more akin to a chess match, with moves and counter-moves.
   ‣ The United States began to expand its nuclear weaponry with bigger bombs, and the Soviets did the same thing.
   ‣ The United States and Soviets began to pour massive amounts of money into military spending.
   ‣ The United States and USSR were involved with moves and counter-moves in Greece, Turkey, Germany, Korea, Vietnam, and Cuba.
   ‣ The race for superiority between the two nations led to the space race, beginning in 1957 with the successful launching of *Sputnik*.
   ‣ NATO and the Warsaw Pact alliance were established.

45. Effect on the U.S. home front with respect to *fears, sympathizers, and threats* (1945–60):
   Fears:
   ‣ The Red Scare.
   ‣ McCarthyism.
   ‣ Communist sympathizers in the government, education field, and Hollywood.

- Those who opposed Senator McCarthy were labeled as communist sympathizers.
- Establishment of loyalty boards.
- Creation of the HUAC to investigate communist infiltration.
- Feared of communism and what it might to do to people's way of life.
- The Rosenburgs, Klaus Fuchs, and the Alger Hiss cases highlighted the scare of communism.

Sympathizers:
- People did not want to be seen or associated with anyone who might appear sympathetic toward communists.
- You could be branded a communist sympathizer for failing to name names of people you knew who might be suspected of communist activities.
- The Hollywood 10 and others in Hollywood were blacklisted for their failure to cooperate and name names.
- No one wanted to appear to be soft on communist and communism.

Threats:
- People such as Nixon and McCarthy were on the forefront attacking the communist threat.
- Arthur Miller wanted people to think about what was happening in the country by relating events of the 1950s to the hysteria of the Salem Witchcraft Trials.
- The Soviet development of a nuclear weapon by 1949 led to the dramatic increase of more and bigger nuclear weapons during the 1950s.
- The United States wanted to be proactive in stopping the advance of Soviet aggression in Europe and Asia.
- The United States felt threatened by the ICBM and *Sputnik*.
- The USSR felt threatened by the U-2 spy plane incident.
- Both the United States and USSR felt threatened by the advance of bigger and more powerful nuclear weapons.

46. Effectiveness of U.S. policy of containment in:
Turkey and Greece:
- The Truman Doctrine of containment attempted to "prevent the spread" of communism.
- Required an increase in military spending and financial support to the region.

Korea:
- North Korea invaded South Korea in 1950; South Korea appealed to the UN for assistance.
- UN response was a "police action" to fight back against the communist invasion.
- A war lasted for nearly three years and ended with a cease-fire agreement, not a formal declaration.
- Tensions still exist between the two nations.

Vietnam:
- The U.S. began to be involved in 1954 when the Geneva Accords divided the region into North and South Vietnam.

▶ Elections were planned but canceled.

▶ The fear was that communist North Vietnam was out to overtake democratic South Vietnam.

▶ The United States began sending over military advisers and began to support the leadership in the South.

Berlin:

▶ Germany and Berlin were divided into four zones following the end of World War II.

▶ Britain, France, and the United States combined their German zones and formed the new country of West Germany and West Berlin.

▶ Berlin became a divided city.

▶ The Soviet zone became East Germany.

▶ The Soviets blockaded Berlin in 1948; the United States countered with a massive 11-month airlift.

▶ The blockade ended in 1949 when the Soviets called an end to the actions.

Chapter 12 Answers

Multiple Choice

1. D	3. C	5. B	7. D	9. B	11. D
2. D	4. A	6. A	8. D	10. D	12. C

Matching

13. L	15. E	17. K	19. C	21. D	23. H	25. M
14. A	16. F	18. B	20. J	22. G	24. I	

Short Answer

26. 1950s *happy days* influence on the U.S. role as a superpower:

▶ Big cities grew.

▶ Suburbs began to grow; Levitt homes were built in many areas.

▶ Inner cities began to struggle with "white flight," as whites moved to the suburbs, leaving behind large groups of mostly poor minorities in the inner city.

▶ Family life grew as the birth rate gave way to the baby boom generation.

▶ Family values became important in the 1950s.

▶ Although there was a lot of prosperity in the 1950s, 20 percent of the population in America still lived below the poverty level.

▶ Evangelists were widely popular, with their gospel messages being delivered in large stadiums and on television.

▶ Church attendance increased.

▶ Programs and pamphlets were developed to educate the public about how to react to the threat of nuclear weapons.

▶ Federal spending was increased as one way to combat Soviet Aggression.

27. Post–World War II domestic challenges:
   ‣ Truman sought to extend the New Deal programs began by FDR.
   ‣ Many conservatives in Congress opposed many of Truman's ideas as "too liberal."
   ‣ Both Truman and Eisenhower attempted to rely on the power of the federal government for a wide variety of programs.
   ‣ Truman and Eisenhower both dealt with foreign and domestic concerns during their presidencies.
   ‣ The threat of the spread of communism was a motivating factor behind government programs, government spending, and so forth.
   ‣ Truman and Eisenhower both appeared to be strong and forceful in their dealing with Soviet aggression.
   ‣ Truman and Eisenhower both wanted to preserve and increase the economic strength of the United States.
   ‣ Education efforts were seen as vital to economic recovery and stability.
   ‣ Both presidents relied on massive amounts of government spending for domestic and foreign programs.
   ‣ The government continued to play a large role in the lives of Americans (a trend that began with FDR and the New Deal program during the Great Depression).

Chapter 13 Answers
Multiple Choice

1. **D**	4. **D**	7. **A**	10. **B**	13. **D**	16. **B**
2. **B**	5. **C**	8. **D**	11. **D**	14. **D**	17. **D**
3. **A**	6. **D**	9. **D**	12. **A**	15. **D**	

Matching

18. **G**	21. **H**	24. **D**	27. **B**	30. **A**	33. **C**	36. **P**
19. **I**	22. **S**	25. **E**	28. **O**	31. **R**	34. **L**	37. **K**
20. **U**	23. **M**	26. **N**	29. **F**	32. **T**	35. **Q**	38. **J**

Short Answer
39. Federal government's role in the 1950s and 1960s Civil Rights struggle:
   ‣ The Civil Rights Acts of 1957 and 1960 were enacted during Eisenhower's administration.
   ‣ Eisenhower ordered National Guard troops to Central High School (Little Rock, Arkansas) in 1957.
   ‣ JFK was ready to send civil rights legislation to congress in 1963.
   ‣ LBJ signed the Civil Rights Acts of 1964 and 1965 into law.
   ‣ The 24th Amendment was passed, banning poll taxes.
   ‣ Black voting rights were secured and more blacks registered to vote.

▶ The Supreme Court ruled in favor of integration in the 1954 *Brown* case.

▶ Although slow to react initially, the federal government could no longer sit back and not take action.

40. The Civil Rights movement and its goals/leaders' success:

▶ Boycotts, sit-ins, marches, and protests achieved measures of success.

▶ Schools, buses, lunch counters, and so on were all integrated.

▶ New laws were enacted to ensure integration.

▶ People from all parts of the country were witnesses to various events either in person or on television.

▶ Whites participated with blacks in several marches, demonstrations, bus rides, and so forth.

▶ Nonviolent measures worked in bringing about lasting change (bus boycott, sit-ins).

▶ MLK and other leaders promoted the continued use of non-violent measures to achieve civil rights.

▶ Other black leaders, such as Malcolm X, became dissatisfied with the rate of civil rights actions and promoted the use of violence to achieve immediate rights and demands.

▶ Several deaths (children, marchers, bus riders, committee members) heightened awareness in the Civil Rights movement.

▶ Progress was being made in the movement, but the 1968 assassination of MLK threw the movement into disarray.

41. Role of the media in the Civil Rights movement:

▶ The media wrote about and televised violent events, powerful tools in the movement.

▶ Pictures often showed calm black students and protestors and violent reactions by whites.

▶ Televised reports about bus bombings, violence in a children's march, and so forth sparked outrage in the general public.

▶ Media reports helped focus attention on the Civil Rights movement.

▶ Reports about the March on Washington in 1963 and MLK's "I Have a Dream Speech" were broadcast across the nation.

Chapter 14 Answers

Multiple Choice

1. A	4. B	7. B	10. D	13. C
2. D	5. A	8. B	11. A	14. A
3. A	6. D	9. D	12. A	15. B

Matching

16. C	20. R	24. D	28. V	32. T	36. Q
17. K	21. E	25. B	29. J	33. S	37. N
18. A	22. I	26. L	30. G	34. P	
19. H	23. M	27. F	31. U	35. O	

Short Answer

38. U.S. achievement of objectives in Vietnam:
    - ▶ JFK and LBJ sent military advisors to Vietnam.
    - ▶ Policy was partially based on Eisenhower's domino theory that stated if one country fell to communism, all would fall.
    - ▶ At first, support for the conflict in Vietnam was popular.
    - ▶ The war in Vietnam was basically ignored by the media, but, once reports began, they conveyed strong patriotic support.
    - ▶ As media coverage continued, the public opinion began to turn against the war.
    - ▶ Politicians and advisors began voicing their discontent with the war effort.
    - ▶ LBJ declined to run for re-election in 1968, becoming a causality of the war himself.
    - ▶ Nixon claimed to have a secret plan to end the war. (This was later proven false.)
    - ▶ After Tet and My Lai, public support for the war dramatically declined.
    - ▶ Peace talks were being held between the U.S. and North Vietnam all the while bombing raids were continuing.
    - ▶ In 1973, the United States withdrew its troops in an attempt at "peace with honor."

39. 1968 is often viewed as a turning point in the nation's history:
    - ▶ The 1968 presidential campaign was thrown into chaos when LBJ declined to run on the Democratic ticket.
    - ▶ Protests broke out over the country during the summer of 1968 over civil rights and the war in Vietnam.
    - ▶ The Tet offensive in January caught American troops and the American public off guard. Even though the United States repelled enemy forces, it still "lost the battle" in the hearts and minds of people back home.
    - ▶ The My Lai massacre in March, which involved the killing of innocent women and children, added to the anti-war sentiment at home.
    - ▶ Martin Luther King, Jr., was assassinated in April.
    - ▶ Robert Kennedy was assassinated in June.

40. Influence of the antiwar movement on policy in Vietnam:
    - ▶ The hippies and counterculture movement used a variety of means to voice their opposition to the war.
    - ▶ Members of the clergy and politicians began voicing their opposition to the war.
    - ▶ LBJ fired his secretary of defense for his lack of support for the war in Vietnam.
    - ▶ The chairman of the Senate Foreign Relations Committee voiced his opposition to the war strategy in Vietnam.
    - ▶ Students at Kent State University and other colleges began protesting the war.
    - ▶ The 1968 and 1972 elections focused heavily on the war in Vietnam.
    - ▶ The war in Vietnam began having a negative impact on the U.S. economy, as resources were drained from other programs in order to finance the war effort, leading to spiraling inflation in the 1970s.
    - ▶ Peace talks began in order to secure "peace with honor" and a U.S. withdrawal from Vietnam.

Chapter 15 Answers
Multiple Choice

1. D	4. B	7. D	10. B	13. C	16. D
2. B	5. D	8. C	11. D	14. D	17. B
3. D	6. D	9. C	12. C	15. C	

Matching

18. C	22. H	26. K	30. G	34. S	38. P
19. A	23. D	27. O	31. I	35. V	39. R
20. U	24. L	28. M	32. Q	36. W	40. T
21. F	25. B	29. J	33. E	37. N	

Short Answer

41. Importance of presidential power in the Watergate scandal:
    ▶ President Nixon ordered the break-in and the cover-up.
    ▶ Nixon denied that anyone on his staff was involved with the break-in.
    ▶ Nixon used money from his campaign (CREEP) to pay off those involved with the break-in.
    ▶ The closer the investigation got to the Oval Office, the more defiant Nixon became.
    ▶ He cited the use of executive privilege in order to avoid turning over taped recorded messages that would implicate him in the scandal.
    ▶ Nixon tried to obstruct the investigation. This abuse of power led the House to draw up three articles of impeachment against him in 1974.
    ▶ Nixon lost his court case with the Supreme Court when it ruled on August 4, 1974, that he must turn over the tapes. (The 28 minutes of "missing tape" that implicated him in the scandal.)
    ▶ Nixon resigned from office on August 9, 1974.

42. Iran hostage crisis and the Carter presidency:
    ▶ Carter was already dealing with the Soviet invasion into Afghanistan when the problems with Iran began.
    ▶ The new regime in Iran held a fierce hatred toward the West, especially the Untied States.
    ▶ Carter's diplomatic attempts to resolve the crisis failed.
    ▶ The rescue attempt failed.
    ▶ Carter worked on gaining the release of the hostages up to the last minutes of his presidency.
    ▶ The Iranians finally released the hostages only after Carter left office and Reagan was sworn in.
    ▶ The nation and the president followed daily development from the television reports on *Nightline*. Ted Koppel numbered the days of the crisis at the beginning of each day's reporting.

43. The Reagan presidency and the 1980s:
    ▸ The country had just finished with the Iran Hostage crisis in January 1981.
    ▸ Reagan survived an assassination attempt in March 1981.
    ▸ Reagan began his program of Reaganomics to sponsor tax cuts to stimulate the economy.
    ▸ Reagan took a tough stance on the Soviets and insisted that Gorbachev tear down the Berlin Wall.
    ▸ Despite the tough stance and rhetoric against the Soviets, Reagan and Gorbachev began a series of summit talks that would open the way for the end of the Cold War during the Bush presidency.
    ▸ Reagan gained the nickname "the great communicator."
    ▸ Reagan's conservative views shaped his presidency.
    ▸ Reagan was an extremely popular president and easily won re-election in 1984.

Chapter 16 Answers

Multiple Choice

1. C	4. B	7. B	10. B	13. A	16. C
2. D	5. D	8. D	11. B	14. D	17. D
3. D	6. A	9. D	12. D	15. C	

Matching

18. H	21. Q	24. J	27. O	30. T	33. R	36. G
19. F	22. D	25. S	28. M	31. K	34. E	37. C
20. L	23. I	26. B	29. N	32. U	35. P	38. A

Short Answer

39. Foreign affairs and the presidency of George H. W. Bush:
    ▸ Continuing summit meetings with Gorbachev that began with Reagan and Gorbachev.
    ▸ The fall of the Berlin Wall in November 1989 and the reunification of Germany in 1990.
    ▸ Seeing the end of the Cold War with the demise of the USSR and the end of communism by December 31, 1991.
    ▸ Seeing democracy spread through Eastern Europe.
    ▸ Persian Gulf War – Operation Desert Shield and Operation Desert Storm to free Kuwait from the Iraq invasion in August 1990.
    ▸ Extreme popularity at home for his dealing with the Persian Gulf War in 1991.
    ▸ Popularity began to decline with the onset of a recession.

40. Significant of Clinton's impeachment:
    ▸ The issue of the affair with Monica Lewinsky came about during a deposition in 1997 about the Paula Jones sexual harassment case.

- ▶ January 1998 denied having 'sexual relations with that woman."
- ▶ August 1998 declared to the American public he had made an error in judgment.
- ▶ December 19, 1998: the House settled on two articles of impeachment against Clinton—perjury and attempting to obstruct justice.
- ▶ Clinton became only the second president in U.S. history to be impeached (Andrew Johnson in 1867; remember, Nixon resigned before he could be impeached).
- ▶ The test for impeachment in the constitution is "high crimes and misdemeanors" – it gives no definition as to "high crimes" or "misdemeanors."
- ▶ In the outcome of the 1998 midterm election, Republicans failed to gain any new seats in the Senate and actually lost five seats in the House (Clinton was still popular!).
- ▶ The Senate trial began in January 1999 and lasted nearly five weeks.
- ▶ In the end, there was a majority of votes but not the 2/3 necessary to remove him from office.
- ▶ The Senate decided that as reprehensible as Clinton's actions were, they still did not meet the Constitutional definition of the "high crimes and misdemeanors" needed to remove a president from office.
- ▶ Clinton expressed sorrow for his actions and faced censure in the Senate for those actions, but remained in office.

Resources

Primary Documents

Primary documents provide a valuable resource for any history student. Although primary documents are not included in this Homework Helpers review text, I am including information where to locate a valuable collection of documents.

"Our Documents: 100 Milestone Documents from the National Archives" is located at *www.ourdocuments.gov/* and has a list of 100 documents that provide a valuable resource of primary documents for any student in a U.S. history course. It would benefit you, as you review the content of your U.S. history course and review material presented in the *Homework Helpers U.S. History* series, to visit the government Website and review several of the primary documents listed here.

Depending on material covered in your class or material anticipated on your exams, you may want to conduct a web search for additional primary documents. You can begin to access more primary documents at The National Archives at *www.archives.gov/historical-docs/*.

The following is a list of the documents that can be found at the National Archive site *Our Documents: 100 Milestone Documents* and that apply to *Homework Helpers U.S. History (1865–Present)*.

41. Check for the Purchase of Alaska (1868)
42. Treaty of Fort Laramie (1868)
43. 14th Amendment to the U.S. Constitution: Civil Rights (1868)
44. 15th Amendment to the U.S. Constitution: Voting Rights (1870)
45. Act Establishing Yellowstone National Park (1872)

46. Thomas Edison's Patent Application for the Light Bulb (1880)
47. Chinese Exclusion Act (1882)
48. Pendleton Act (1883)
49. Interstate Commerce Act (1887)
50. Dawes Act (1887)
51. Sherman Anti-Trust Act (1890)
52. *Plessy v. Ferguson* (1896)
53. De Lôme Letter (1898)
54. Joint Resolution to Provide for Annexing the Hawaiian Islands to the United States (1898)
55. Platt Amendment (1903)
56. Theodore Roosevelt's Corollary to the Monroe Doctrine (1905)
57. 16th Amendment to the U.S. Constitution: Federal Income Tax (1913)
58. 17th Amendment to the U.S. Constitution: Direct Election of U.S. Senators (1913)
59. Keating-Owen Child Labor Act of 1916 (1916)
60. Zimmermann Telegram (1917)
61. Joint Address to Congress Leading to a Declaration of War Against Germany (1917)
62. President Woodrow Wilson's 14 Points (1918)
63. 19th Amendment to the U.S. Constitution: Women's Right to Vote (1920)
64. Boulder Canyon Project Act (1928)
65. Tennessee Valley Authority Act (1933)
66. National Industrial Recovery Act (1933)
67. National Labor Relations Act (1935)
68. Social Security Act (1935)
69. President Franklin Roosevelt's Radio Address unveiling the second half of the New Deal (1936)
70. President Franklin Roosevelt's Annual Message (Four Freedoms) to Congress (1941)
71. Lend-Lease Act (1941)
72. Executive Order 8802: Prohibition of Discrimination in the Defense Industry (1941)
73. Joint Address to Congress Leading to a Declaration of War Against Japan (1941)
74. Executive Order 9066: Resulting in the Relocation of Japanese (1942)
75. General Dwight D. Eisenhower's Order of the Day (1944)
76. Servicemen's Readjustment Act (1944)
77. Manhattan Project Notebook (1945)
78. Surrender of Germany (1945)
79. United Nations Charter (1945)
80. Surrender of Japan (1945)
81. Truman Doctrine (1947)
82. Marshall Plan (1948)

83. Press Release Announcing U.S. Recognition of Israel (1948)

84. Executive Order 9981: Desegregation of the Armed Forces (1948)

85. Armistice Agreement for the Restoration of the South Korean State (1953)

86. Senate Resolution 301: Censure of Senator Joseph McCarthy (1954)

87. Brown v. Board of Education (1954)

88. National Interstate and Defense Highways Act (1956)

89. Executive Order 10730: Desegregation of Central High School (1957)

90. President Dwight D. Eisenhower's Farewell Address (1961)

91. President John F. Kennedy's Inaugural Address (1961)

92. Executive Order 10924: Establishment of the Peace Corps. (1961)

93. Transcript of John Glenn's Official Communication with the Command Center (1962)

94. Aerial Photograph of Missiles in Cuba (1962)

95. Test Ban Treaty (1963)

96. Official Program for the March on Washington (1963)

97. Civil Rights Act (1964)

98. Tonkin Gulf Resolution (1964)

99. Social Security Act Amendments (1965)

100. Voting Rights Act (1965)

Bibliography

American Experience: Eyes on the Prize.
www.pbs.org/wgbh/amex/eyesontheprize/

American Experience: The Murder of Emmet Till.
www.pbs.org/wgbh/amex/till/

American Experience: Race for the Super Bomb.
www.pbs.org/wgbh/amex/bomb/

American Experience: Reconstruction the Second Civil War.
www.pbs.org/wgbh/amex/reconstruction/

American Experience: The Rockefellers. *www.pbs.org/wgbh/amex/rockefellers/*

American Experience: Scottsboro, An American Tragedy.
www.pbs.org/wgbh/amex/scottsboro/

American Experience: Theodore Roosevelt. *www.pbs.org/wgbh/amex/tr/*

The American Presidency Project. *www.presidency.ucsb.edu/*

American President: An Online Reference Resource.
www.millercenter.virginia.edu/academic/americanpresident/

The Century: America. Videocassette. Buena Vista Home
Entertainment, 1999.

Clark, Christopher, et. a;. *Who Built America: Working People and the
Nation's Economy, Politics, Culture, and Society*. New York: Worth, 2000.

Divine, Robert, et. al. *America: Past and Present*. New York: Pearson, 2005.

Faragher, John, et. al. *Out of Many: A History of the American People*.
Englewood Cliffs, N.J.: Prentice Hall, 2005.

Goldfield, David. *The American Journey: A History of the United States*.
Upper Saddle River, N.J.: Prentice Hall, 2001.

The History Channel. *www.history.com*

A Hypertext on American History from the colonial period until Modern Times. *www.let.rug.nl/usa/index.htm*

Jennings, Peter, and Todd Brewster. *The Century.* New York: Doubleday, 1998.

Jones, Jacqueline. *Created Equal: A Social and Political History of the United States.* New York: Longman, 2003.

Outline of U.S. History. *www.usinfo.state.gov/products/pubs/histryotln/index.htm*

Teacher Oz's Kingdom of History. *www.teacheroz.com*

Index

About the Author

RON OLSON, co-teacher leader and faculty member of the Achiever School at Clover Park High School in Lakewood, Washington, has been teaching for 25 years. His experience includes extensive work with AP U.S. history, regular U.S. history, American literature, AP government, and humanities courses. He earned his B.A. in history and English from New Mexico State University in 1981, and he earned his M.A. in secondary education from Adams State College in 1993. In addition, he serves as a faculty consultant for the College Board and is currently a candidate pursuing his National Board Teacher Certification. He resides in Bonney Lake, Washington.

HOMEWORK HELPERS™

The Essential Help You Need When Your Textbooks Just Aren't Making the Grade!